P9-DVU-693

GREAT AMERICAN QUILTS 1989

GREAT AMERICAN QUILTS 1989

Compiled and Edited by

Sandra L. O'Brien

Oxmoor House®

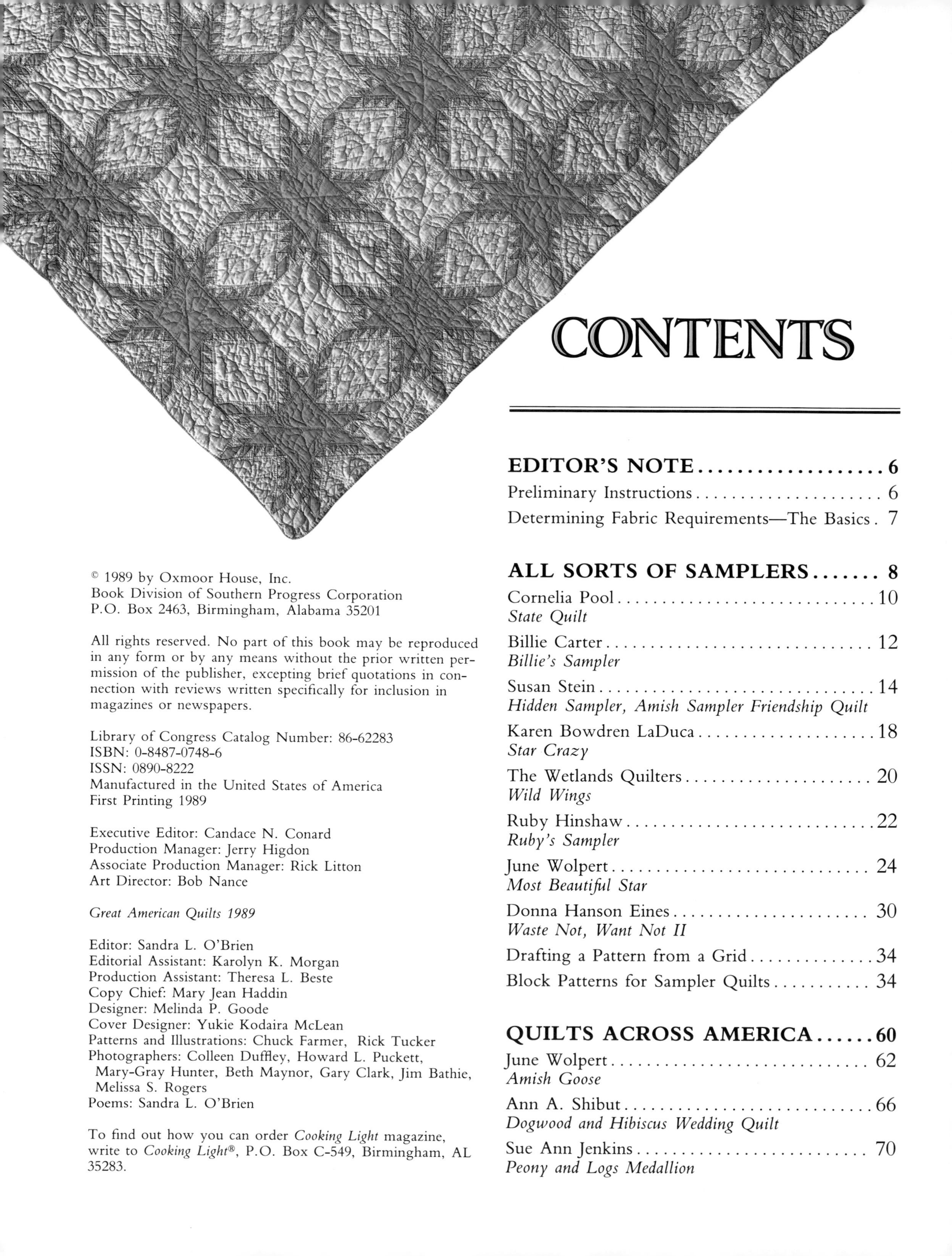

CONTENTS

Book Division of Southern Progress Corporation
P.O. Box 2463, Birmingham, Alabama 35201

Library of Congress Catalog Number: 86-62283
ISBN: 0-8487-0748-6
ISSN: 0890-8222
Manufactured in the United States of America
First Printing 1989

Executive Editor: Candace N. Conard
Production Manager: Jerry Higdon
Associate Production Manager: Rick Litton
Art Director: Bob Nance

Great American Quilts 1989

Editor: Sandra L. O'Brien
Editorial Assistant: Karolyn K. Morgan
Production Assistant: Theresa L. Beste
Copy Chief: Mary Jean Haddin
Designer: Melinda P. Goode
Cover Designer: Yukie Kodaira McLean
Patterns and Illustrations: Chuck Farmer, Rick Tucker
Photographers: Colleen Duffley, Howard L. Puckett, Mary-Gray Hunter, Beth Maynor, Gary Clark, Jim Bathie, Melissa S. Rogers
Poems: Sandra L. O'Brien

EDITOR'S NOTE

A potpourri of spectacular quilt block patterns awaits you in our "All Sorts of Samplers" chapter. There are block patterns from the early 1900s and patterns of twinkling stars and indigenous wildlife, as well as patterns from the quilters' personal drawing boards.

You will find more than 100 block patterns in this chapter, each one on its own grid. "Why grids?"—you ask. Or, "Oh no, grids!" you lament. Or, "Oh boy! grids!" you shout.

So, why grids? Well, we used grids to accommodate the large number of block patterns in one book. The choice was either to publish quilts with full-size patterns and, therefore, fewer quilts and fewer patterns; or to publish quilts with gridded patterns and, therefore, more quilts and more patterns. We thought you would prefer the latter.

For those of you who tremble at the thought of anything that vaguely resembles mathematics, we have especially prepared directions on how to draft patterns from a grid. (See Drafting a Pattern from a Grid, page 34.) Take a moment to digest them and, with a few supplies—ruler, graph paper, and pencil, you will find the procedure simple and rather gratifying. If this still doesn't persuade you to try it, take a trip to your local photocopy store, and they can enlarge or reduce the pattern to your specifications.

Now, for you grid fans (and we don't mean football!), you know the benefits. It's the freedom of choice offered by grids that makes them so appealing. You can make block patterns in a multitude of sizes, and mix and mingle them from several quilts.

To get you started, we give you the finished quilt size, block size, and sashing and border widths (if applicable) for each quilt as the original quilter made it. You will also find block piecing and setting diagrams for every quilt. Because you may choose to make your blocks in a size different from the size chosen by our quilter, we felt that listing fabric requirements would be confusing. You may find it helpful to review Determining Fabric Requirements—The Basics, which follows on the next page.

Our "Quilts Across America" chapter is bubbling with new stories, quilt chatter, and patterns from your quilting friends. In addition, we are excited about introducing you to the art of papermaking so that you can make a paper facsimile of your favorite fabric quilt.

The Bees have been buzzing with activity (as usual!) to produce the finest of quilts. The "Bee Quilters" chapter offers a variety of techniques—from piecing, to trapunto, to leaf printing. There's something for everyone.

"Traditions in Quilting" crystallizes the past and brings it into the present via shared memories and quilts to make. And while your hands are busy quilting, take a moment to feast your eyes upon the powerful quilted statements of color and fabric made by today's quilting innovators in our "Designer Gallery" chapter.

Preliminary Instructions

All pattern pieces include ¼" seam allowance. All measurements for pieces and sashing and border strips are given *with* seam allowances, unless noted otherwise. Some oversize pieces are placed on a grid, with scale information noted. (See Drafting a Pattern from a Grid, page 34.)

Fabric requirements are based on 44"/45"-wide fabric with trimmed selvages. Fabric requirements for backing are based on a three-panel backing for bed quilts. *Generous fabric allowances are given for fabric requirements to account for fabric shrinkage and individual differences in fabric cutting.* Fabric requirements are given for one-piece borders. Finished quilt size is the size of the quilt before quilting. Prepare fabrics before marking and cutting by washing, drying, and pressing.

Determining Fabric Requirements—The Basics

These directions are for quilts with very simple block settings that use solid-colored fabrics with no sheen or nap that might interfere with the customary template grain-line direction. They are intended to introduce you to the basics and to help you get started.

If you are using fabrics with complex or one-way patterns, stripes, plaids, or the like, *or* if you are using a quilt pattern with unusual shapes and sizes, determining fabric requirements can be a little more involved. In addition, in these instances grain-line direction may be contrary to what is customarily used.

Never hesitate to use graph paper and a calculator to determine fabric requirements before purchasing fabric. And most of all, as we do with our fabric requirements, add a ⅛ to ¼ yard margin of error to each fabric calculation. You will be glad you did, and any excess fabric can go into the bin for a scrap quilt.

1. Select block size and quilt size.
2. Select quilt setting, that is, whether the blocks will be set perpendicular to each other or on the diagonal. Will they be set with or without sashing, and will they be framed with a border or with multiple borders? Once the block size, quilt size, and setting are determined, you will know the number of blocks you need.
3. Make a sketch of your quilt on graph paper.
4. Calculate the number of each template needed by multiplying the number of times the template is used per block by the number of times the block is used in the quilt. For example, if template A is used twice in each block, and there are 24 blocks in your quilt, then the number of template A required is 48 (2 x 24 = 48). Make a list of the number of each template needed for each color of fabric.
5. Measure templates and determine sashing and border dimensions (if applicable). Include ¼″ seam allowances with each measurement.
6. If you are using one-piece sashing and/or borders, determine the length of fabric needed for these first. These will be cut on the lengthwise grain of the fabric. (See Example of Fabric Layout.) A calculator and graph paper are very handy at this point.

However, if there is a sheen or nap to your fabric, cut top and bottom borders on the crosswise grain so that all grain lines are going in the same direction. (See Diagram for Quilt Borders with Nap or Sheen.)

As a rule of thumb, we use 42″ as a standard-width measurement for 44″/45″ fabric to adjust for trimmed selvages, fabric-width discrepancies from bolt to bolt, and shrinkage.

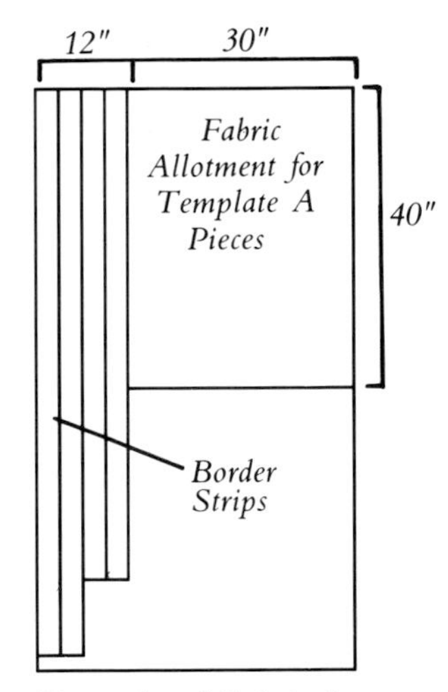

Example of Fabric Layout

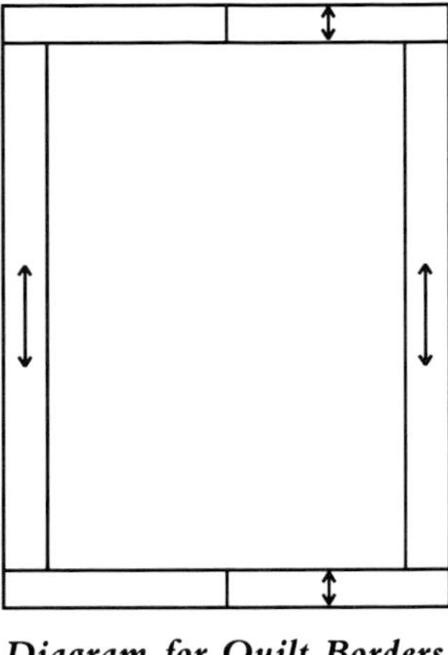

Diagram for Quilt Borders with Nap or Sheen

7. Deduct the widths of the borders from 42″ to determine the remaining width of fabric. (See Example of Fabric Layout.) For our example, it would be 42″ - 12″ = 30″.
8. Divide the measurement of your template into the width of the remaining fabric to determine the number of templates that will fit across that width. For example, if template A equaled a 5″ square, six templates would fit across the fabric (30″ ÷ 5″ = 6).
9. Divide the total number of pieces required for each template by the number that can be cut from the fabric width to determine the number of rows needed. For example, if you needed 48 of template A, you would need 8 rows (48 ÷ 6 = 8 rows).
10. Multiply the number of rows by the measurement of your template to determine the length of fabric you need. In our example, you would need 40″ of fabric (8 rows x 5″ = 40″ of fabric). (See Example of Fabric Layout.)
11. Continue in this manner for each template and for each fabric color.
12. If you are making a bed quilt, calculate the backing-fabric requirement based on a three-panel backing with vertical seams.
13. For bias binding, one 36″ square of fabric will make 13 yards of 2½″ double-fold binding, and one 43″ square, 20 yards.

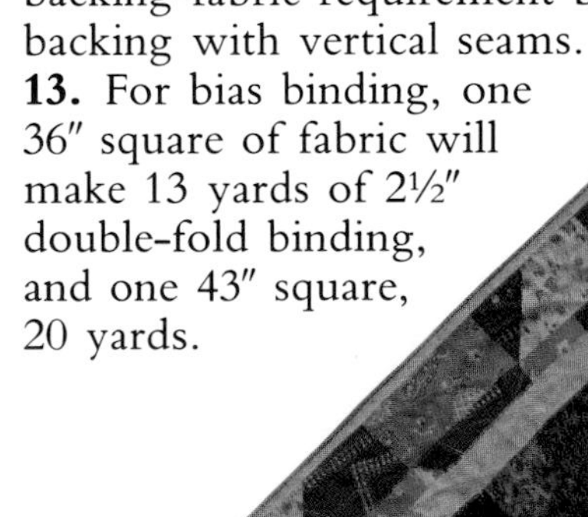

ALL SORTS OF SAMPLERS

Folded in a chest, for many a decade,
rests the first quilt I ever made.
A sampler quilt, they called it—
the quilter's cup of tea.
I chuckled a bit, I must admit;
it was all Greek to me.

It was a smorgasbord of patchwork,
a kingdom of orderliness;
I made every stitch so carefully;
I wanted to do my best.

Many quilts I've made since then,
so my sampler's been left behind.
And yet, I use it often to recall
a favorite block of mine.

I think I'll make another, because
I like this one so well,
For I'm a sampler fanatic, giving
lonely blocks a place to dwell.

N.DAK
ILL
CAL
N.H.
ALA
IND
OHIO
TEX
CONN
W.VA
LA

Cornelia Pool

Vienna, New Jersey

Quilting bees were regular events in Vienna, New Jersey, at the turn of the century. A frequent member of those quilting bees was Joan Nahass's great-grandmother, Cornelia Pool. Cornelia was born in Vienna and lived there all her life, even after her marriage. There was much camaraderie at those bees, and the *State Quilt*, below, can attest to the fact that they were sources of many attractive quilts.

Joan's love for quilting began when she was a teenager and was taught to make a nine-patch block by her grandmother, Susan Gulick. In fact, Joan's grandmother later gave her *State Quilt* (which she had inherited from her mother, Cornelia) because Joan was the only grandchild who was a quilter. Joan tells us that presently she has no set time for quilting, but "when I do find the time," says Joan, "then it's gung ho!" Quiltmaking is done among her other activities—square dancing with her husband, gardening, playing the organ, and keeping the books for a bus her husband drives.

Joan Nahass
Park Ridge, New Jersey

State Quilt

1910

The recycling of commodities may have become the noble and fashionable thing to do today, but not so long ago, Cornelia Pool and her friends considered the recycling of fabrics a part of their daily routine. Flour sacks and feed bags were excellent sources of muslin and cotton fabrics. Fabrics from old dresses were reused until threadbare.

State Quilt was one of the many quilts that Cornelia, her sister, various other relatives, and friends made from recycled fabrics. We believe these block patterns were obtained from a popular farm magazine at that time, *Hearth & Home*. (See "Resources.")

Block patterns, quilt dimensions, and diagrams for State Quilt *begin on page 34.*

Billie Carter

Mansfield, Arkansas

Hampered by commitments to a full-time job and a family, it seemed to Billie that there was only time to read about quilts—not to make them. But in spite of these time limitations, her determined spirit and love for quilts motivated her to make one. Says Billie, "It went a little slow, but I find you can stay up almost all night when you want to do something so much."

Three years and four quilts later, Billie enrolled in her first quiltmaking class. "I enjoyed the class and the other quilters so much, and from that class we started our local guild, The Belle Point Quilter's Guild," Billie recalls.

Billie's Sampler

1984

You can almost smell the aroma of budding springtime when looking at *Billie's Sampler* quilt. The floral striped sashing and small-flowered prints in warm shades of lilac and green evoke a garden ready to burst into bloom. This quilt is a reminder, too, that traditional blocks lend themselves very well to nontraditional colors.

Billie's Sampler is the fifth quilt she has made, but the first one she made in a quiltmaking class. (See "Resources.") "I wanted to get instructions on how to make all kinds of blocks," says Billie. Later that same year, 1984, *Billie's Sampler* won Sweepstakes and First Place ribbons at the Scott County Fair, Waldron, Arkansas, and a first place ribbon at the Arkansas/Oklahoma State Fair, Ft. Smith, Arkansas.

Block patterns, quilt dimensions, and diagrams for Billie's Sampler *begin on page 38.*

Susan Stein

St. Paul, Minnesota

"Quilting is my consuming passion," says Susan. "Eleven years ago, I went bonkers over quilting! I joined the Minnesota Quilters, read quilting books and magazines, enrolled in classes, and attended shows." And proof of her continued enthusiasm is seen in the more than 100 quilts she has made since then. Needless to say, every room in her house has a quilt in it. "I love quilting—alone in my studio, sharing it with guild members, teaching it, and reading about it," says Susan.

Susan has become well-known for her special interest in sampler quilts. (See "Resources.") She loves to lecture on what she calls "blockbuster" quilts. As Susan puts it, "Those are the quilts that get away from rows of blocks with standard setting arrangements."

Hidden Sampler

1987

Susan's *Hidden Sampler* teaches us that a sampler doesn't necessarily mean rows of blocks framed by strips of contrasting fabric. And a sampler doesn't have to represent your first attempt at quiltmaking, either. Instead, it can bring all your creative juices to attention and challenge you to invent a sampler that "isn't a sampler."

The continuity and dominance of the green blocks over the contrasting red blocks deceive our eyes and mind into thinking the background is all the same. Take a second look, and you will see that each red block is different. In effect, by using shades of the complementary colors red and green, Susan was able to camouflage 13 unique blocks among green-on-green pieced blocks.

But Susan is still not finished deceiving us. Though each red block looks different, in reality all blocks (including the green blocks) in this quilt are made from one template, the same small triangle. It is Susan's color usage and arrangement of the triangles that make the blocks look different.

Block patterns, quilt dimensions, and diagrams for Hidden Sampler *begin on page 46.*

Amish Sampler Friendship Quilt

1985

The Split Bar variation is a quilt setting most often associated with many Pennsylvanian Amish quilts. Susan found its design appealing and a perfect opportunity to incorporate a dozen of her favorite block patterns in an uncustomary sampler setting.

It also gave her a chance to have a little fun with color placement. "I feel perfection in color placement makes boring quilts," says Susan. "So, I purposely added 'mistakes' in color placement while making the Pinwheel and Flying Geese blocks."

The fact that the signature of a friend is penned in each of Susan's sampler blocks, following the custom of friendship quilts, makes this an extra-special quilt for her.

One last thing—when making this quilt, Susan reminds you to be sure and add a few of your own color mistakes!

Block patterns, quilt dimensions, and diagrams for Amish Sampler Friendship Quilt *begin on page 48.*

Karen Bowdren LaDuca

Pittsford, New York

"I haven't stopped sewing since my aunt taught me at the age of seven," says Karen. At that time Karen's aunt, a home economics teacher, decided it was time her niece learned how to use a sewing machine. "After three days of sitting on a telephone book so I could reach the machine," says Karen, "I had completed a pair of pajamas for my cousin. I still remember the fabric—pink flannel with white snowmen!"

Quilting came much later in Karen's life, but once it did, she found the fabric selection and piecing involved in quiltmaking a source of greater satisfaction than making garments to wear. "The challenge of sewing precise seams with tiny stitches made the process interesting," says Karen. "I could choose many fabrics and give a flat design depth and movement by the placement of color and quilting lines." Enjoy seeing more of Karen's precise piecing and design innovation in our "Quilts Across America" chapter.

Star Crazy
1984

This star-studded galaxy of patchwork octagons is a dazzling display of Karen's love for star designs. "I am intrigued by the variety and intricacy of designs possible using simple geometric shapes," explains Karen, who majored in mathematics in college. To make *Star Crazy*, Karen started with the Star of Bethlehem block and eliminated the corner squares to form an octagon. She adapted and rearranged other star blocks, such as Carpenter's Wheel and Blazing Star, to fit her octagon motif.

"*Star Crazy* represents many of my feelings about quilting and star designs in general," says Karen. "For me stars symbolize joy, achievement, and celebration, emotions I associate with quilting."

Karen's *Star Crazy* won First Place at the Vermont Quilt Festival in 1984, and an Honorable Mention at the 15th Annual Quilt Show of the National Quilting Association in 1984.

Block patterns, quilt dimensions, and diagrams for Star Crazy *begin on page 50.*

The Wetlands Quilters enjoy an afternoon of quilting. They are (clockwise, beginning in foreground with the quilter in the white sweater)—*Ruth Murphy, Betty Ward, Frances Maher, Alice Skoland, Olive Prout, Letty Parks, Edith Soltis, Myrtle Wilson, Mary Heyneker, Marion Glaspey, Elsie Snyder, and Elsie Mott.*

The Wetlands Quilters

Stone Harbor, New Jersey

Seven years ago Marion Glaspey rather casually mentioned in *The Wetlands Institute Newsletter* that the Institute would be having a meeting once a week for afternoon tea and quilting. "To our amazement, a number of ladies already known to each other arrived in a group, bringing with them quilting expertise, goodies for tea, and a wonderful camaraderie," says Marion. "Seven years and seven quilts later, they are still coming."

What enticed them to come, besides quilting, was The Wetlands Institute. The Wetlands Institute is a private, nonprofit organization dedicated to scientific research and public education concerning intertidal salt marshes and other coastal eco-systems and their plant and animal life. A Wings 'n Water Festival is held each year, featuring a quilt show and benefit raffle, organized by The Wetlands Quilters; a bird carving show and sale; aquarium workshops; salt marsh safaris; and other related shows and activities. The quilt raffles to date have netted approximately $3,000 each year for the educational programs of The Wetlands Institute.

Enjoy another of The Wetlands Quilters' lively quilting projects, *Leaf Prints,* in our "Bee Quilters" chapter.

Wild Wings

1987

In indigenous marshland colors of greens, browns, and sand, a flock of bird and wildlife blocks parade in formation around a pair of Canada geese. *Wild Wings* is the sixth quilt made by The Wetlands Quilters for the annual raffle to benefit the educational programs of The Wetlands Institute.

The Wetlands Quilters were inspired to make a sampler quilt after they saw one made by one of their members. Since the quilt was being made to benefit the Institute, a bird and wildlife theme seemed fitting. "A diligent search of wildlife books and magazines yielded ideas for 14 blocks," says group leader Marion Glaspey. Each member pieced and quilted one or more blocks and joined them to the 12" setting triangles to form the border strips.

"Before we knew it, the cart-before-the-horse dilemma was in effect," remembers Marion. "We had a border but no center!" The dominant center panel of The Wetlands Quilters' quilts had become an expected tradition by their fans and patrons. And as Marion explains, "Our border made several of my nebulous ideas for the panel impossibly wishy-washy." After doing a little more research, Marion designed, appliquéd, and quilted the central panel with flying Canada geese. The geese provided that bold center of interest needed to balance the prominence of the border. The free-form quilting on the center panel represents currents of air flowing around the geese and a marshy foreground. Members who worked on *Wild Wings* were Marion Glaspey, Mary Heyneker, Frances Maher, Elsie Mott, Ruth Murphy, Letty Parks, Olive Prout, Alice Skoland, Elsie Snyder, Edith Soltis, Betty Ward, and Myrtle Wilson.

Block patterns, quilt dimensions, and diagrams for Wild Wings *begin on page 52.*

Ruby Hinshaw

Haviland, Kansas

Ruby's favorite quiltmaking activity is designing her own blocks. That also makes sampler quilts her favorite since it is the best way to display all of her different designs.

After her retirement from teaching school, Ruby took up the craft she had learned as a child from her mother and grandmother. "Creating quilts is an expression of myself," says Ruby. "It is so rewarding to have a lovely heirloom made by my own hands."

Ruby's Sampler

1986

Ruby's goal was to make a quilt with every idea and stitch her very own. Every block was either designed by Ruby or a traditional one changed to fit her plans. Block patterns include a few pieced ones, some appliquéd, and several with a combination of both. "I wanted to have a balance of pattern techniques," says Ruby.

The best part of the designing was that while Ruby was making one block, she would start searching for the next one to make—with the only criterion being that she liked it! The Little Country Church block is a real eye-catcher that Ruby designed herself. The doors open and close with a button latch, and folded fabric gives the roof that authentic shingled look.

"I am very proud to have made it," says Ruby. "My husband was critically ill during that time and having the quilt to work on really was an inspiration. Fortunately, my husband recovered, so I have happy memories of it and the satisfaction of accomplishing my goal."

Block patterns, quilt dimensions, and diagrams for Ruby's Sampler *begin on page 55.*

June Wolpert

Nashville, Indiana

June's Indiana license plate reads, "I QUILT." And, as she tells us, it never fails to start a conversation about quilting. June has been a dedicated quilter for the last ten years, and presently she teaches specialty quilting classes throughout Indiana. "I've collected fabric all my life," says June, "and now that I quilt, it's become a passion. I buy fabric everywhere I go!"

For June, ideas for quilts are everywhere—on billboards, in phone books, the countryside, newspapers, books, and magazines. You'll find another of June's inspiring quilts, *Amish Goose*, in our "Quilts Across America" chapter.

Most Beautiful Star

1983

For June, the most beautiful star is the feathered star. For you, it may be one of the other 30 stars found in *Most Beautiful Star*'s border. (You will count 32 star blocks in the border because Star in a Star and Rolling Star are used twice.)

June enlarged a 6″ feathered star pattern to a 24″ feathered star to create her feathered star-within-a-feathered star medallion. Framed by strips of coordinating fabric and stacked arrows pointing toward the center, June's feathered star takes prominence over all the other stars.

Soon after *Most Beautiful Star* was finished, it won the Viewer's Choice ribbon at the Brown County Historical Society Quilt Show, Nashville, Indiana, in June, 1983, and in September of that year won the blue ribbon in the medallion category at the Bloomington Festival of Quilts, Bloomington, Indiana.

Block patterns, instructions for border assembly, and diagrams for Most Beautiful Star *begin on page 42.*

Most Beautiful Star (Medallion Only)

Finished Medallion Size
61″ x 61″

Fabric Requirements for Feathered Star Medallion Only

Navy paisley	— ¾ yd.
Navy print I	— ¼ yd.
Navy print II	—2 yd.
Navy print III	—1⅞ yd.
Rose print	—1¾ yd.
Maroon print	—1⅞ yd.
Red paisley	—1¾ yd.
Beige	—1¾ yd.

Number to Cut

Template A	—4 navy paisley 1 rose print
Template B	—64 navy print I 8 rose print 80 beige
Template C	—4 navy paisley
Template D	—8 rose print
Template E	—4 maroon print
Template F	—64 maroon print 80 beige
Template G	—4 maroon print
Template G★	—4 maroon print
Template H	—4 navy paisley
Template I	—4 navy paisley
Template J	—8 navy paisley
Template K	—4 navy print I
Template L	—4 navy print I
Template L★	—4 navy print I
Template M	—4 beige
Template N	—4 beige
Template O	—4 maroon print
Template O★	—4 maroon print
Template P	—24 beige
Template Q	—4 navy paisley
Template R	—4 rose print
Template S	—4 beige

★ — Flip or turn over template if fabric is one-sided.

Feathered Star Medallion Assembly

1. Refer to Medallion Piecing Diagram I and join rose print triangles (B) to navy paisley piece C to form a pieced square. Make 4. Join 2 pieced squares to opposite sides of rose print square (A) to form a row. Join 2 navy paisley squares (A) to sides of pieced square to form a row. Make 2. Join rows, as shown in Medallion Piecing Diagrams I and II.

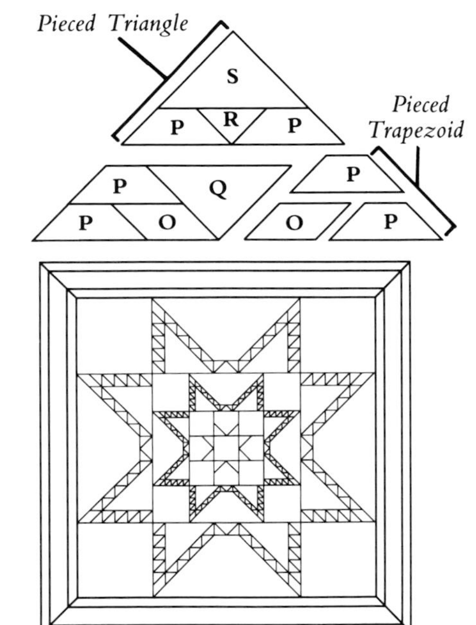

Medallion Piecing Diagram II

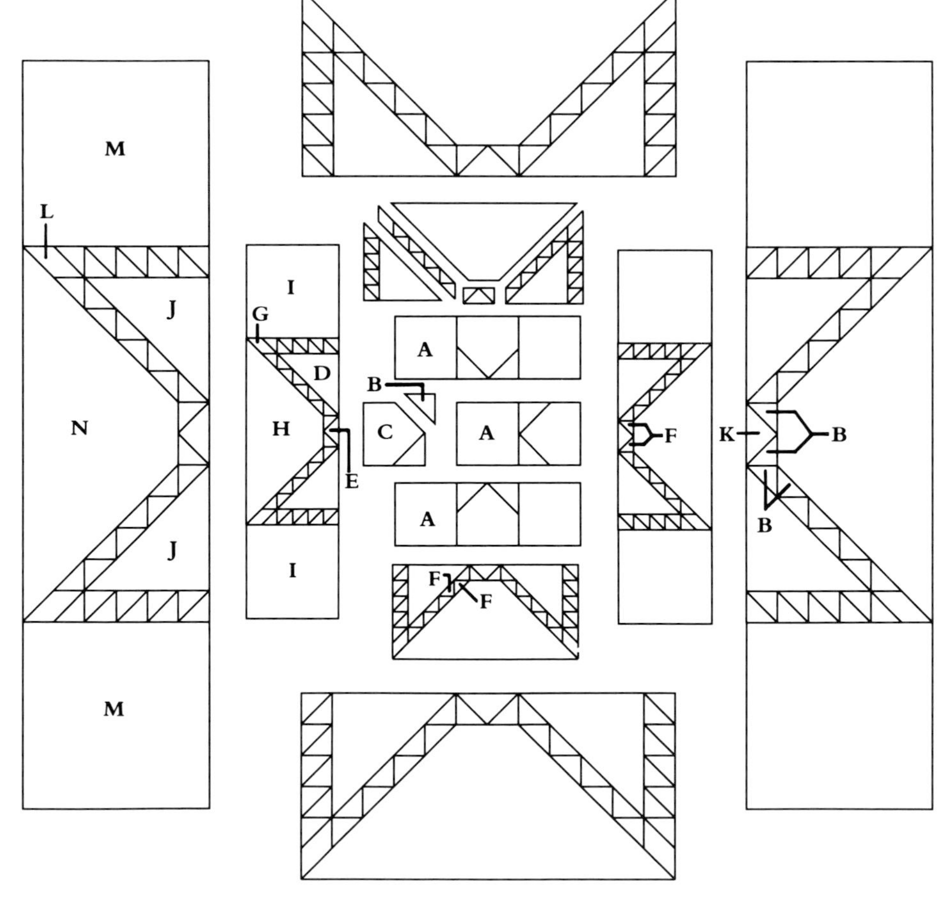

Medallion Piecing Diagram I

2. Join 4 maroon print triangles (F) to 5 beige triangles (F) to form a strip, as shown in Feathered Star Piecing Diagram. Join strip to side of rose print triangle (D).

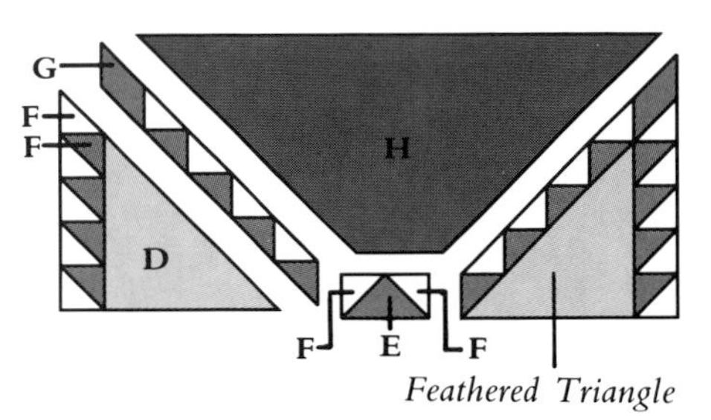

Feathered Star Piecing Diagram

Join 4 maroon print triangles (F) to 4 beige triangles (F) at sides to form a strip. Join 1 maroon print parallelogram (G) to beige triangle at the end of strip. Join strip to bias edge of triangle (D), as shown in Feathered Star Piecing Diagram, to complete feathered triangle. Make 2 feathered triangles.

Join beige triangles (F) to the sides of maroon print triangle (E) to form a pieced rectangle, as shown in Feathered Star Piecing Diagram. Join feathered triangles to sides of pieced rectangle, as shown in Medallion Piecing Diagram I.

Set in navy paisley trapezoid (H) to complete pieced rectangle, as shown. Make 4 pieced rectangles.

3. Join pieced rectangles to top and bottom of star block, made in Step 1.

4. Join 2 squares (I) to the opposite sides of pieced rectangle to form a column, as shown in Medallion Piecing Diagram I. Make 2 columns. Join columns to sides to complete feathered star, as shown.

5. Join pieces B, J, K, L, and N to form a pieced rectangle, as done in Step 2 and as shown in Medallion Piecing Diagram I. Make 4.

Join pieced rectangles to top and bottom of feathered star.

6. Join squares (M) to opposite sides of pieced rectangle to form a column, as shown. Make 2 columns. Join columns to sides of feathered star.

7. Cut 4 strips, 1¼" wide, from navy print II. Join to medallion, as shown in Medallion Piecing Diagram II, and miter corners.

8. Cut 4 strips, 2½" wide, from red paisley. Join to medallion, as shown in Medallion Piecing Diagram II, and miter corners.

9. Cut 4 strips, 1¼" wide, from navy print II. Join to medallion, as shown in Medallion Piecing Diagram II, and miter corners.

10. Join pieces O, P, and Q to form a pieced trapezoid, as shown in Medallion Piecing Diagram II. Join pieces P, R, and S to form a pieced triangle. Join pieced triangle to pieced trapezoid, as shown in Medallion Piecing Diagram II. Make 4. Join one to each side of medallion.

11. Cut 4 strips, 1¼" wide, from navy print II. Join to medallion and miter corners. (Refer to quilt photograph for Steps 11 through 19.)

12. Cut 4 strips, 2½" wide, from red paisley. Join to medallion and miter corners.

13. Cut 4 strips, 1¼" wide, from navy print II. Join to medallion and miter corners.

14. Cut 4 strips, 2" wide, from beige. Join to medallion and miter corners.

15. Cut 4 strips, 2" wide, from rose print. Join to medallion and miter corners.

16. Cut 4 strips, 1¼" wide, from navy print II. Join to medallion and miter corners.

17. Cut 4 strips, 1½" wide, from navy print III. Join to medallion and miter corners.

18. Cut 4 strips, 1¼" wide, from navy print II. Join to medallion and miter corners.

19. Cut 4 strips, 1¼" wide, from maroon print. Join to medallion and miter corners.

Quilting

June quilted her medallion as shown in Quilting Diagram.

Quilting Diagram

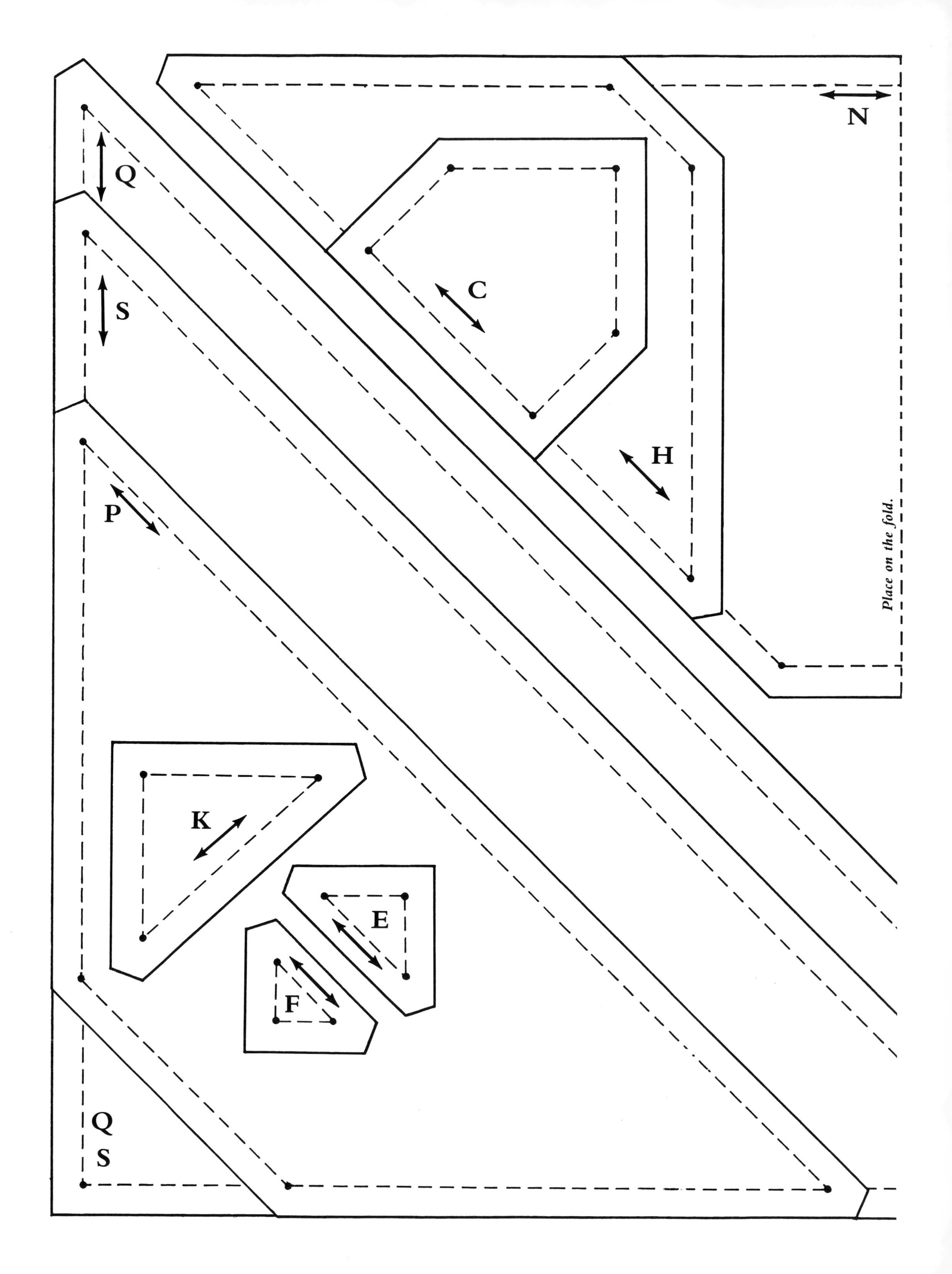

N
Q
C
S
H
P
Place on the fold.
K
E
F
Q
S

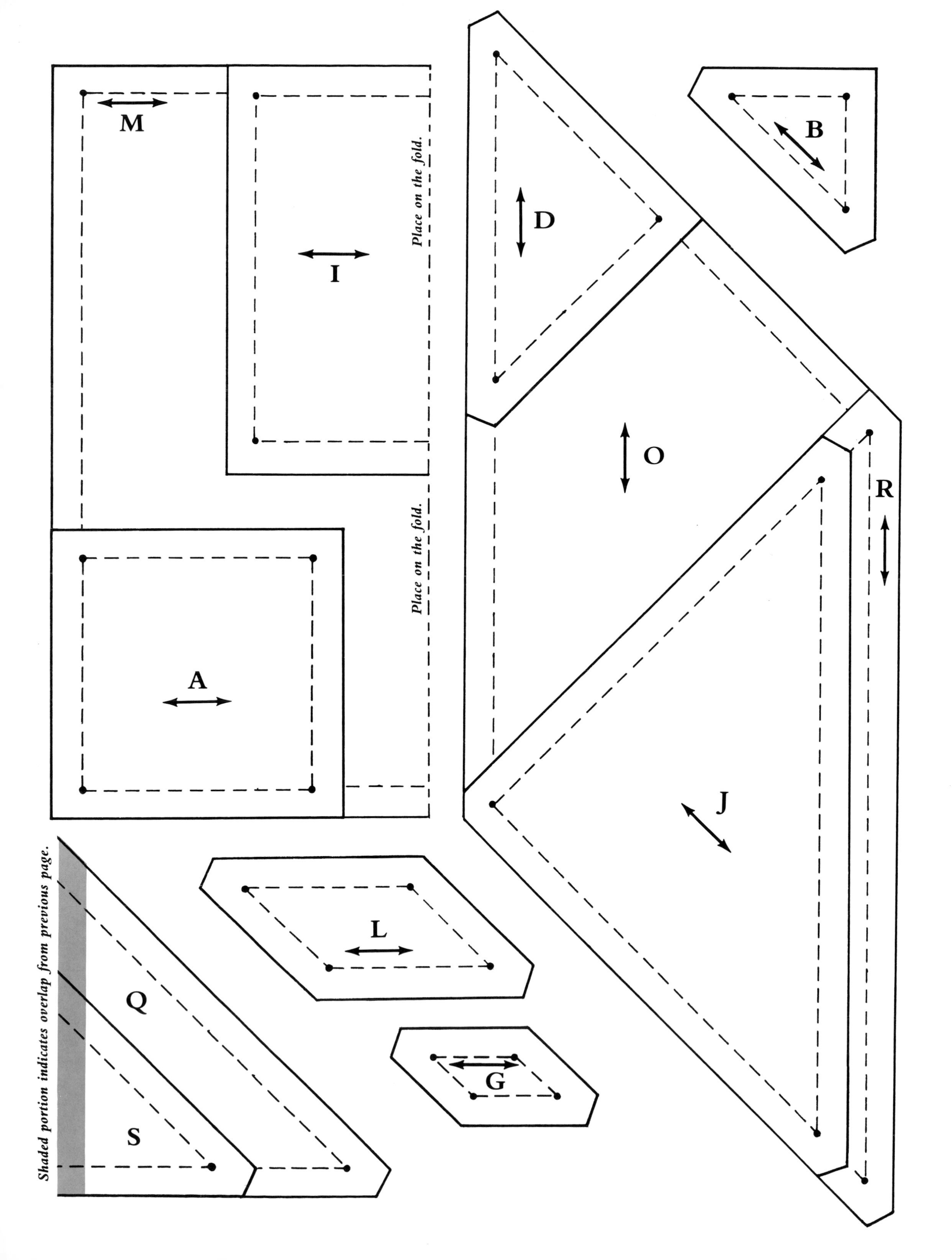
M
I
Place on the fold.
Place on the fold.
A
D
B
O
R
J
L
G
Q
S
Shaded portion indicates overlap from previous page.

Donna Hanson Eines

Edmonds, Washington

As a young girl, Donna was taught stitchery by her Norwegian-born grandmother and developed a love for it that remains today. But it was not until a few decades later that she was personally introduced to quilting. After making her first quilt in 1974, a cathedral window, "I was hooked!" Donna exclaims. Donna's favorite subjects in college were art appreciation courses. "So," says Donna, "quilting became the medium that allowed me to express myself in an artistic way with color and texture."

Quilting is much more than a pastime for Donna. "Quilting has led me to research earlier times, to gain an appreciation for those days, and to observe the contributions made by women, demonstrated in their art," says Donna. Why does she quilt? Says Donna, "For my own great pleasure, to express my own creativity, and to pass on to my children a heritage of my being."

Waste Not, Want Not II
1988
Donna summoned her fellow quilters with a call for all their unwanted blocks—incorrect size, horrible colors—in other words, MISTAKES! In response, loads of blocks were sent her way, enough to make two quilts. Blocks were sorted and overdyed by Donna with a household dye so that the hues would match. Sections for accent strips and backing were also dyed to match.

Says Donna, "Years ago, quilters made do with what they had. It was a challenge and great fun to do just that in 1988." We hope that it will be the same kind of challenge for you—to take your scrap sampler blocks and do just that!

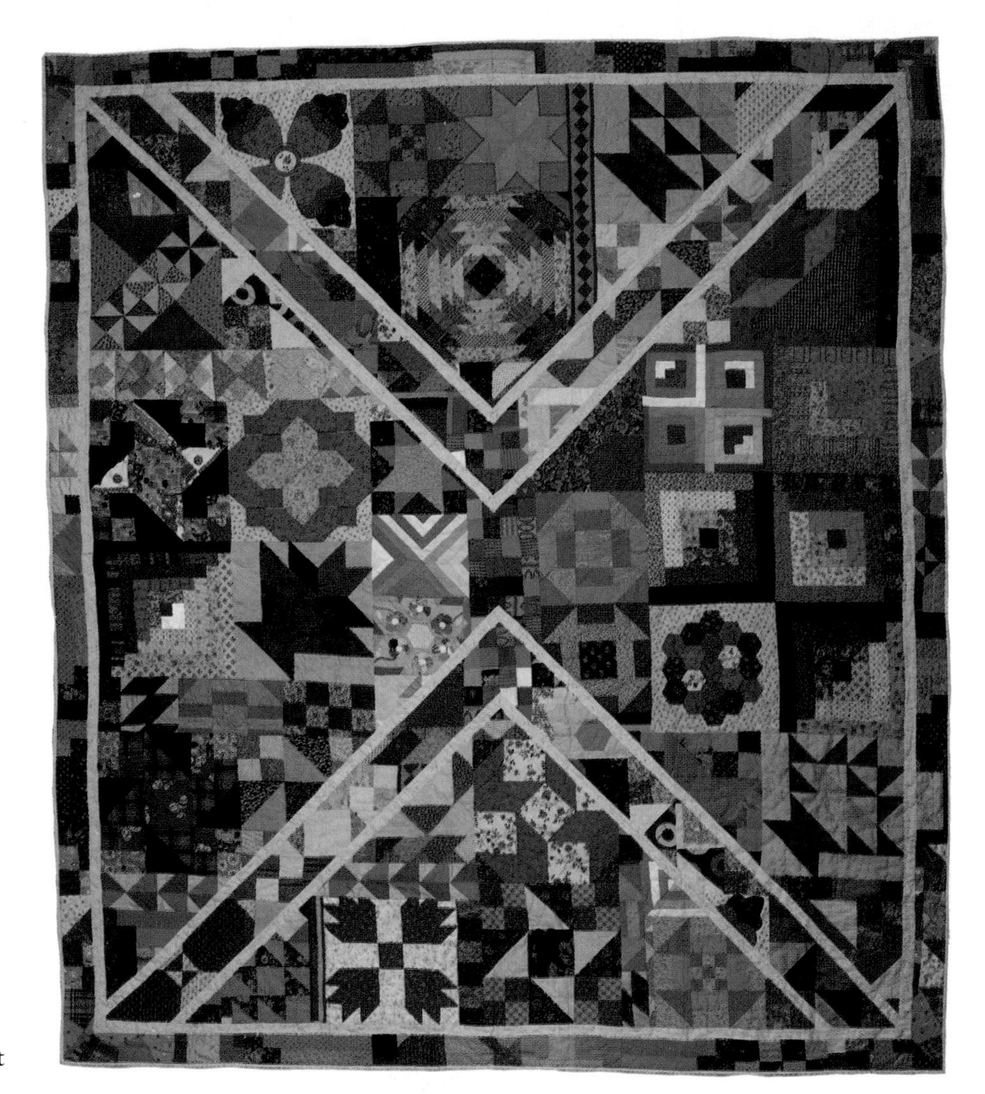

Waste Not, Want Not II

Finished Quilt Size
69″ x 81″

Fabric Requirements

Fabric for accent and border strips	—2⅓ yd.

Other Materials
Plenty of unwanted sampler blocks
Household fabric dye — wine

Quilt Top Assembly
1. Overdye blocks and accent-strip fabric with wine-colored dye.
2. Join blocks in random fashion at sides to form rows and join rows. Make a piece at least 64″ x 76″.
3. Cut right angles into piece, as shown in Setting Diagram I.

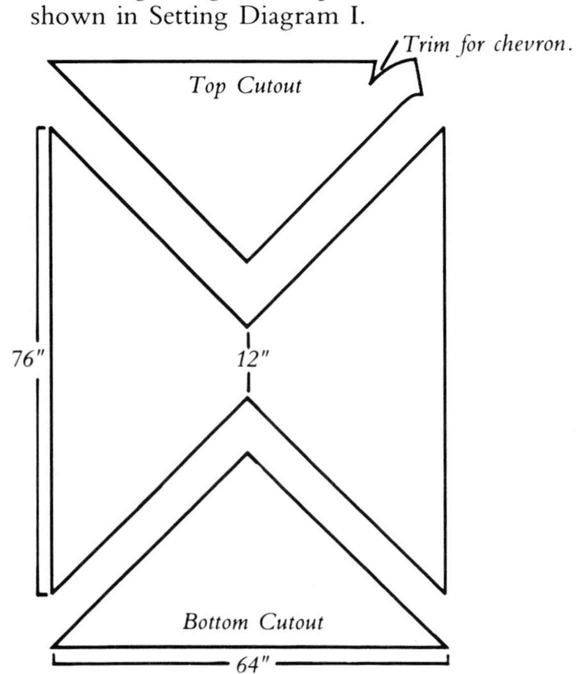

Setting Diagram I

Chevron Piecing Diagram

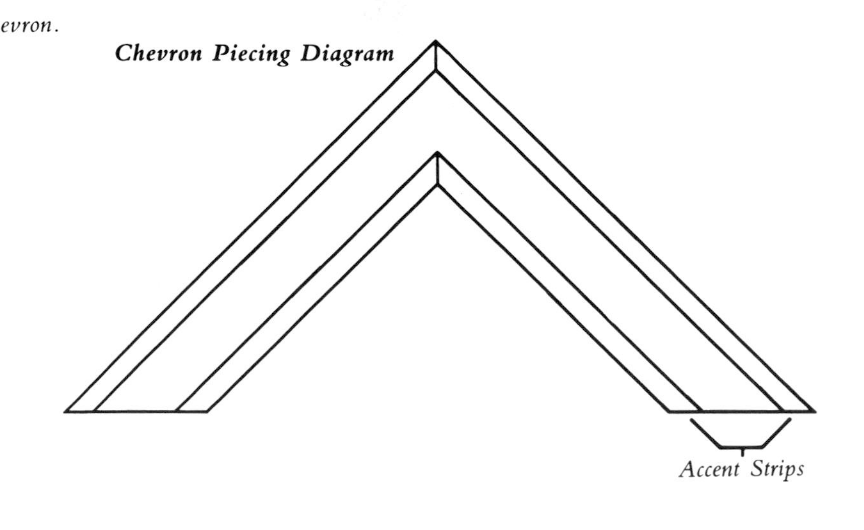

4. From each right-angle cutout, cut a 4½"-wide strip for chevrons, as shown.

Cut strips, 1½" wide, from accent fabric and join to sides of chevrons, mitering strips, as shown in Chevron Piecing Diagram.

5. Join chevrons to quilt piece, as shown in Setting Diagram II. To add interest, Donna sewed the chevron made from the top cutout to the bottom of the quilt and vice versa. (See Setting Diagrams.)

Join cutouts to quilt, as shown. Trim cutouts even with quilt edge, as shown.

6. Cut 4 border strips, 1½" wide, from accent fabric. Join to quilt and miter corners.

7. Cut 4 border strips, 2½" wide, from miscellaneous blocks joined at the sides. Join to quilt and miter corners. (See quilt drawing and photograph.)

Quilting

Donna quilted an overall fan design for *Waste Not, Want Not II.*

Finished Edges

Bind with accent fabric.

Chevron from Bottom Cutout
Top Cutout
Trim.
Bottom Cutout
Chevron from Top Cutout

Setting Diagram II

Drafting a Pattern from a Grid

On all of our grids, each grid square equals 1″. Each gridded block can be reduced or enlarged by making adjustments in the scale, as shown in Step 1.

1. Determine Block Scale

When each grid square equals 1″, a 12″ block can be reduced or enlarged as follows:

For a 3″ block, each grid square equals ¼″.
For a 6″ block, each grid square equals ½″.
For a 9″ block, each grid square equals ¾″.
For a 12″ block, each grid square equals 1″.
For a 15″ block, each grid square equals 1¼″.
For an 18″ block, each grid squares equals 1½″.

And a 16″ block can be reduced or enlarged as follows:

For a 4″ block, each grid square equals ¼″.
For an 8″ block, each grid square equals ½″.
For a 12″ block, each grid square equals ¾″.
For a 16″ block, each grid square equals 1″.
For a 20″ block, each grid square equals 1¼″.
For a 24″ block, each grid square equals 1½″.

2. Select a Method

Graph paper—The graph paper method is one of the most frequently used and least expensive. Purchase graph paper with a grid square size that is in proportion to the grid square size you selected above. For example, if you want to make the 3″ block, purchase graph paper with ¼″ grid squares. (Since all of our scales increase or decrease in increments of ¼″, this graph paper can be marked to match any of the scales listed above.) Before purchasing graph paper, measure the grid square for accuracy.

Other materials that can be used in place of graph paper are *gridded freezer paper, gridded vinyl, or a self-drawn grid.* With gridded vinyl, you will want to draw each piece separately and add seam allowance, since you are transferring the pattern and making the template in one step.

Photocopy—A gridded pattern can be easily enlarged or reduced by using a photocopy machine. Measure each copy for accuracy, because enlargements or reductions can vary from copy to copy and from machine to machine.

3. Transfer the Pattern

Number grid squares vertically and horizontally on both the pattern and your grid. Use the numbers as a guide to copy the pattern outline from the original, square by square. Now the pattern is ready for template making.

Remember, when enlarging or reducing patterns from a grid, you are changing the *numerical value* that one grid square represents (the scale), not the number of grid squares. The number of grid squares *always* remains the same. For example, if the side of a shape equals 4 grid squares, it will always equal 4 grid squares, whether one grid square equals ¼″ or ½″.

State Quilt

Finished Quilt Size
80″ x 80″

Number of Blocks and Finished Size
25 blocks—13″ x 13″

Finished Width of Sashing—2½″
Sashing strips are set with 2½″ accent squares.

Finished Width of Border—2½″

Each square equals 1".

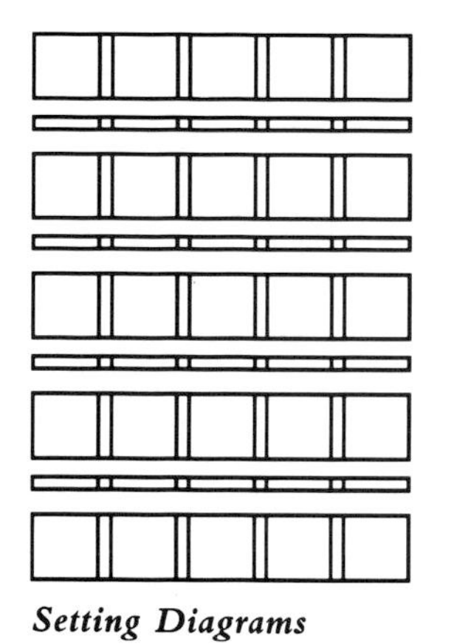

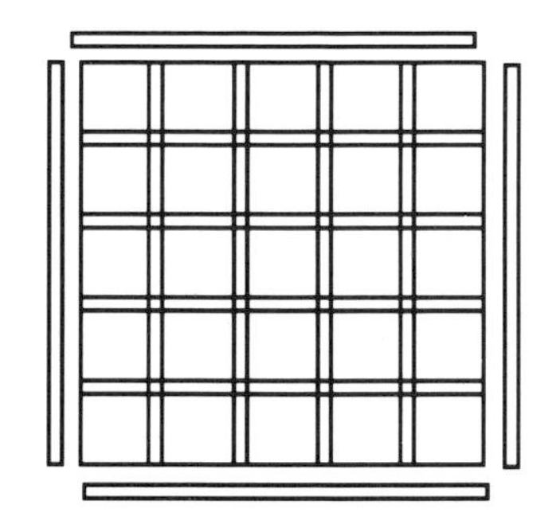

Setting Diagrams

Massachusetts

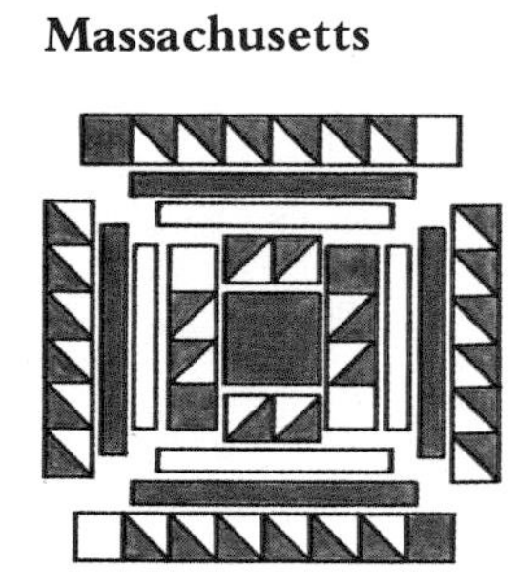

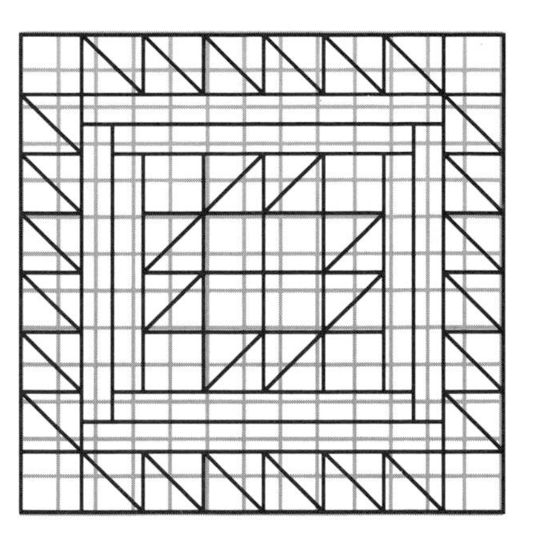

North Dakota

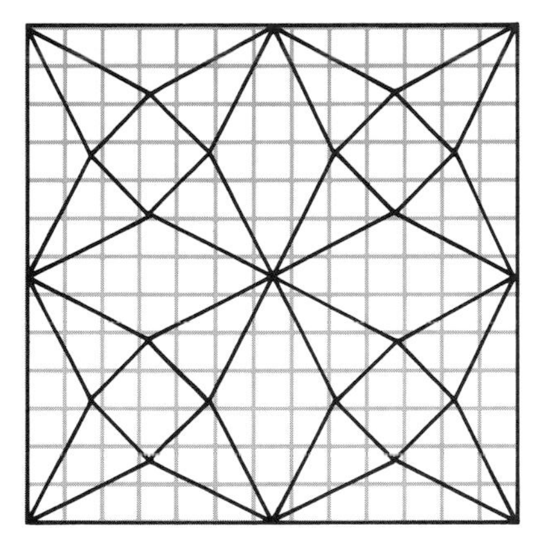

Pennsylvania

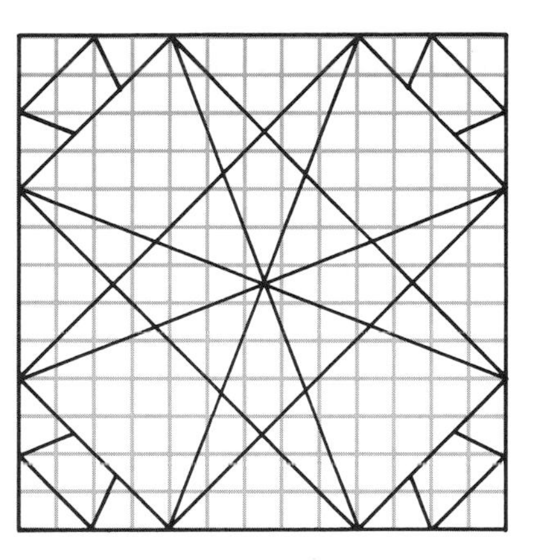

Alabama

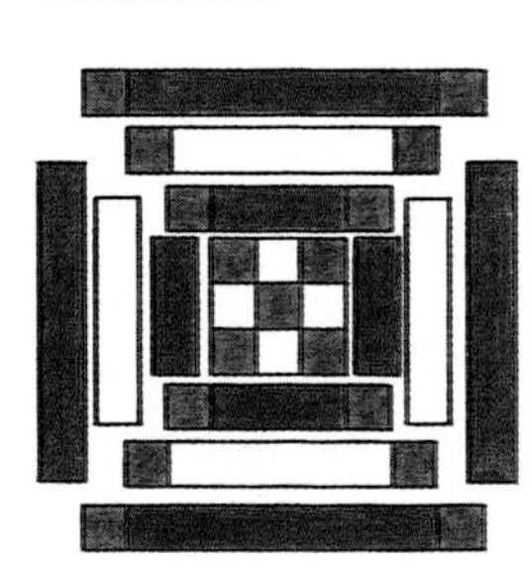

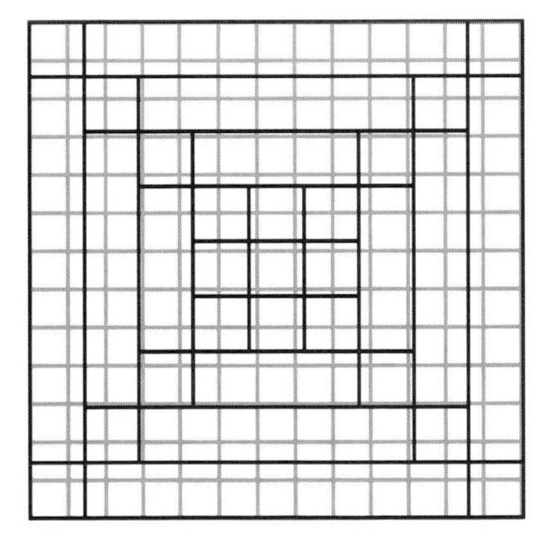

Illinois

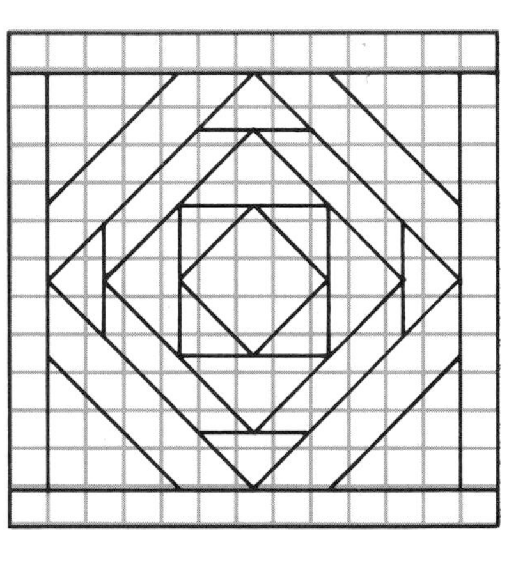

New Jersey

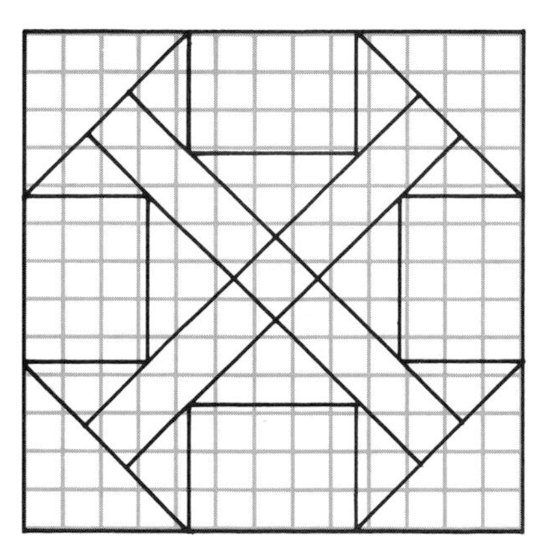

Appliqué pieces to background block.

Indiana

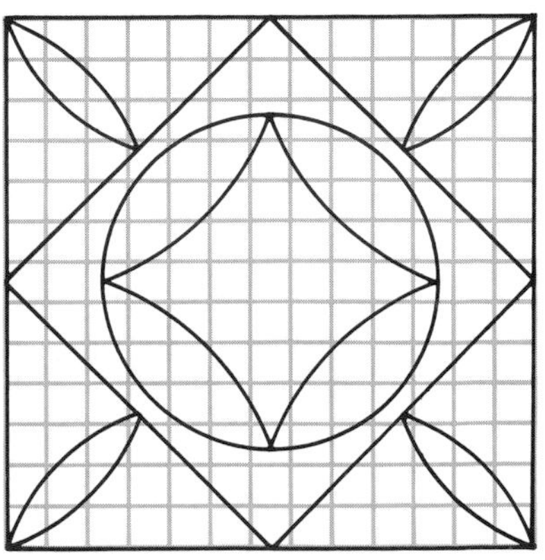

continued

Each square equals 1".

New Mexico

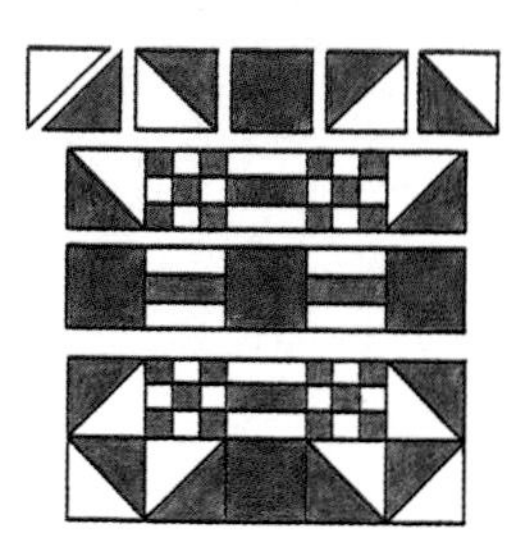

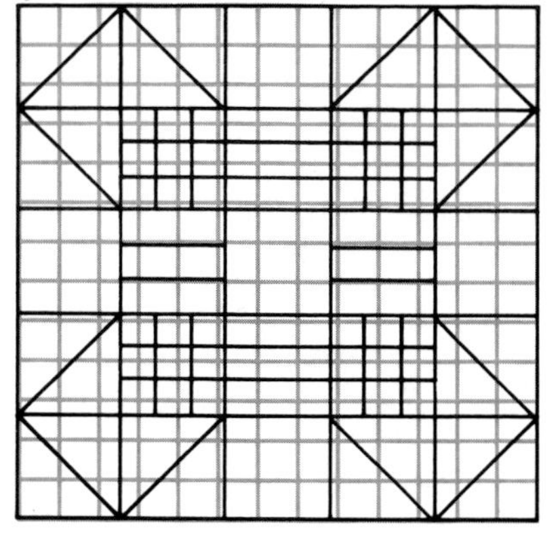

Maine

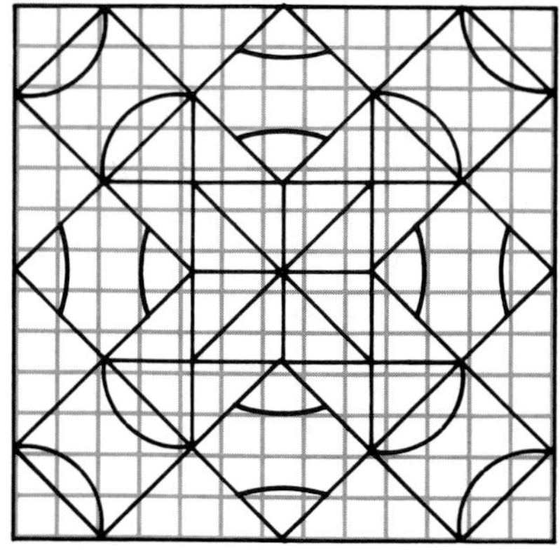

Connecticut

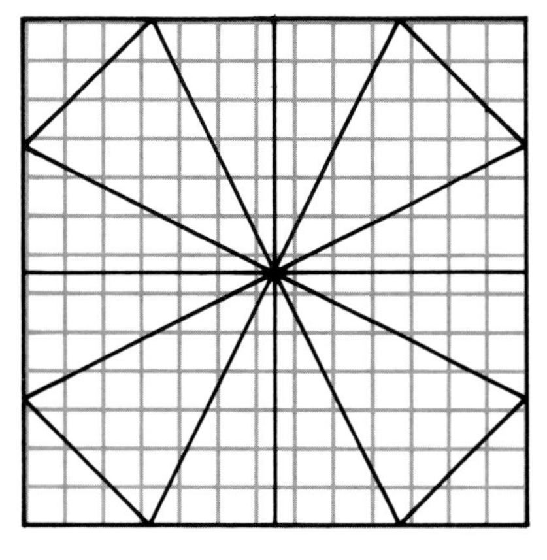

Join pieces to star and then appliqué to background block.

Texas

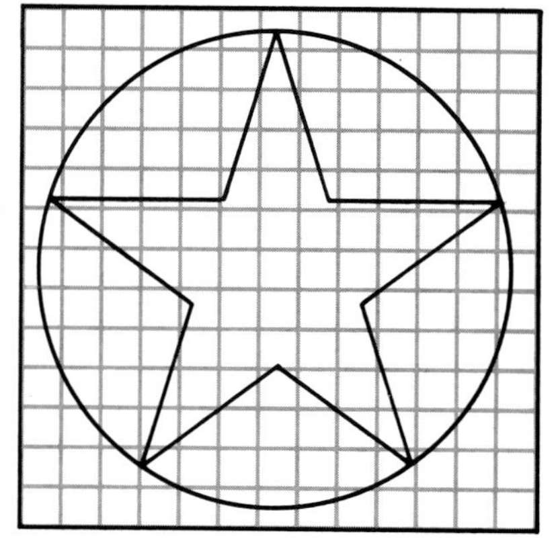

Washington, D.C.

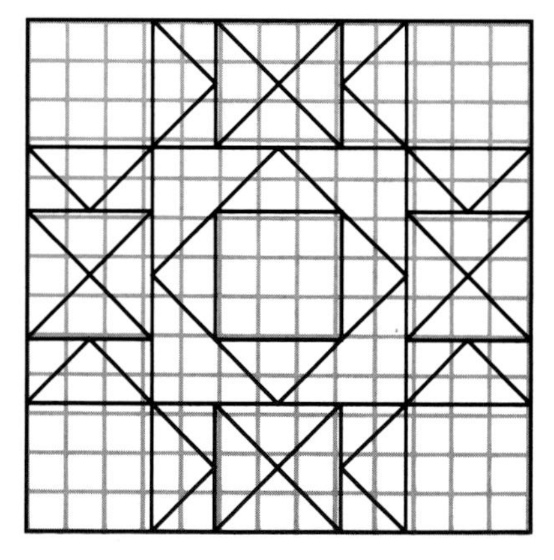

West Virginia

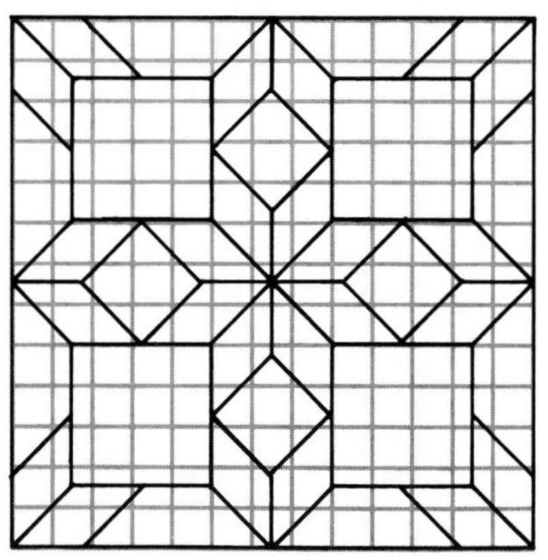

California

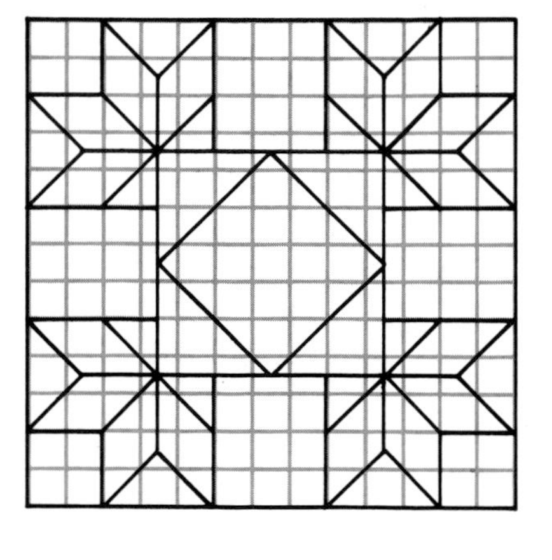

Vermont

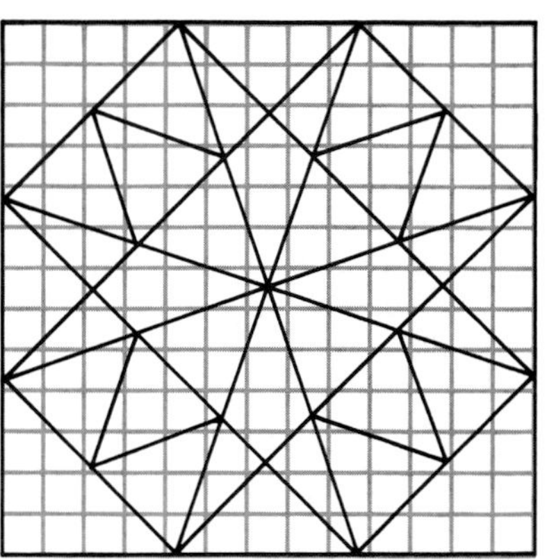

Each square equals 1″.

New Hampshire

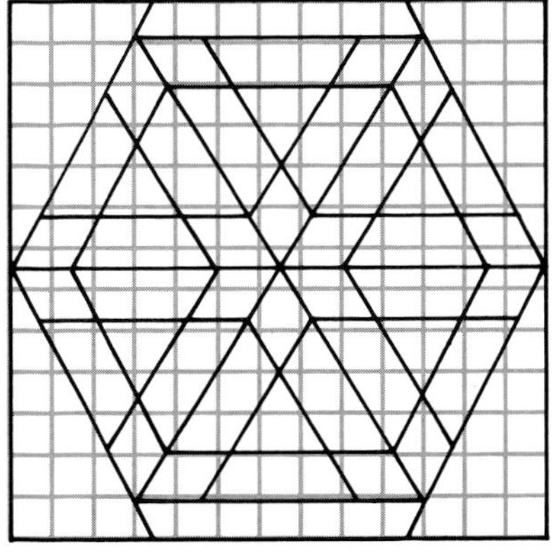

Tennessee

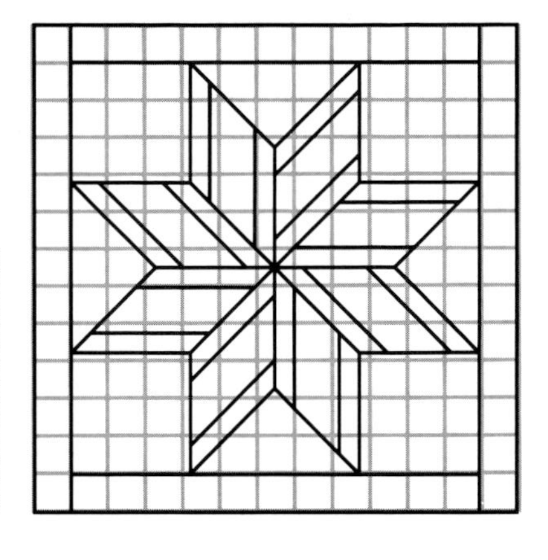

Ohio

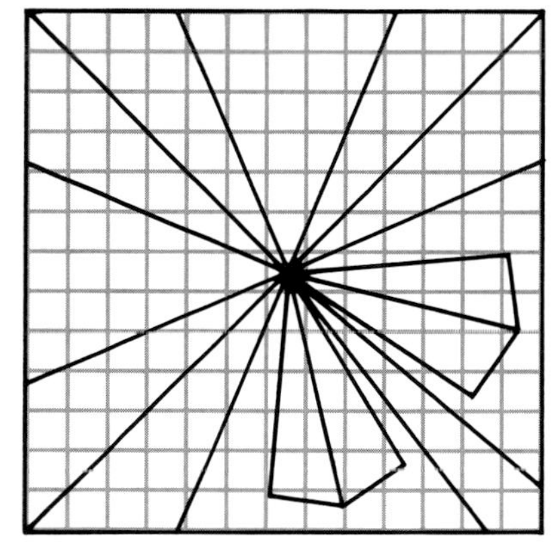

Kentucky

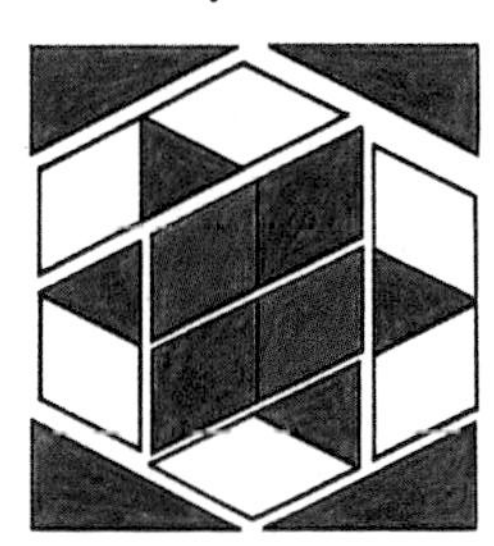

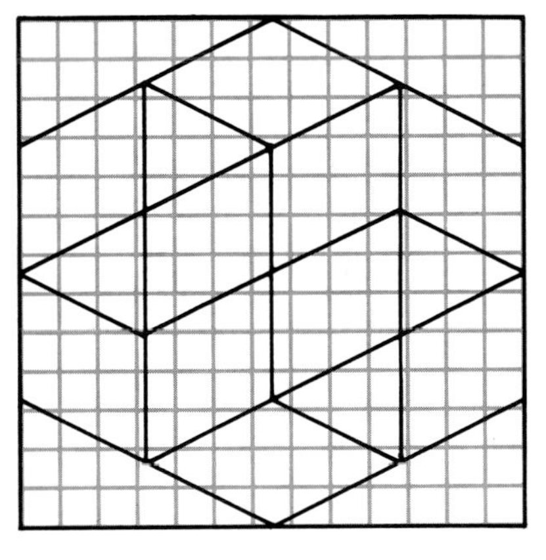

South Dakota

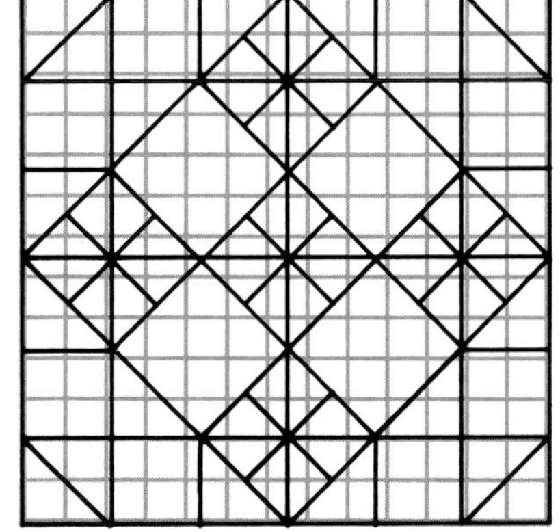

Rhode Island

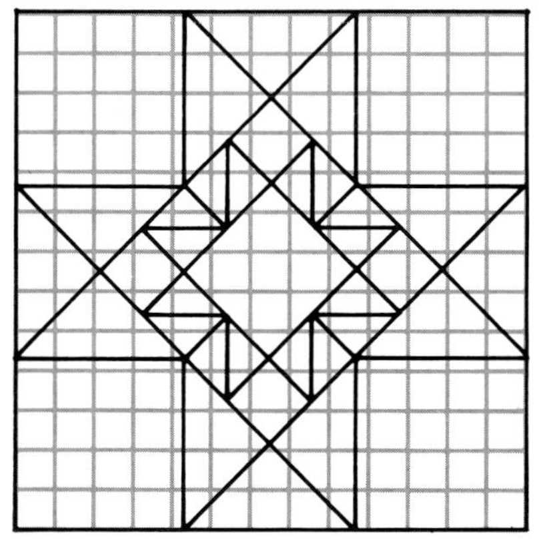

Kansas

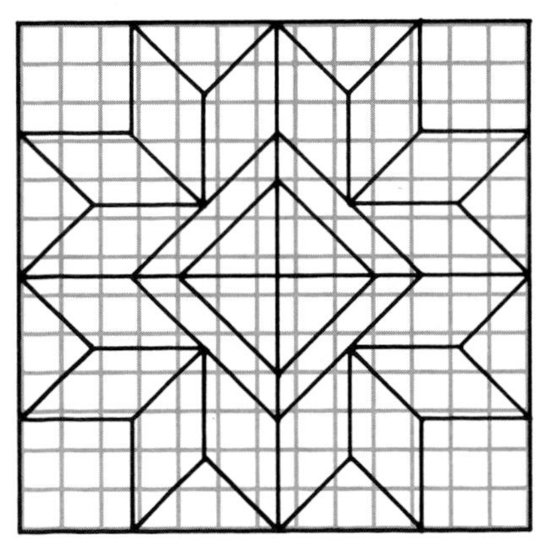

Michigan

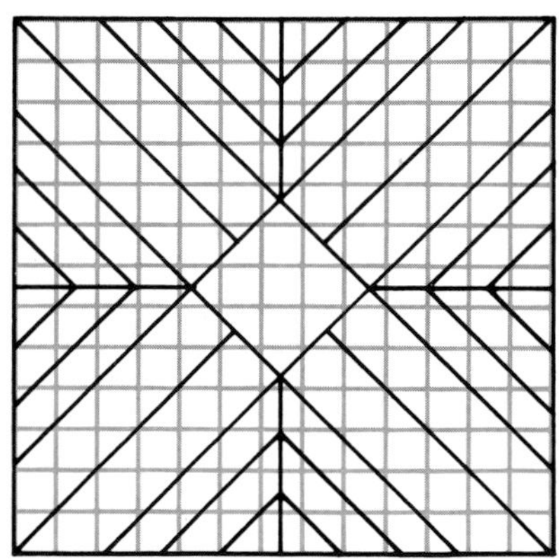

continued

Each square equals 1".

Louisiana

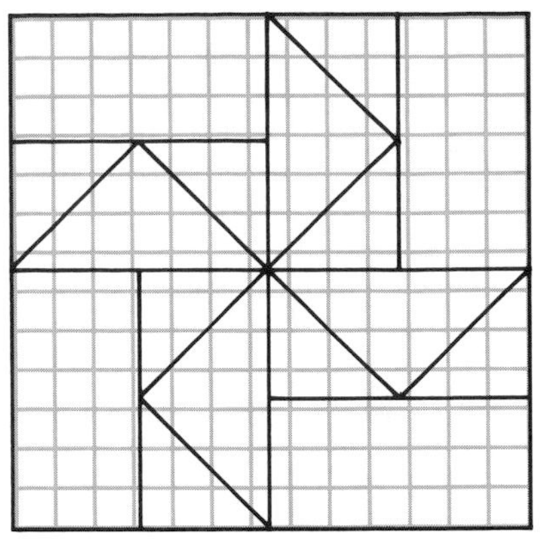

Nebraska

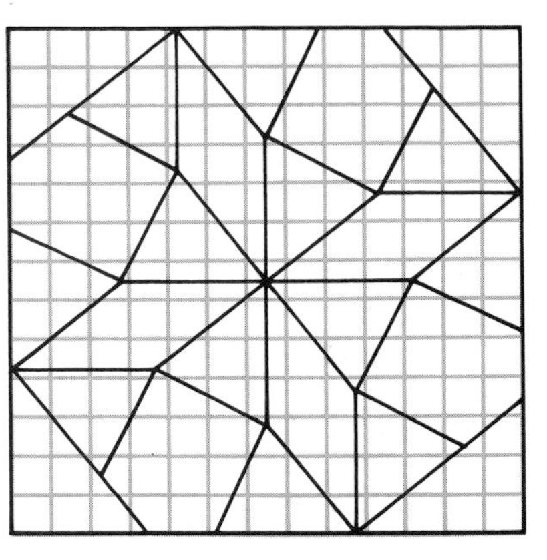

Billie's Sampler

Finished Quilt Size
84" x 114"

Number of Blocks and Finished Size
24 blocks—12" x 12"

Finished Width of Sashing—3"

Finished Width of Border—10½"

Finished Width of Top Border—7"

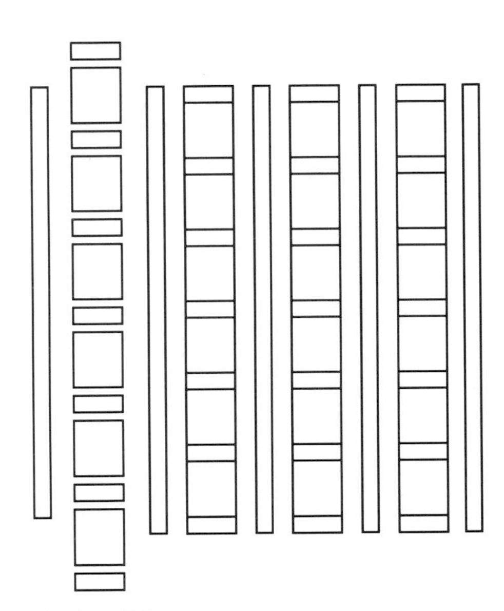

Setting Diagram

Each square equals 1".

Join pieces and then appliqué to background block.

Flower Garden

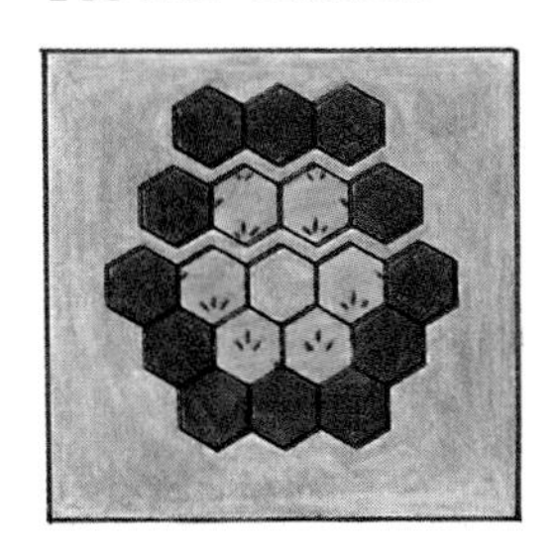

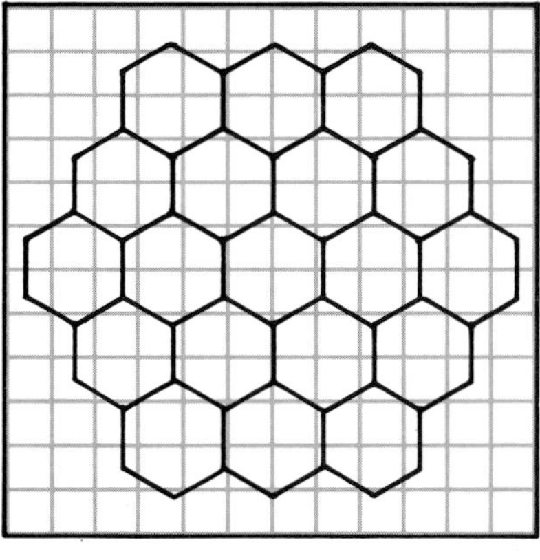

Grandmother's Fan

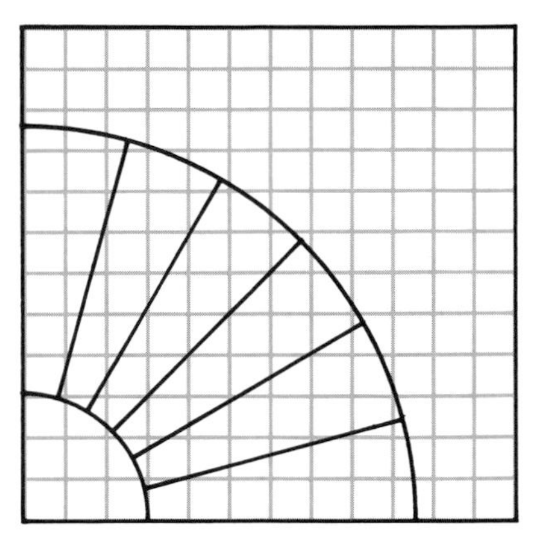

Honey Bee

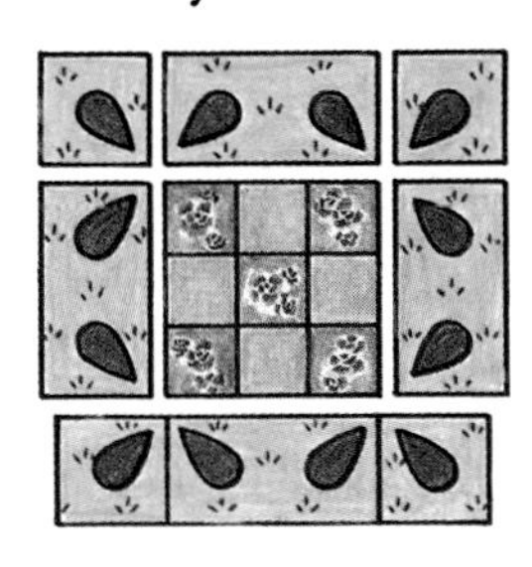

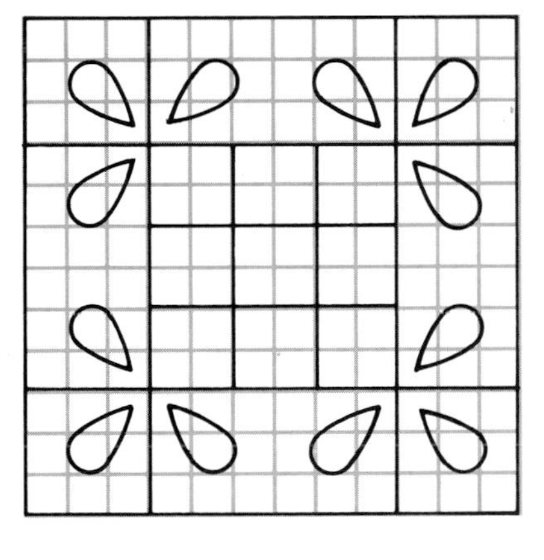

Mexican Star

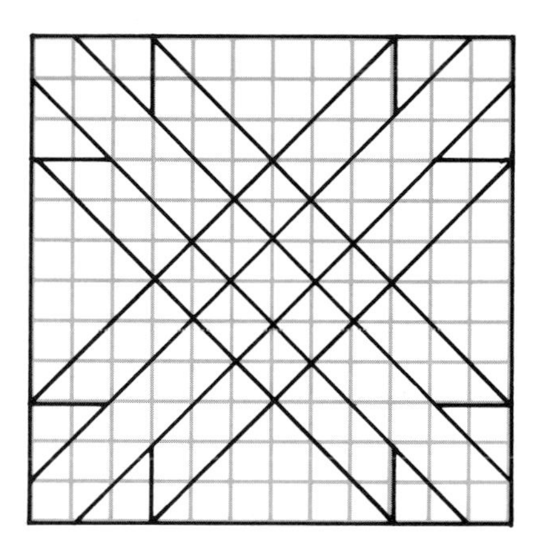

Jacob's Ladder

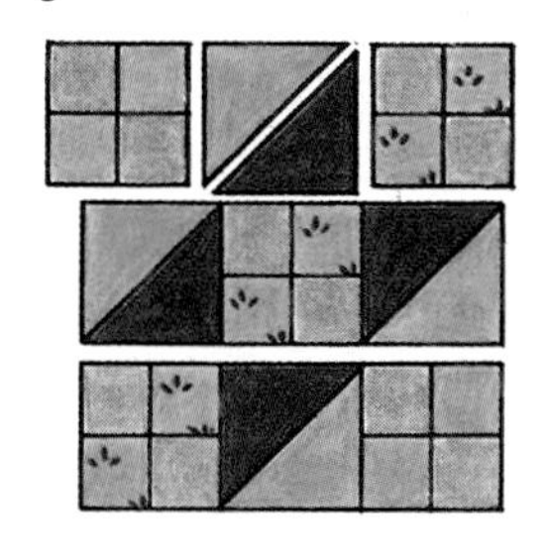

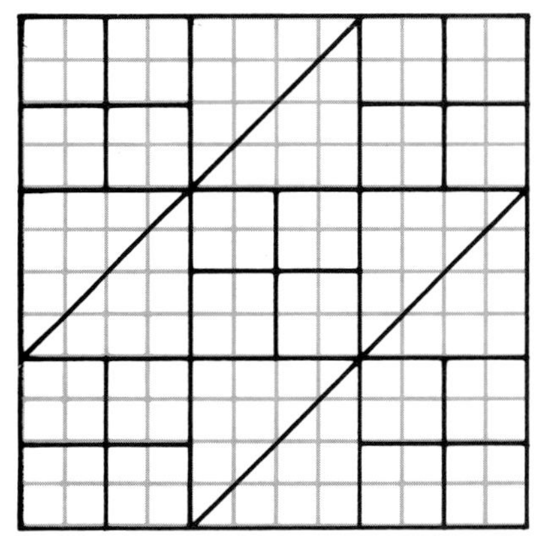

Monkey Wrench

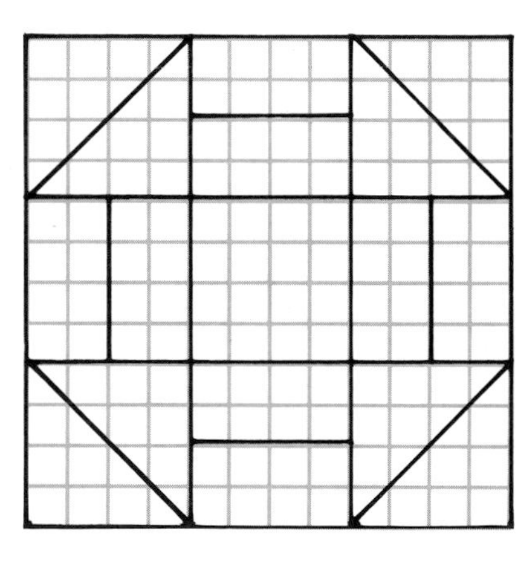

Bright Hopes

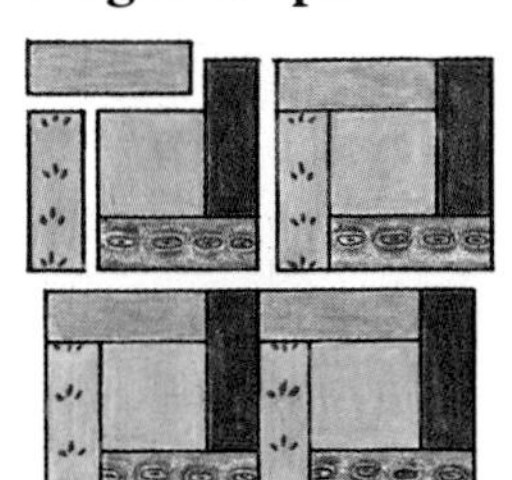

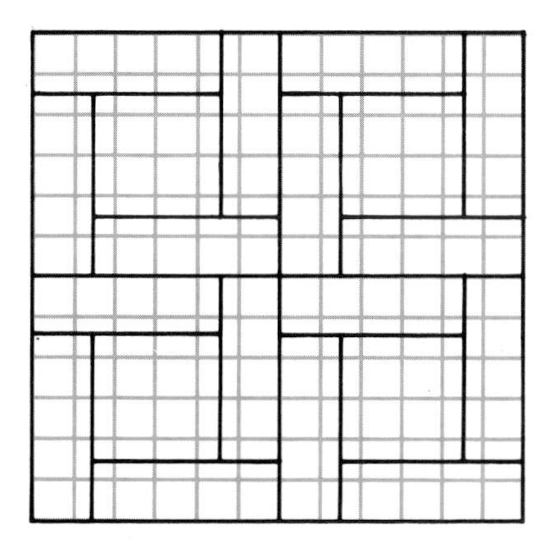

King's X

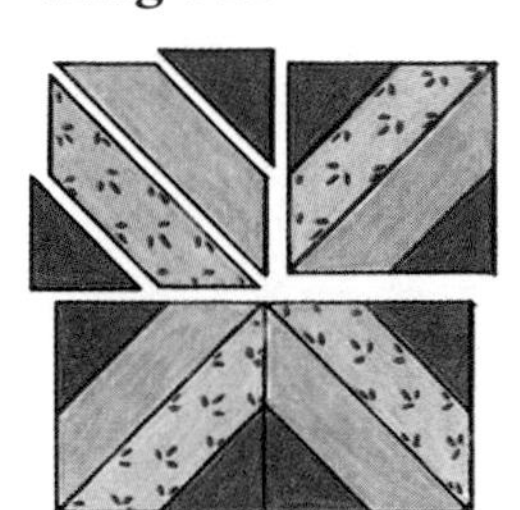

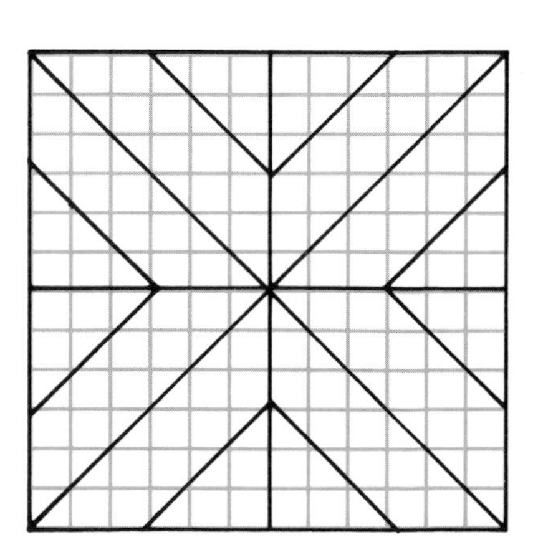

continued

Each square equals 1″.

Garden Path

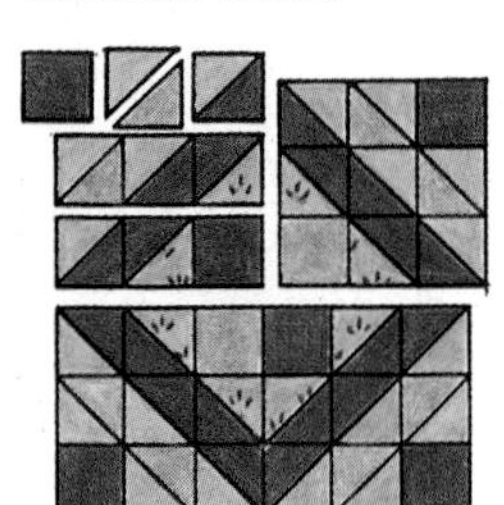

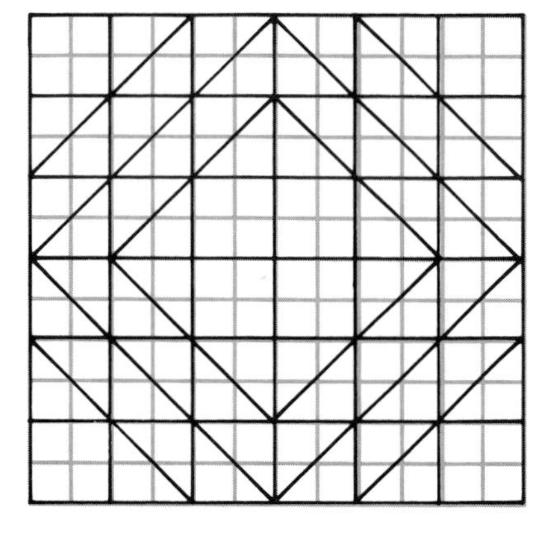

Ohio Star

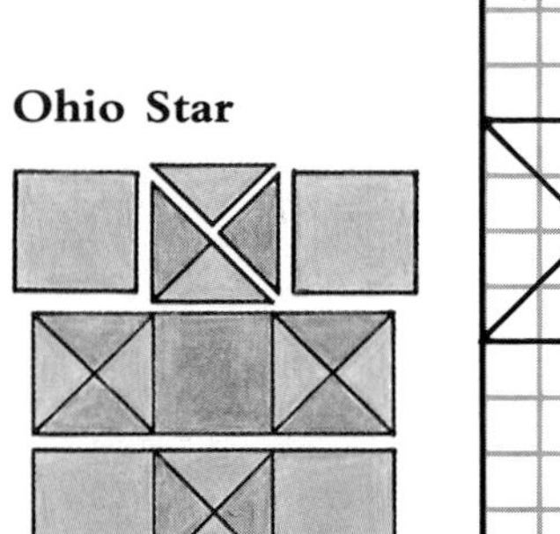

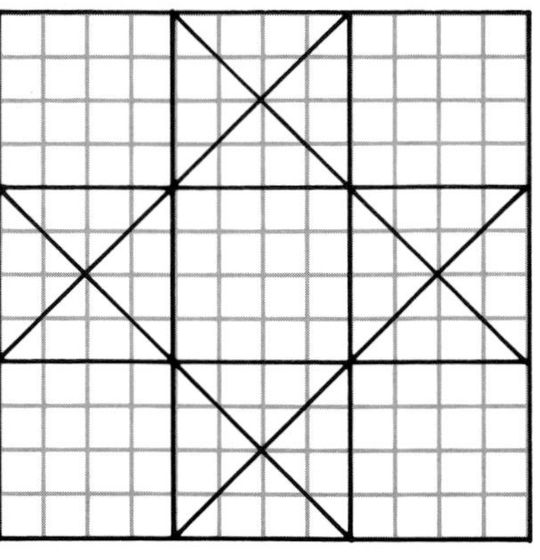

Rail Fence

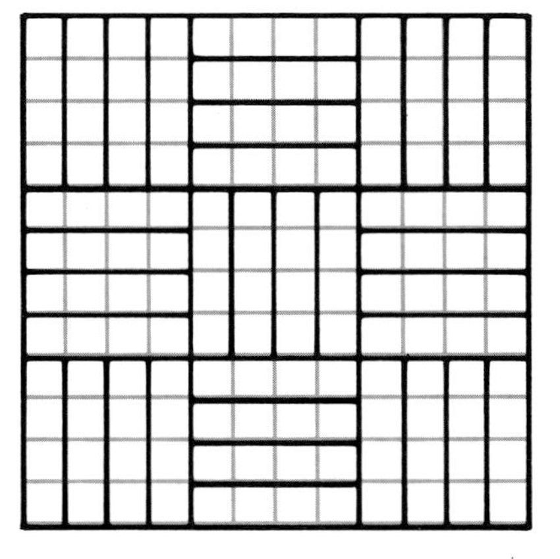

First join segments. Next appliqué to background block. Then appliqué circle to block.

Dresden Plate

Dutchman's Puzzle

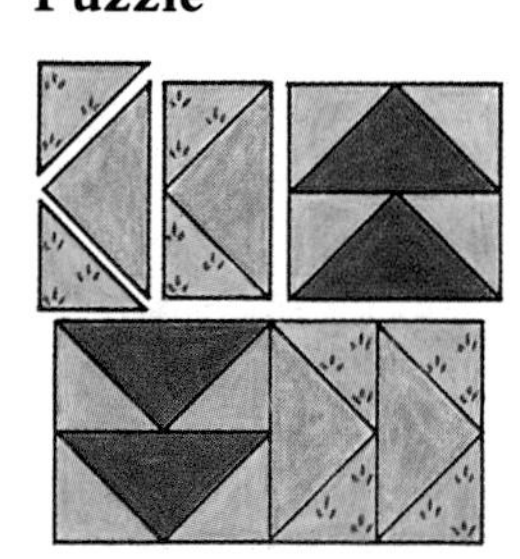

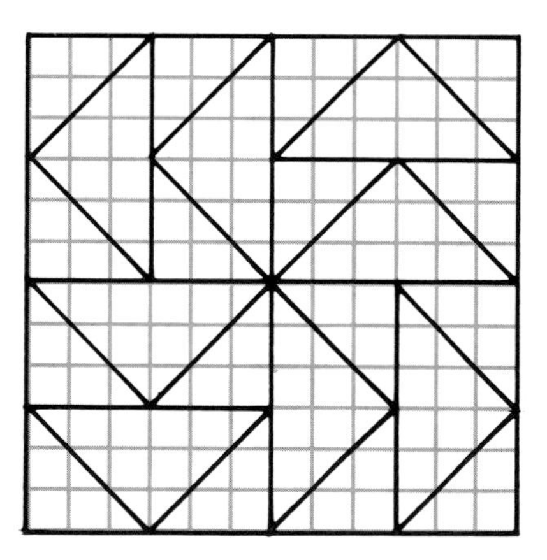

Night and Noon

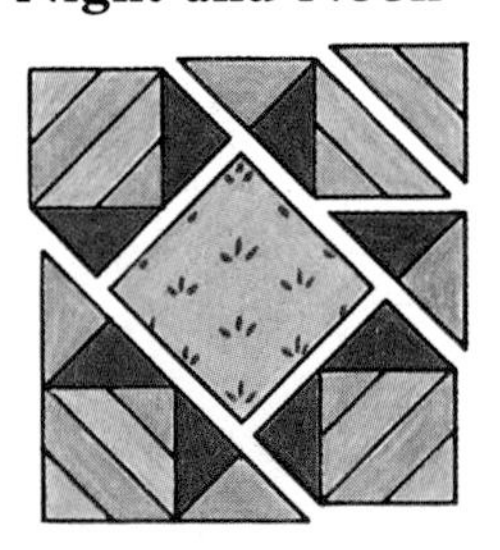

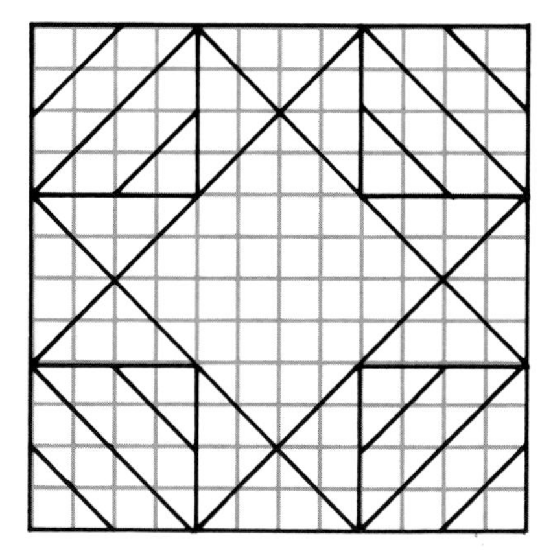

Kansas Dugout

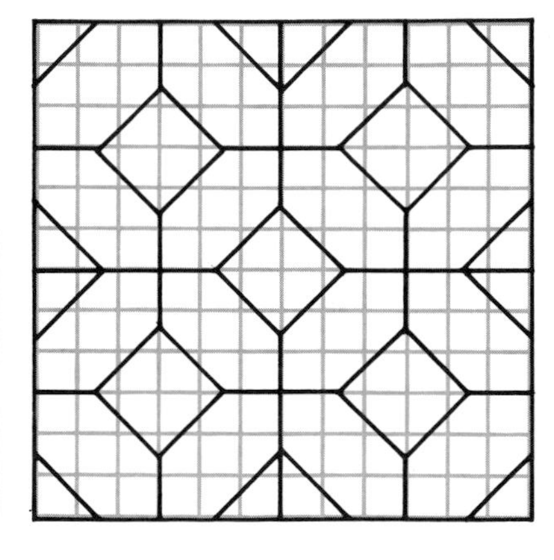

Windmill Variation

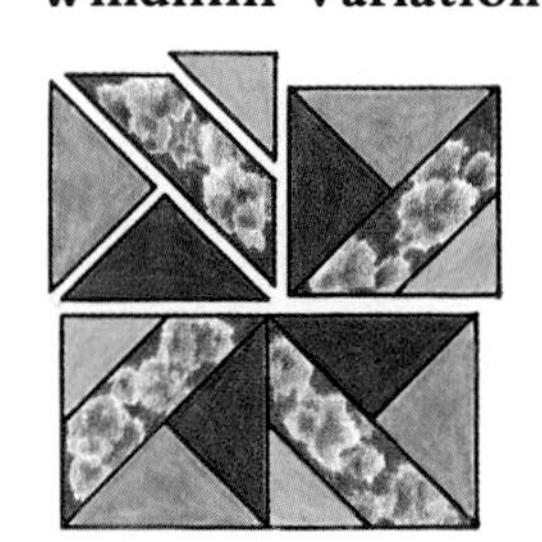

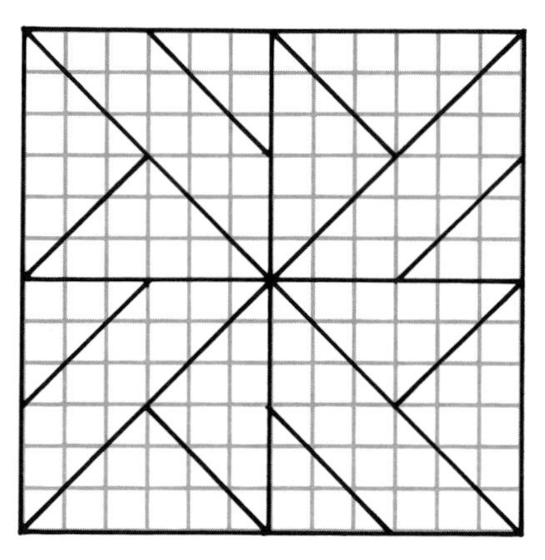

Each square equals 1".

Appliqué pieces to background block.

Bridal Wreath

Patience Corner

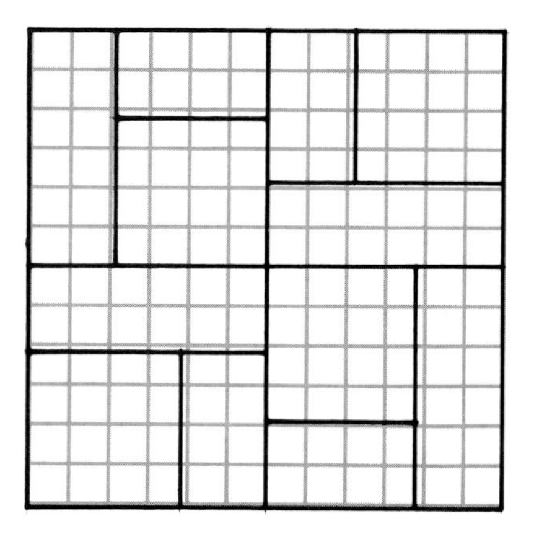

Framed Square

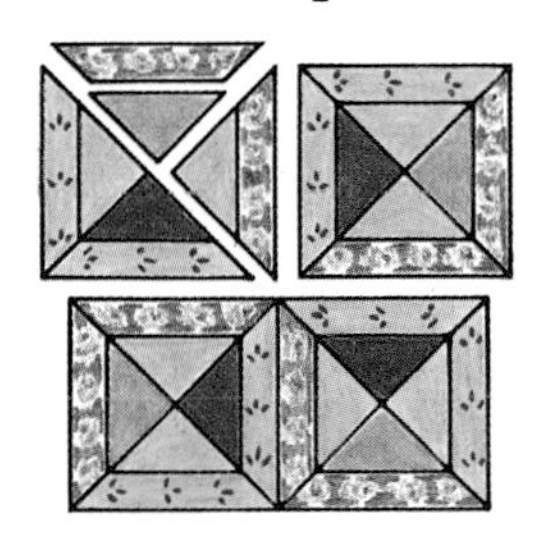

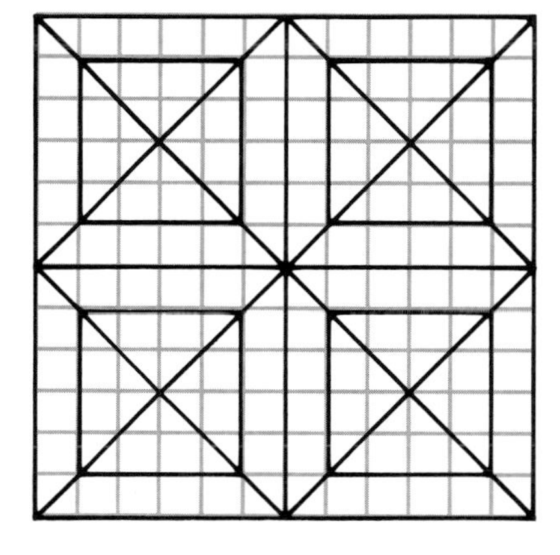

Morning Star

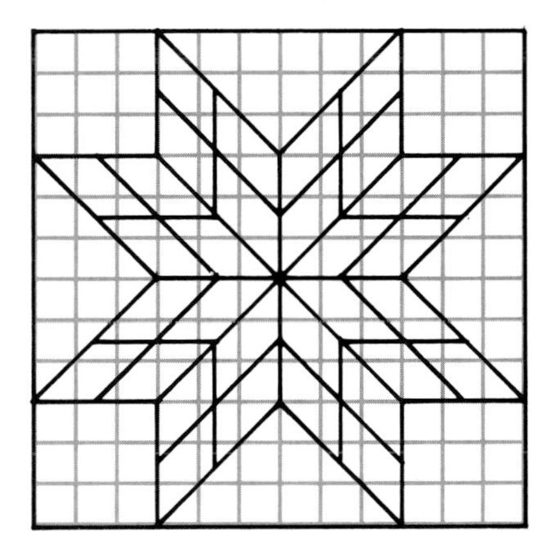

Drunkard's Path

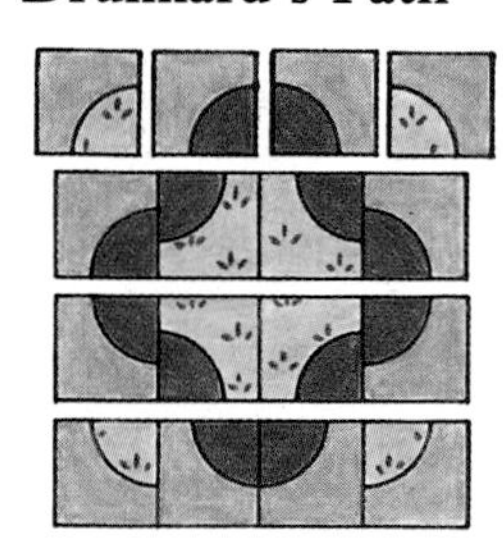

Card Trick

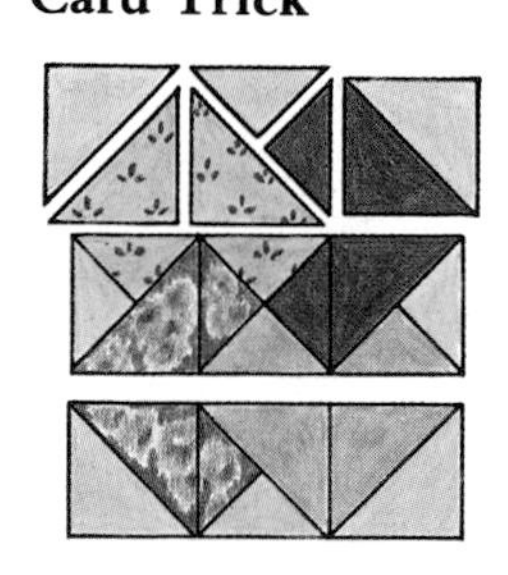

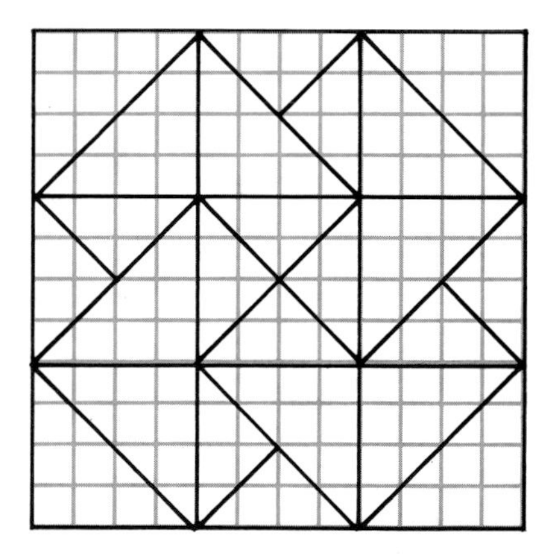

Flying Geese

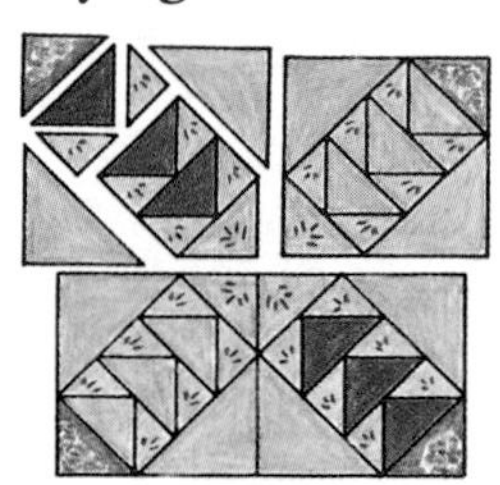

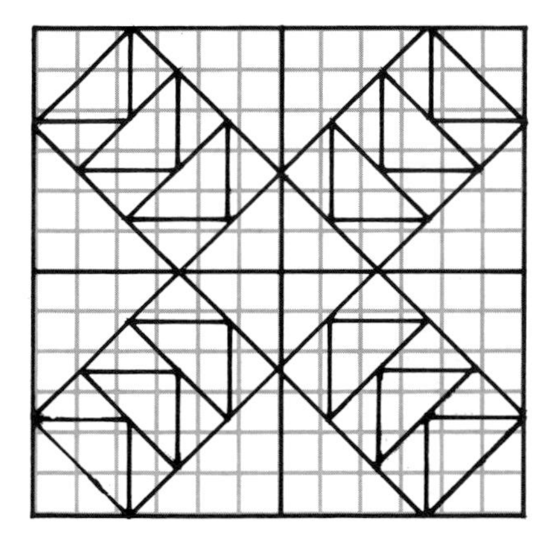

Tree

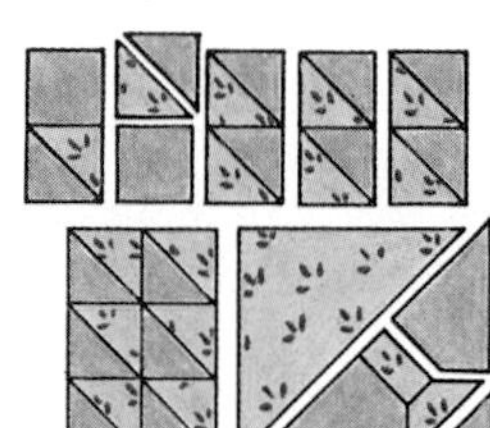

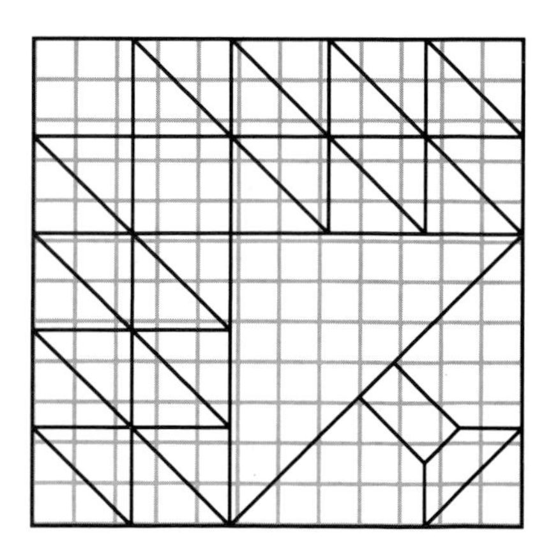

Most Beautiful Star

Sampler Block Border

Number of Blocks and Finished Size
32 blocks—6" x 6"

Finished Width of Border Strips—¾"

Sampler Block Border Assembly
Set sampler blocks of equal size between navy paisley triangles, as shown in Sampler Block Border Piecing Diagram. Make 4 borders and 4 corner sections, as shown. Join to medallion.

Join narrow border strips of maroon print and navy print II, respectively, to quilt, as shown in quilt photograph.

Finished Edges
Bind with navy paisley fabric.

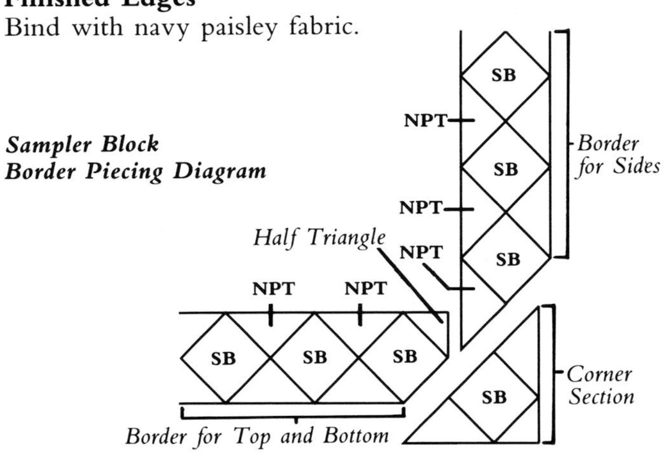

Sampler Block Border Piecing Diagram

SB = Sampler Block
NPT = Navy Paisley Triangle

Each square equals 1".

Morning Star

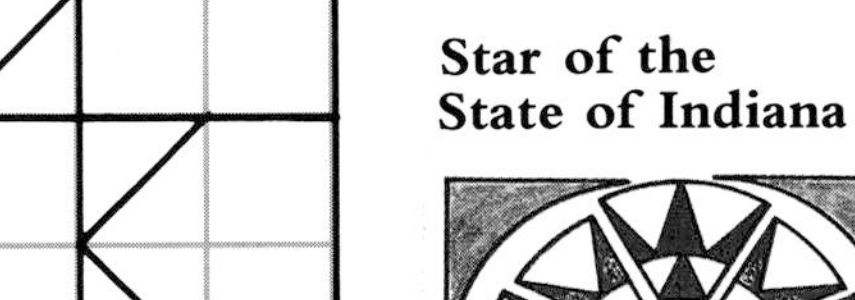

Star of the State of Indiana

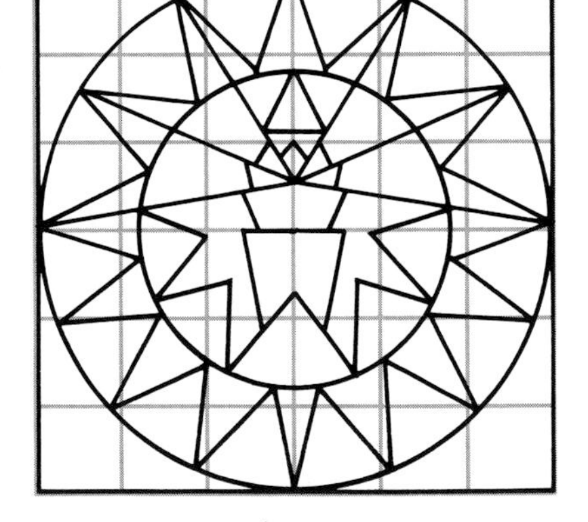

Blocks and Star

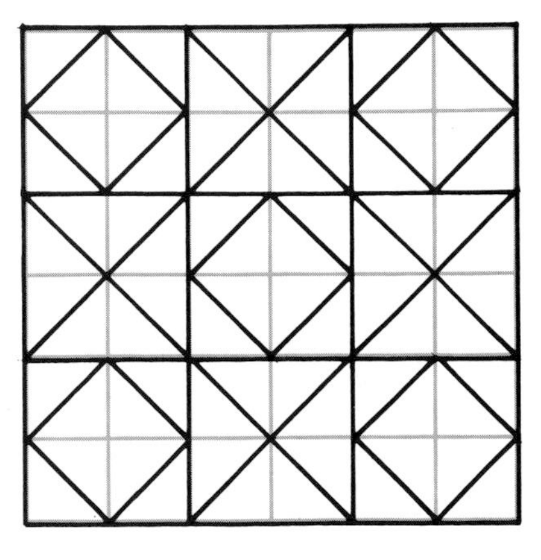

Stardust

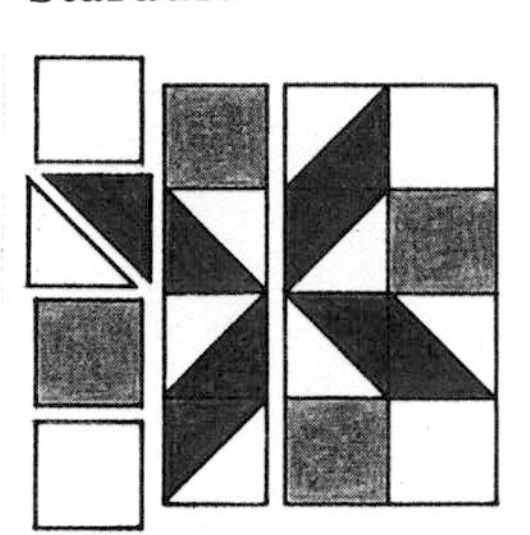

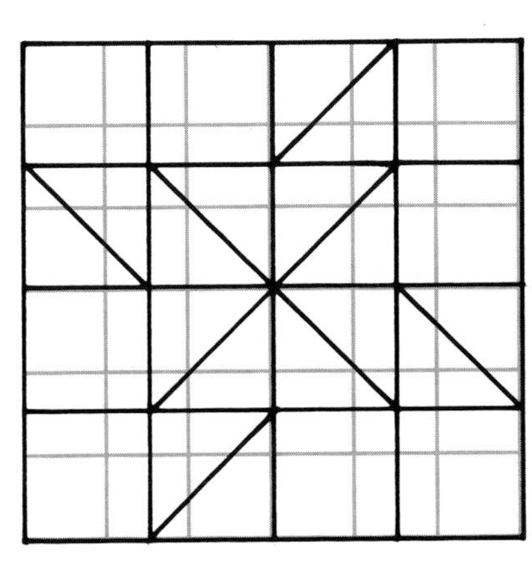

Each square equals 1".

Mexican Star

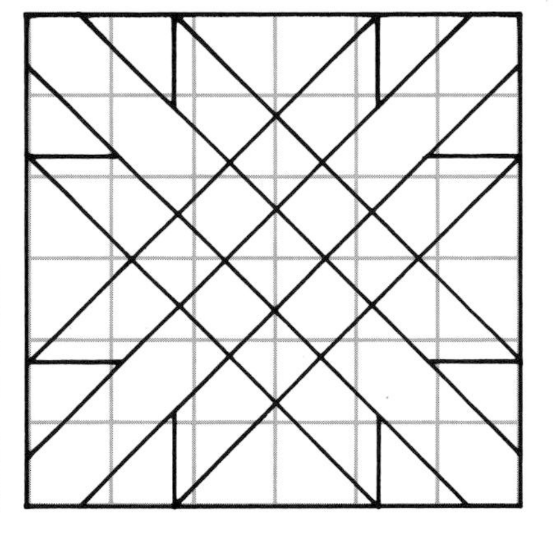

Friendship Star

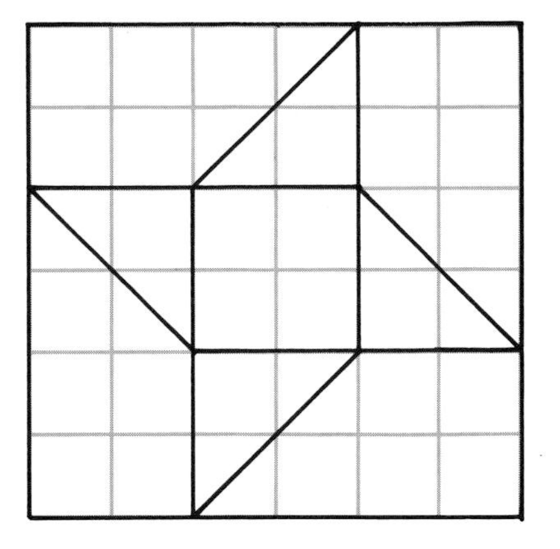

Morning Star

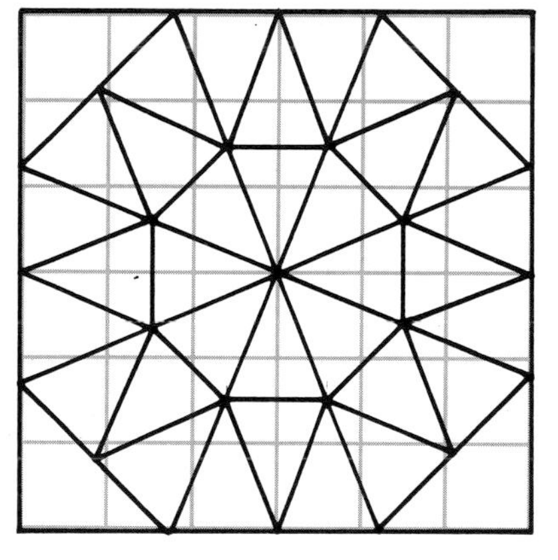

Maltese Star

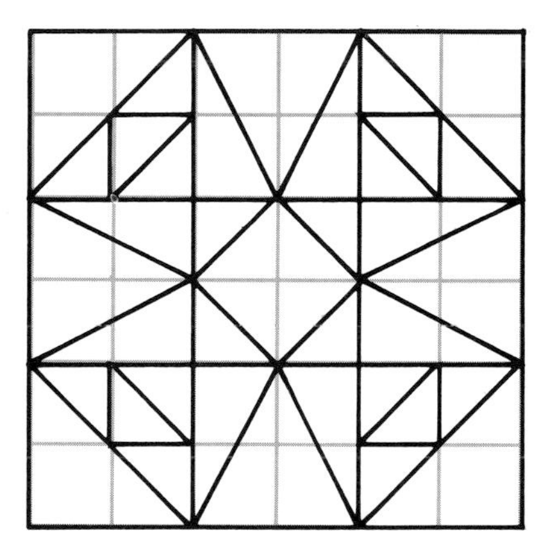

Star of the City of Indianapolis

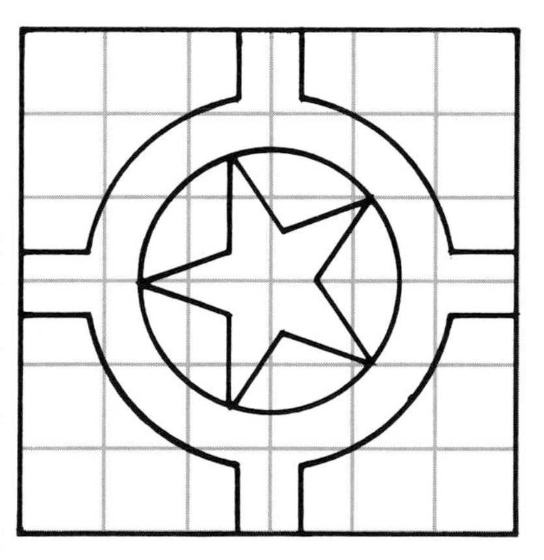

Star of the Milky Way

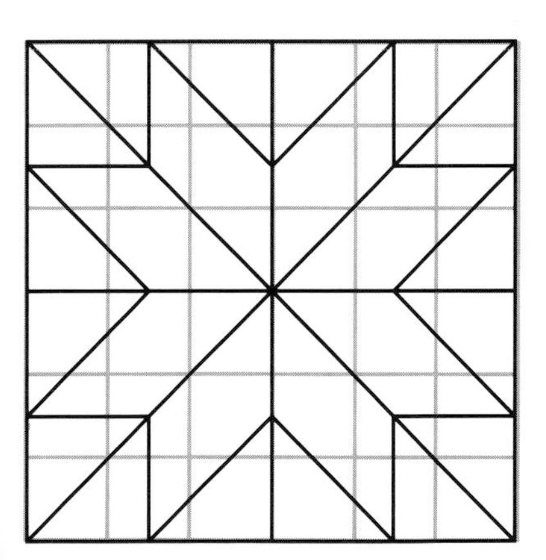

Summer Stars

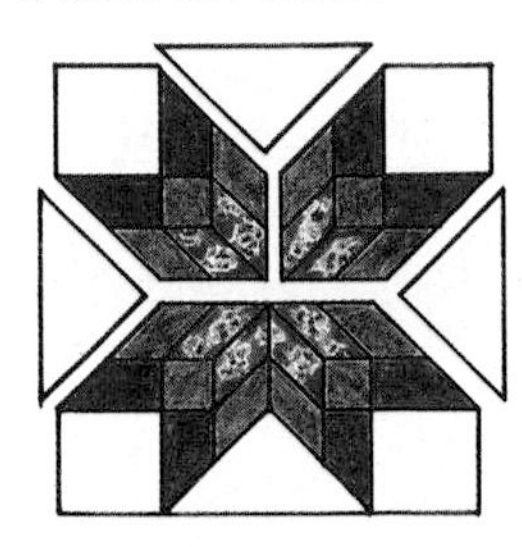

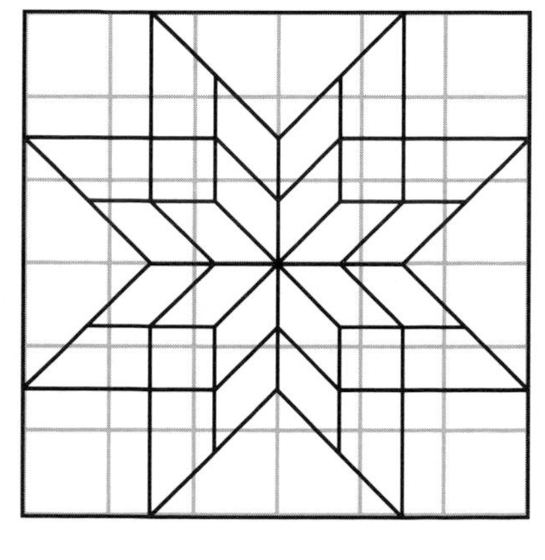

French Star

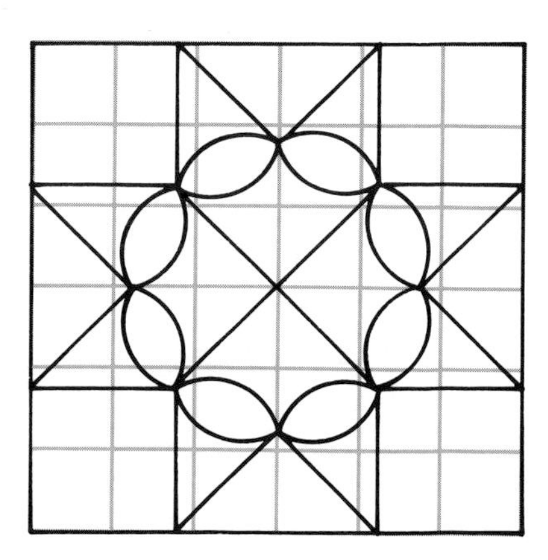

continued

Each square equals 1".

LeMoyne Star

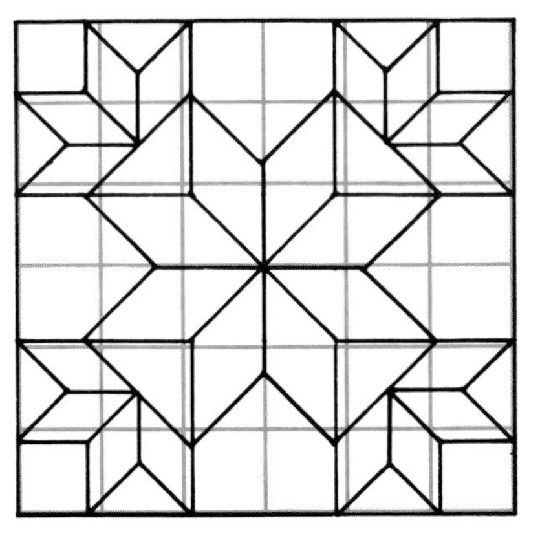

Star in a Star

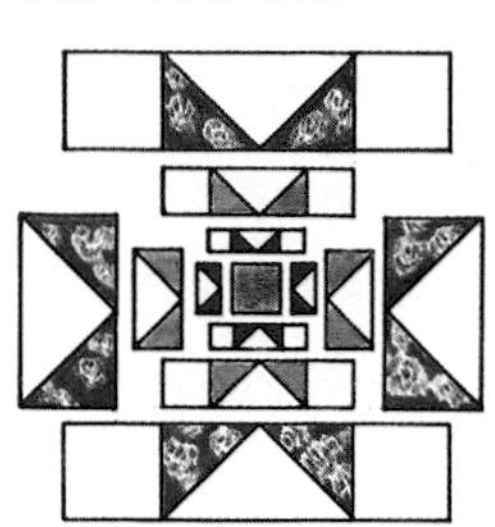

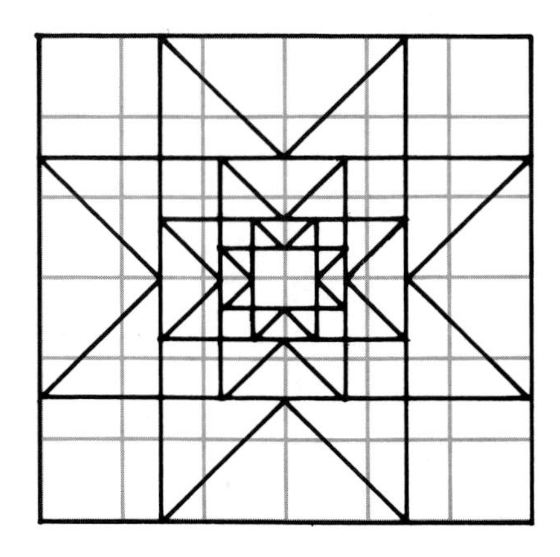

Star of White River Park

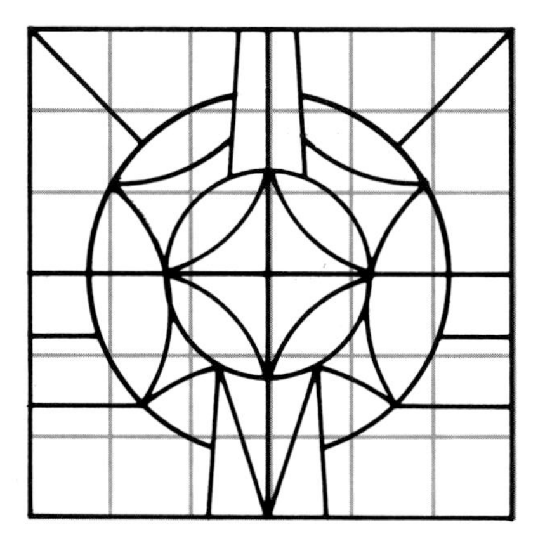

Falling Star

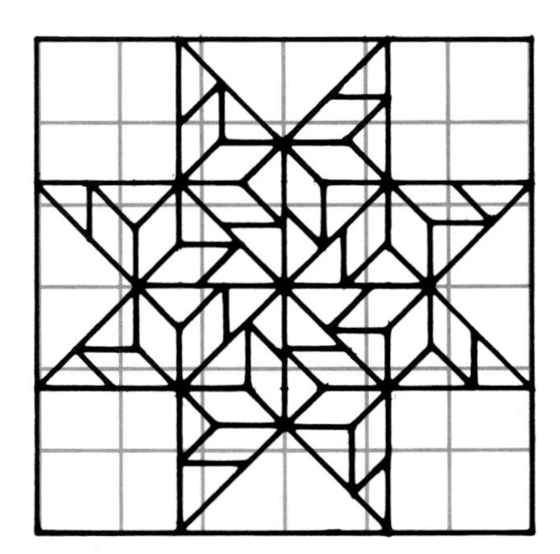

Lemon Star

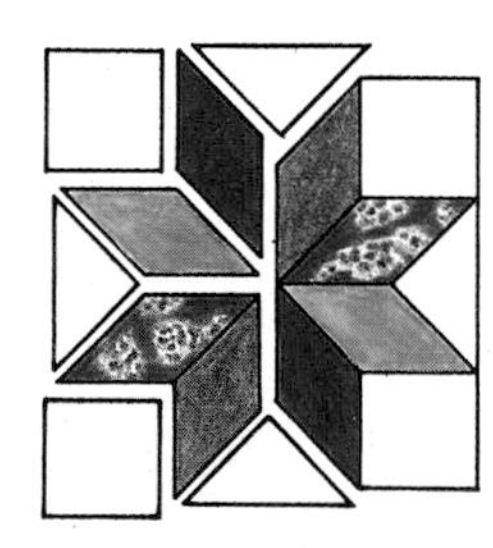

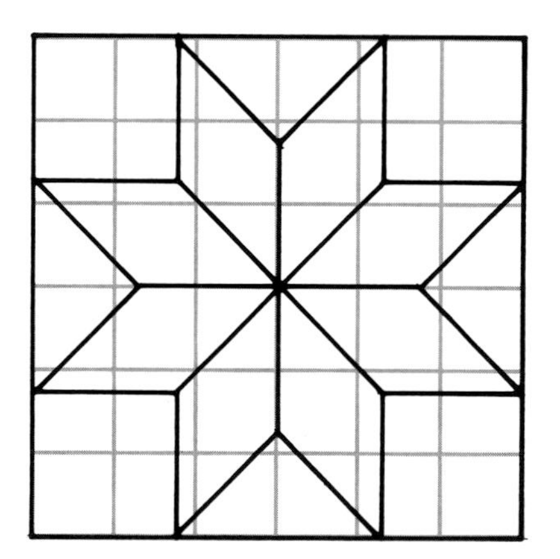

Royal Star

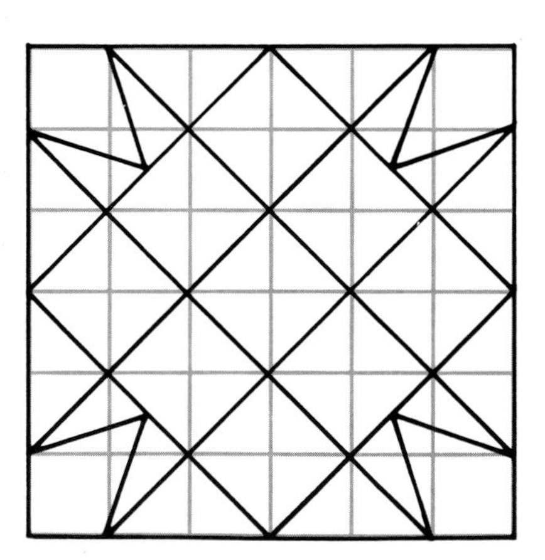

Variable Star

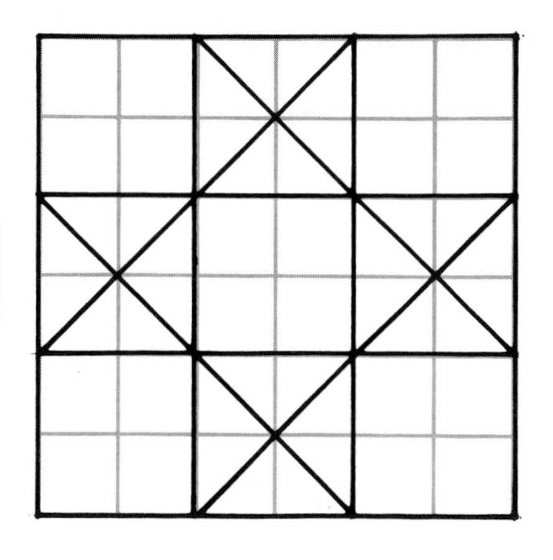

Bright Star

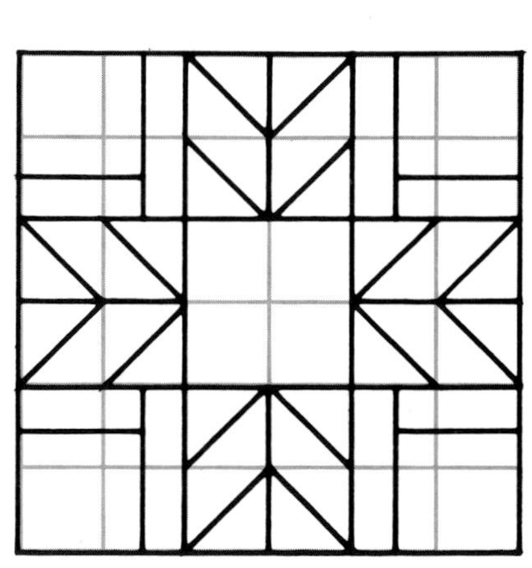

Each square equals 1".

Blazing Star

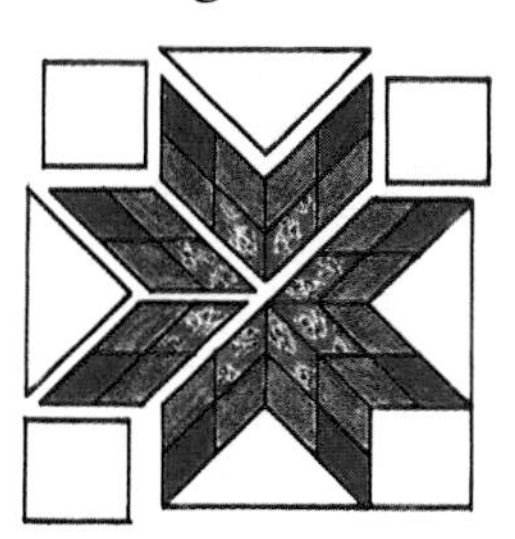

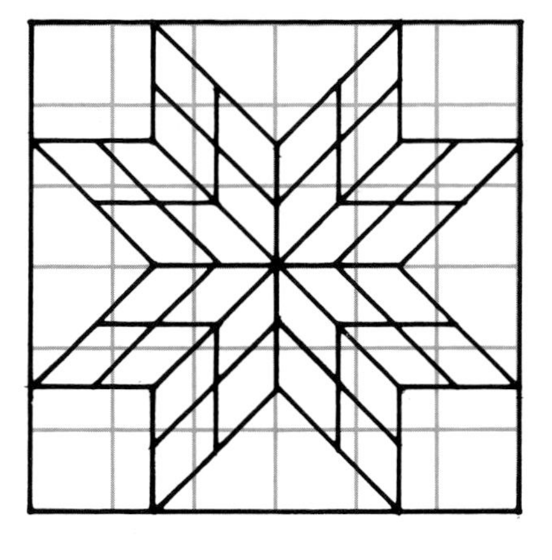

Log Cabin Star

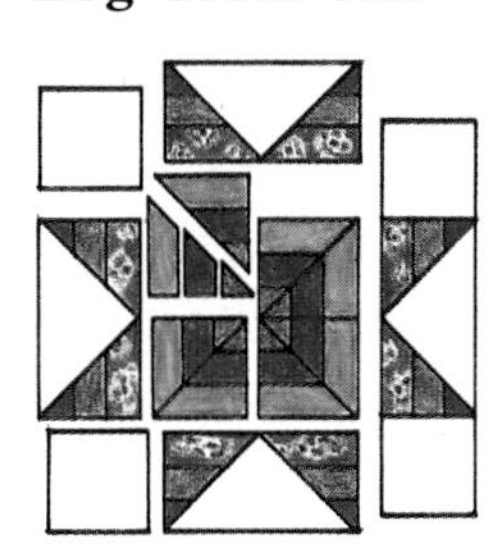

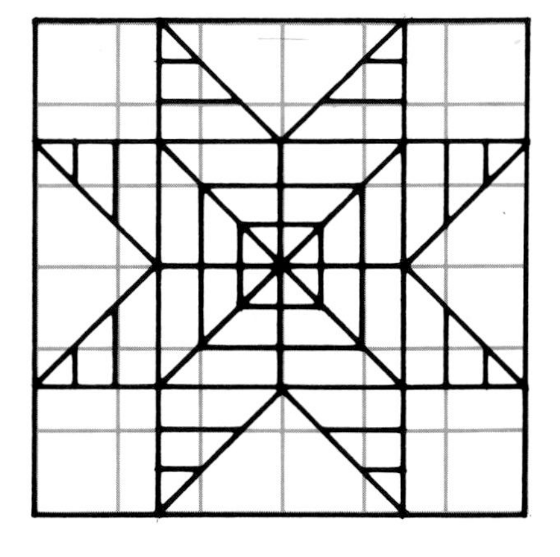

Rolling Star

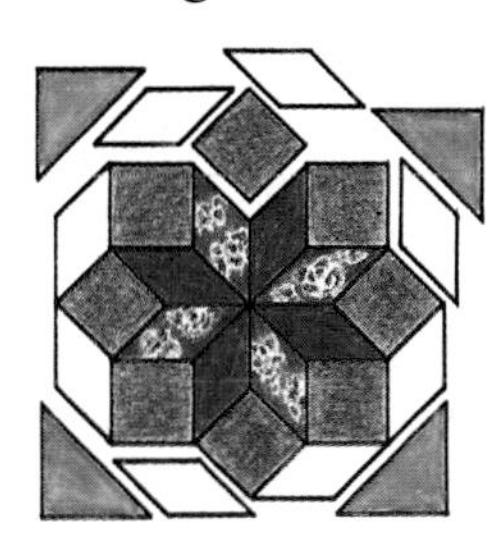

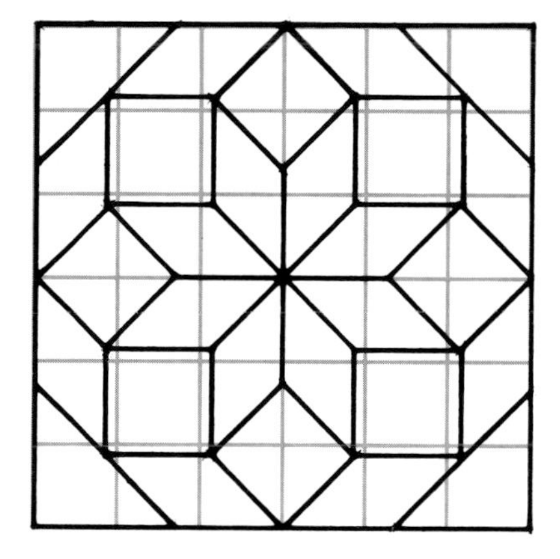

Eccentric Star

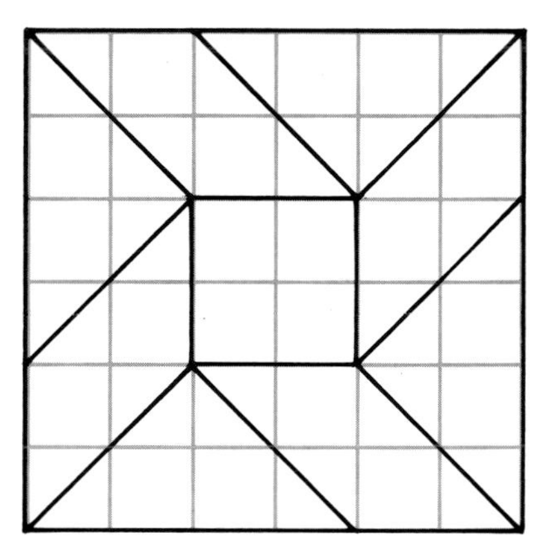

Feathered Star

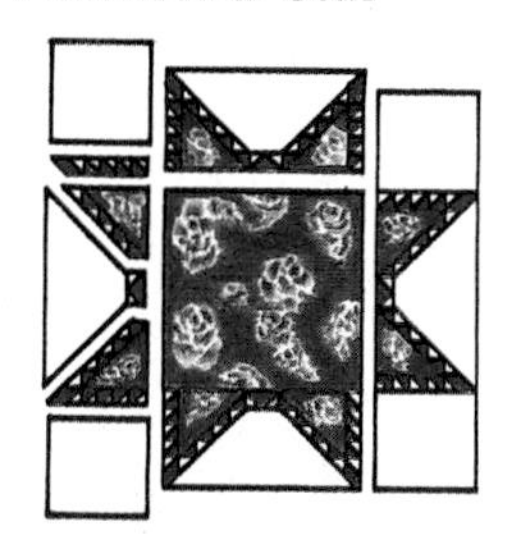

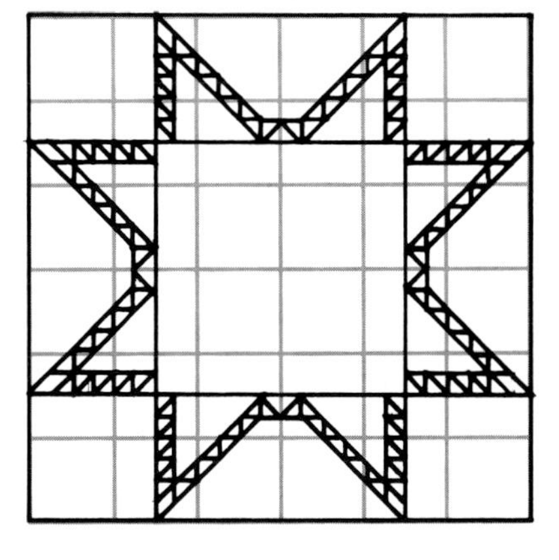

Mother's Fancy Star

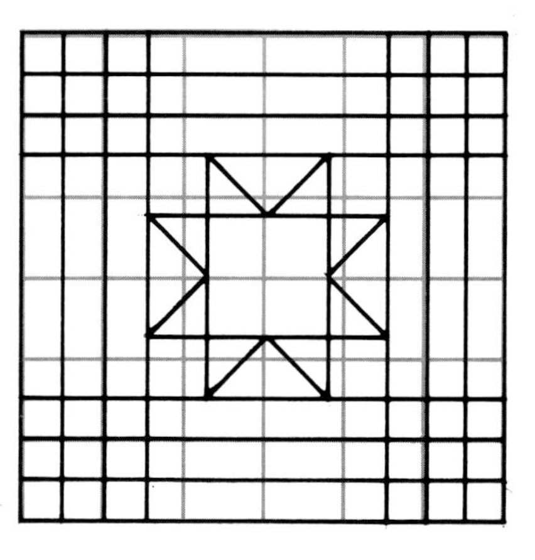

Beautiful Star

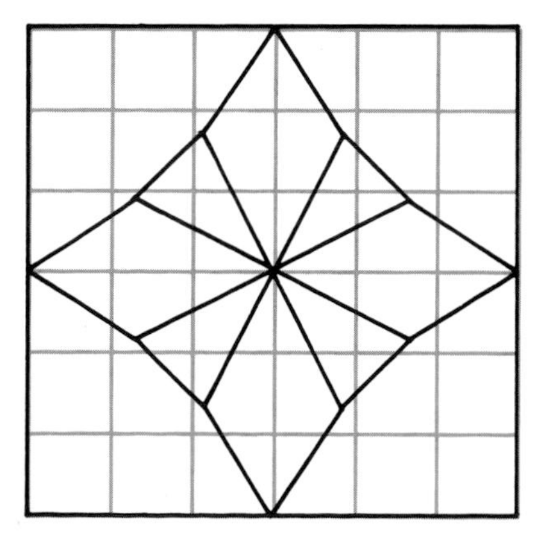

Liberty Star

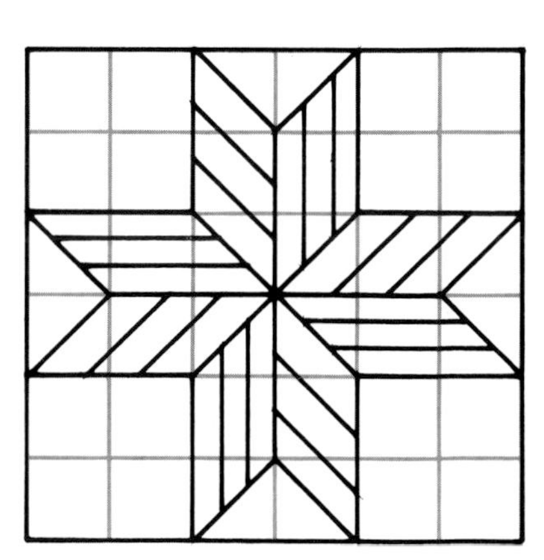

continued

Each square equals 1″.

Pieced Star

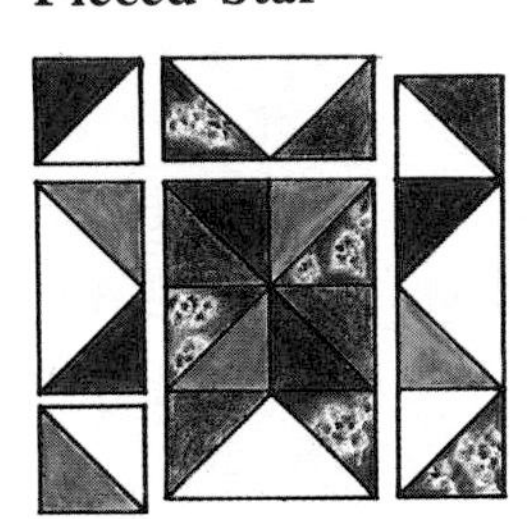

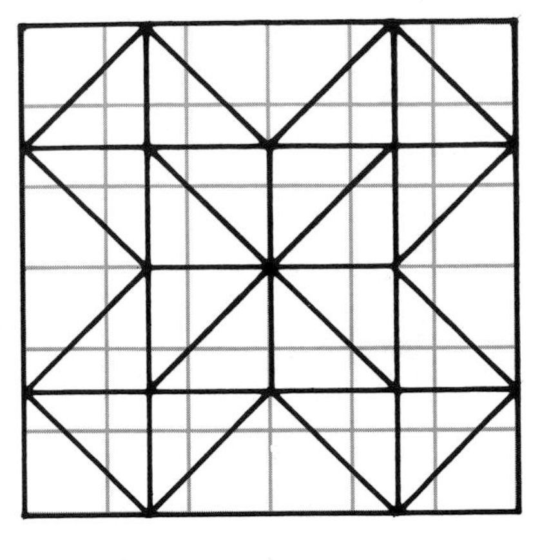

Four X Star

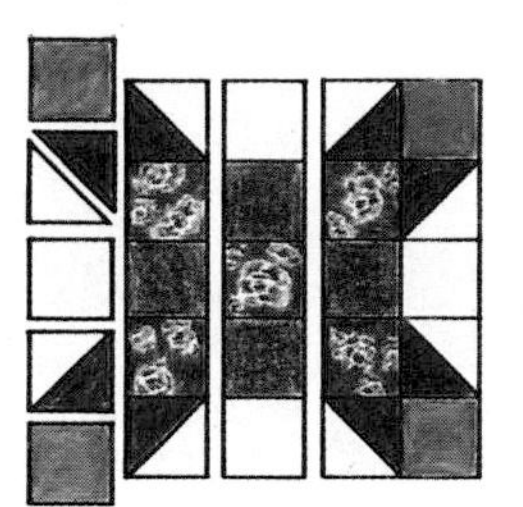

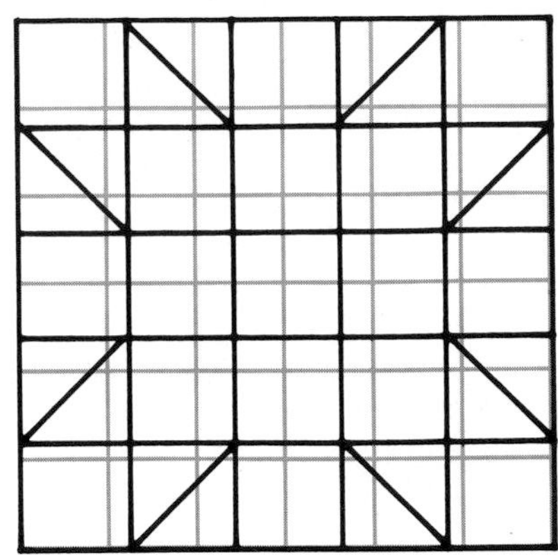

Block Setting Diagram

1	2	7	2	12
2	5	2	10	2
3	2	8	2	13
2	6	2	11	2
4	2	9	2	14

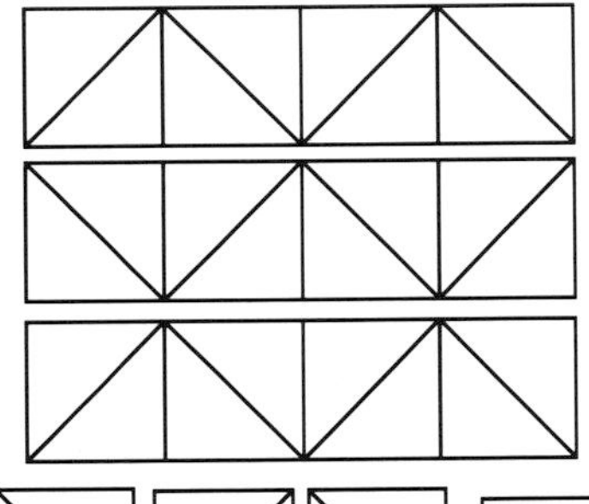

Basic Block Piecing Diagram
The pieced-squares arrangement shown here is for blocks 1, 7, 9, 12, 13, and 14.

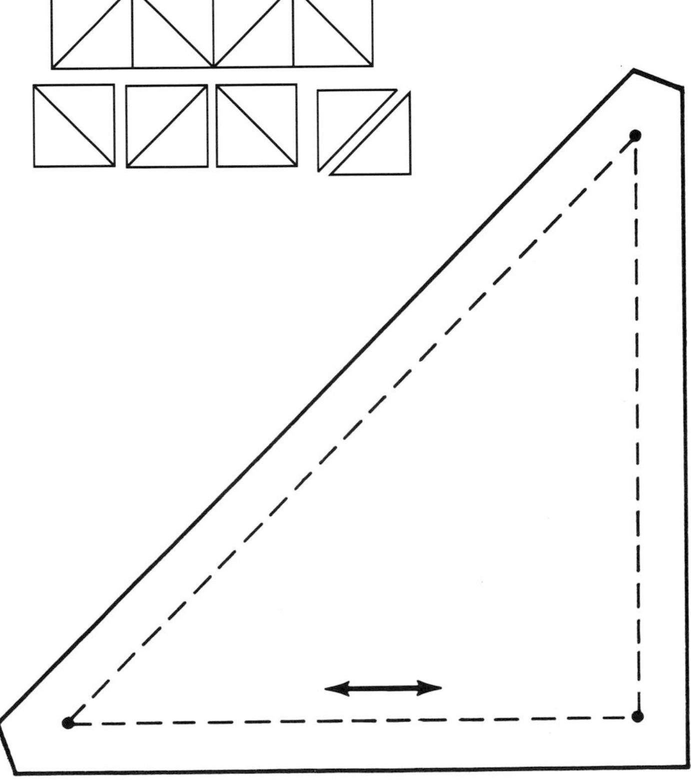

Hidden Sampler

Finished Quilt Size
66″ x 66″

Number of Sampler Blocks and Finished Size
13 blocks—12″ x 12″

Number of Green Blocks and Finished Size
12 blocks—12″ x 12″

Finished Width of Border—3″

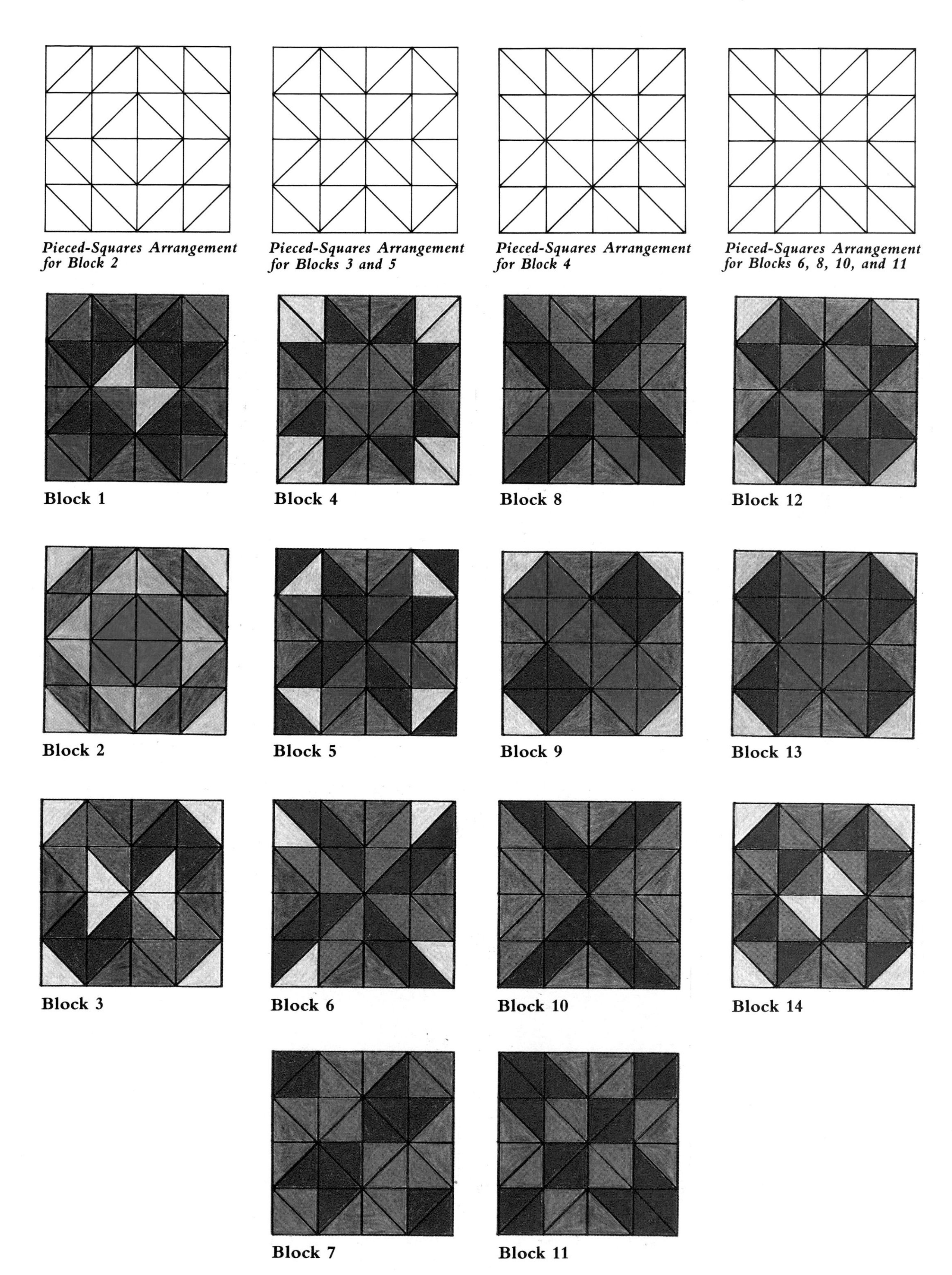
Pieced-Squares Arrangement for Block 2
Pieced-Squares Arrangement for Blocks 3 and 5
Pieced-Squares Arrangement for Block 4
Pieced-Squares Arrangement for Blocks 6, 8, 10, and 11
Block 1
Block 4
Block 8
Block 12
Block 2
Block 5
Block 9
Block 13
Block 3
Block 6
Block 10
Block 14
Block 7
Block 11

Amish Sampler Friendship Quilt

Finished Quilt Size
86″ x 95″

Number of Sampler Blocks and Finished Size
12 blocks—12″ x 12″

Finished Width of Sashing—3″

Finished Width of Border—4″

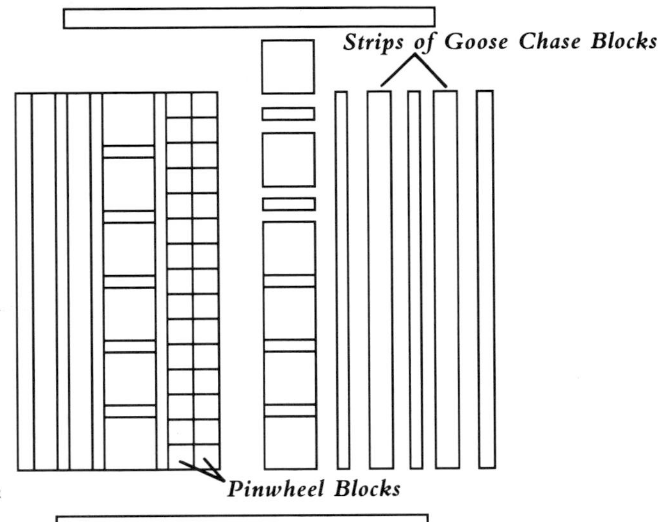

Setting Diagram

Each square equals 1″.

Weather Vane

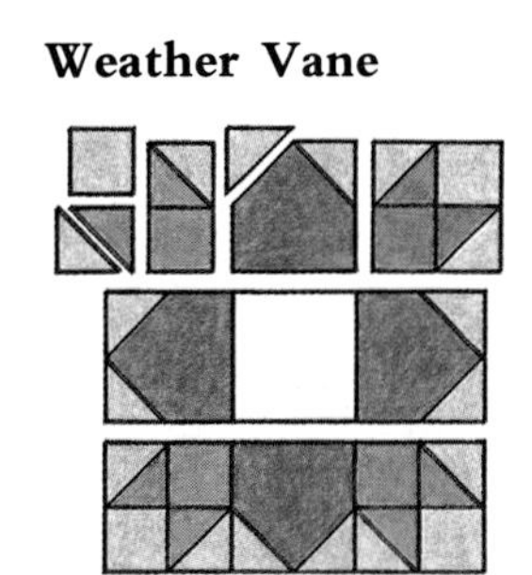

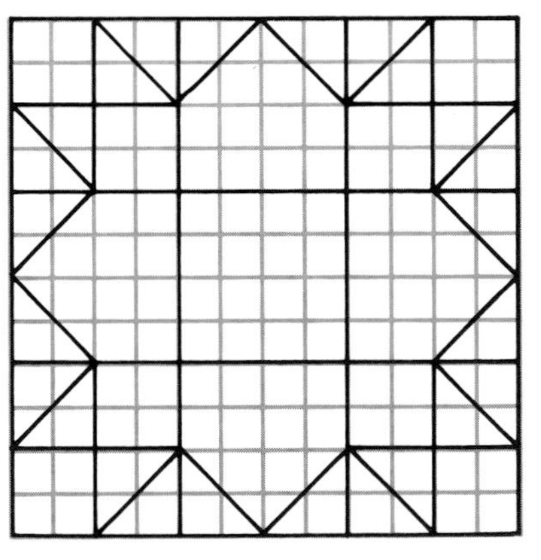

Rising Sun

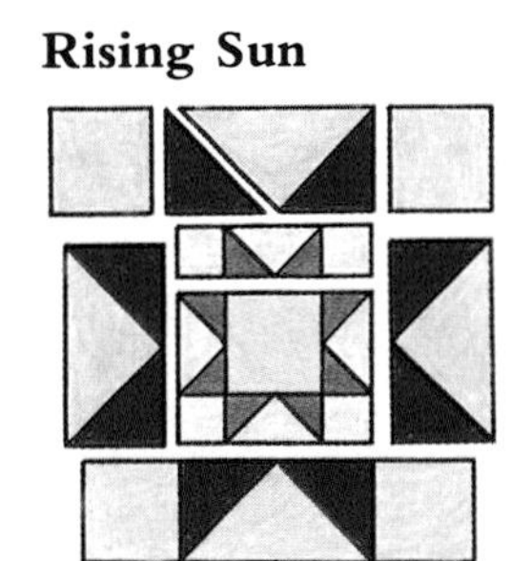

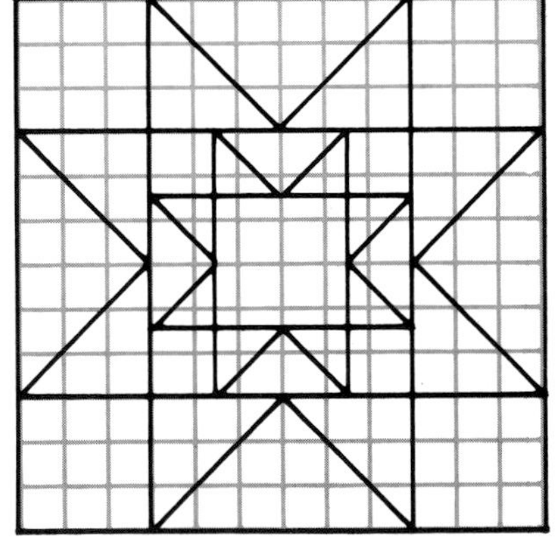

Stepping Stones

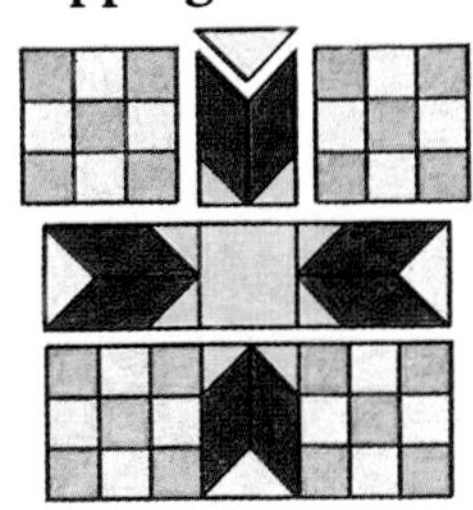

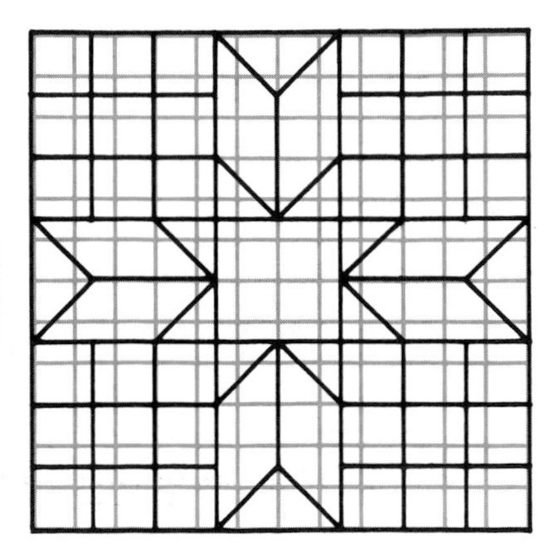

Five Patch Star

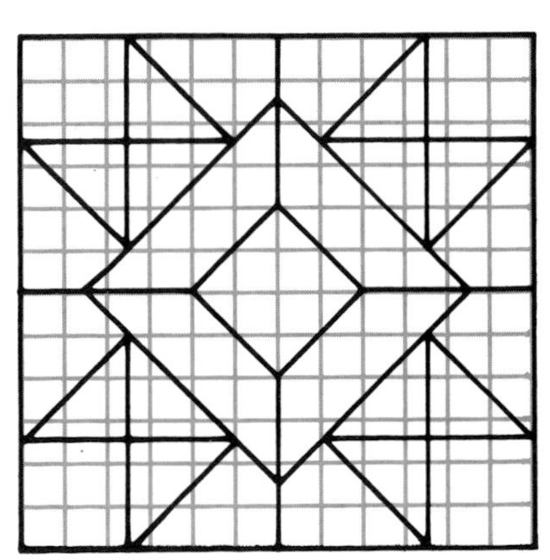

Each square equals 1".

Many-Pointed Star

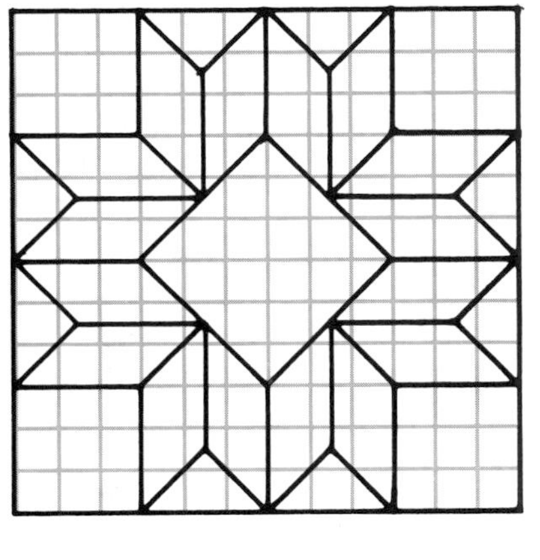

Union Square Variation

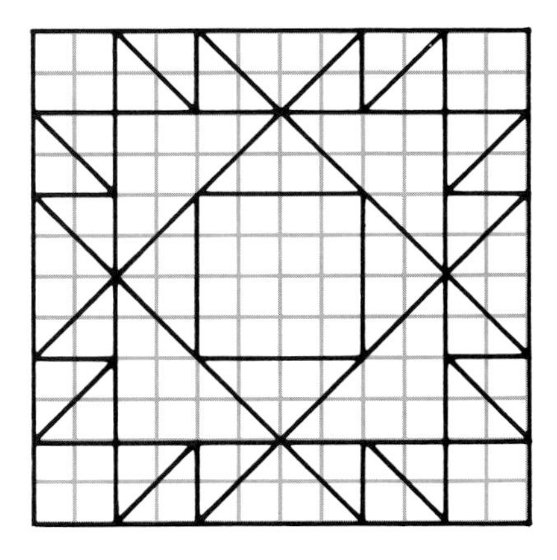

Puss in the Corner

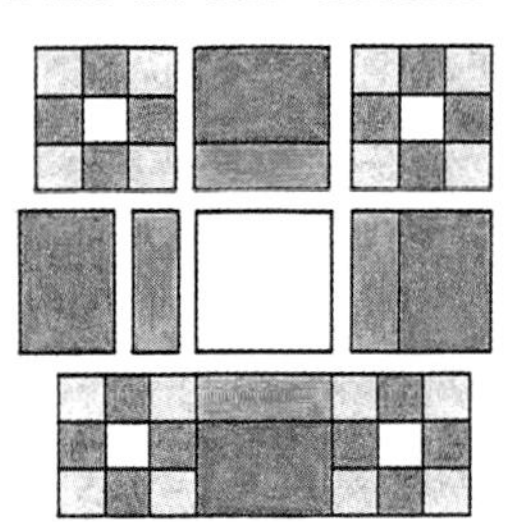

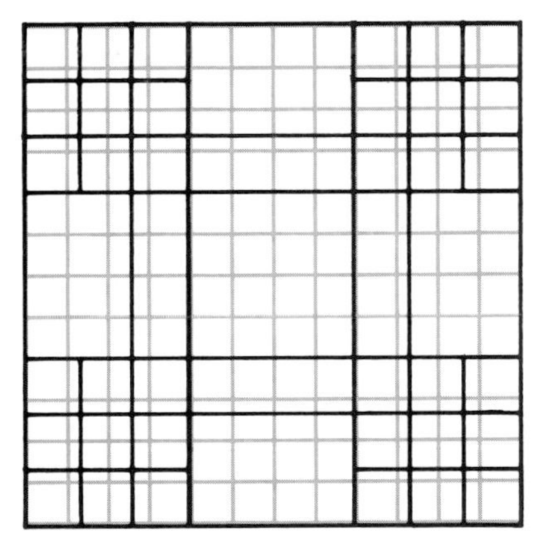

Beggar's Block

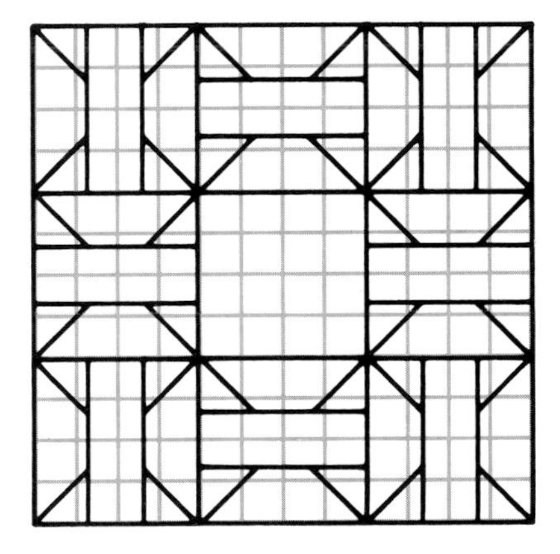

Lotus Star

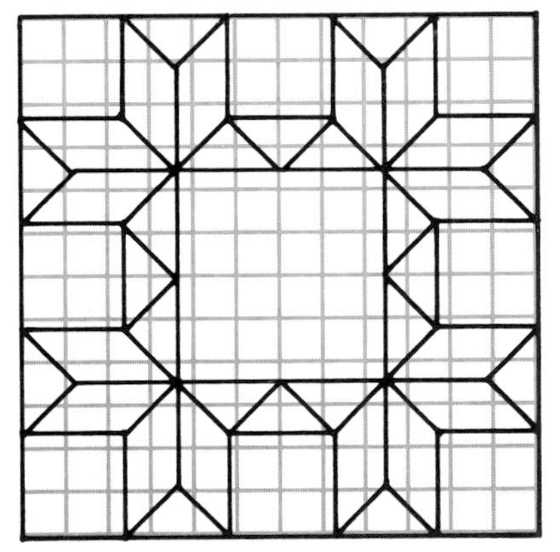

Single Irish Chain

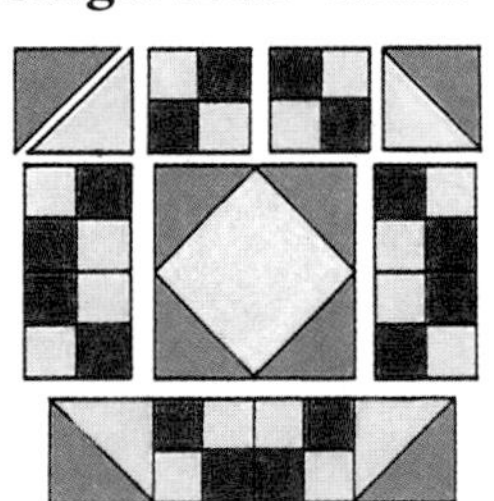

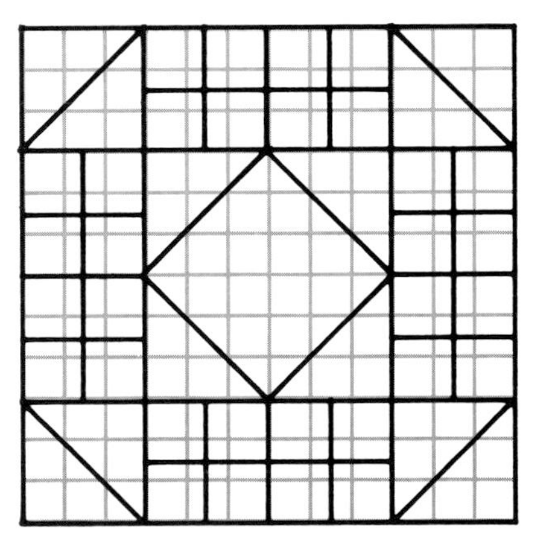

Album

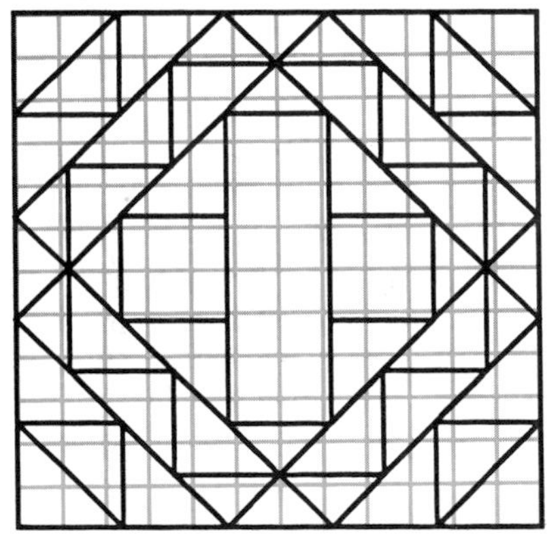

Jefferson City

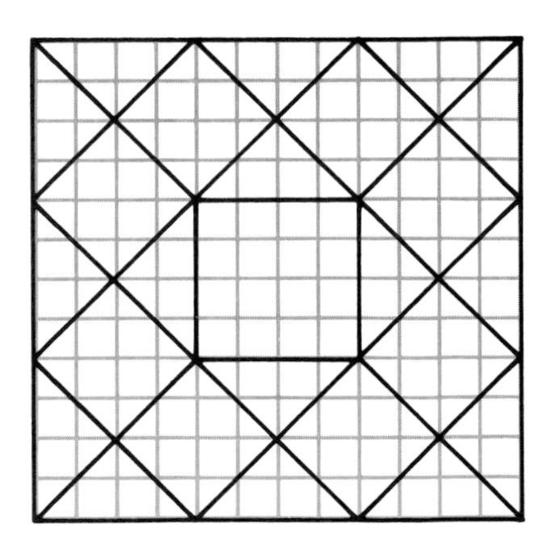

Star Crazy

Finished Quilt Size
32″ x 46″

Number of Blocks and Finished Size
6 octagons—12″ across

Finished Width of Sashing—1″

Finished Width of Border—2″

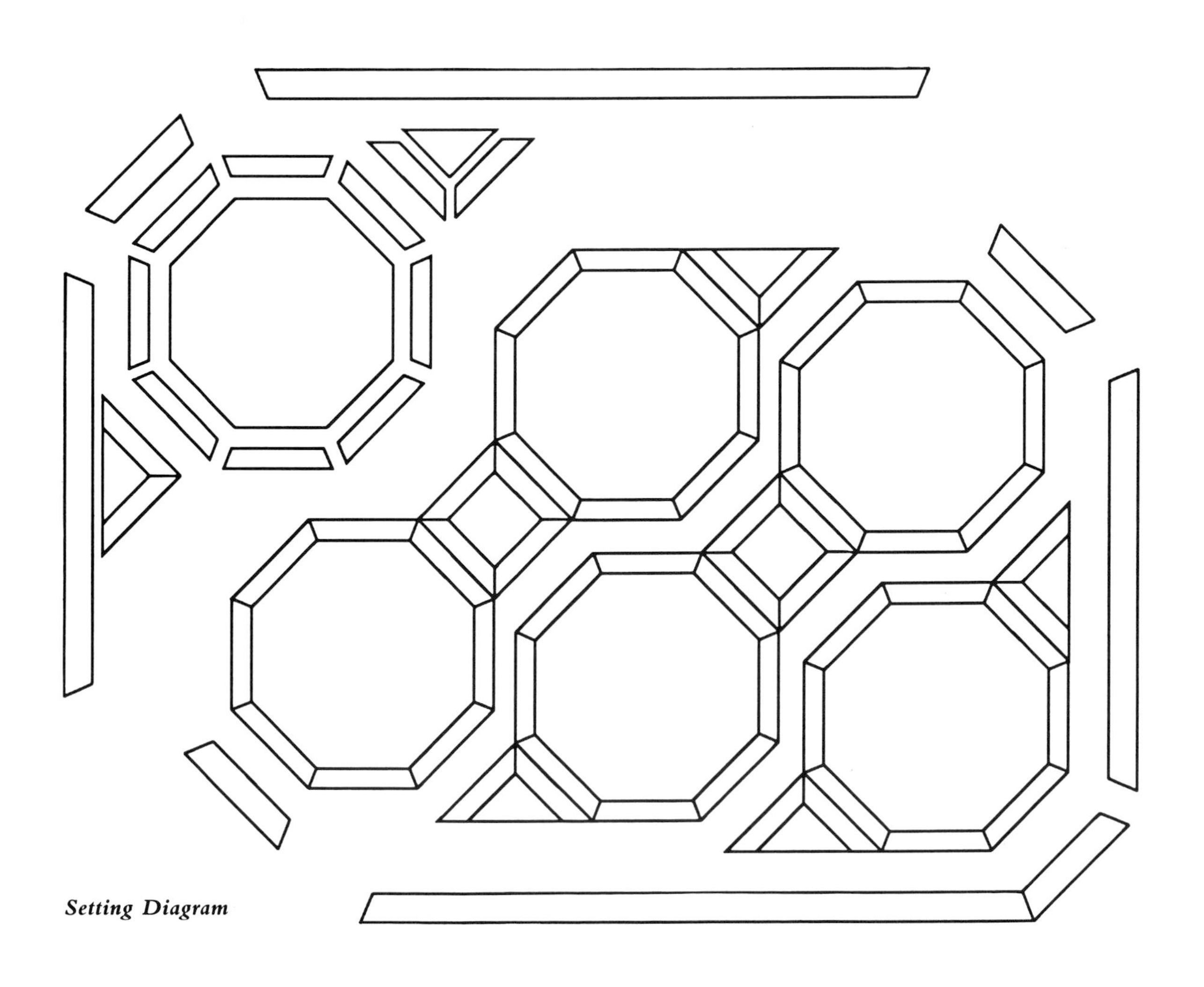

Setting Diagram

Each square equals 1″.

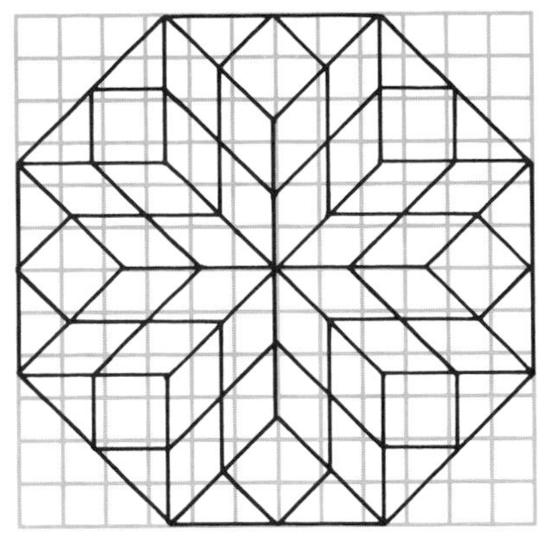

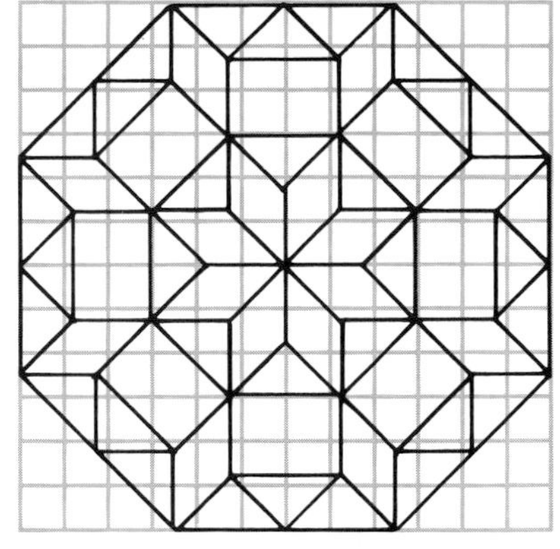

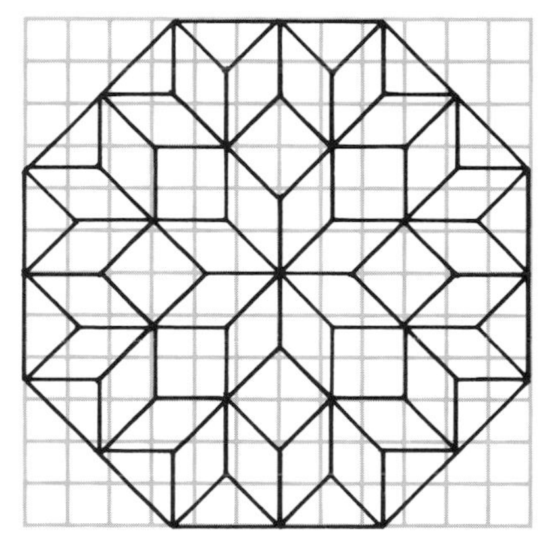

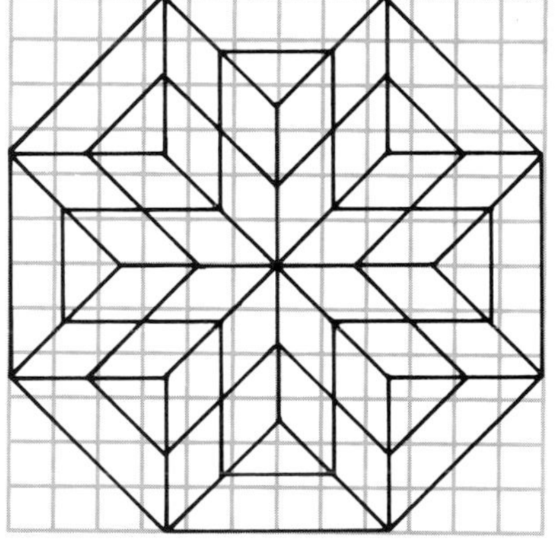

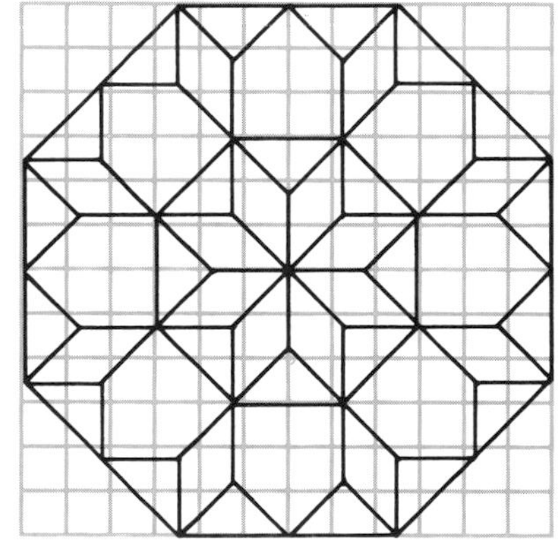
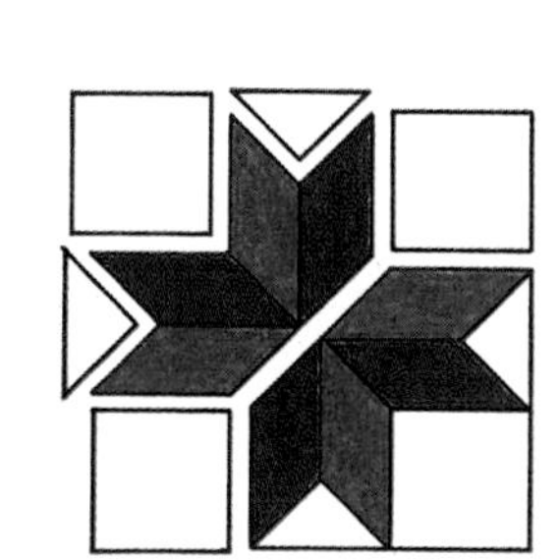
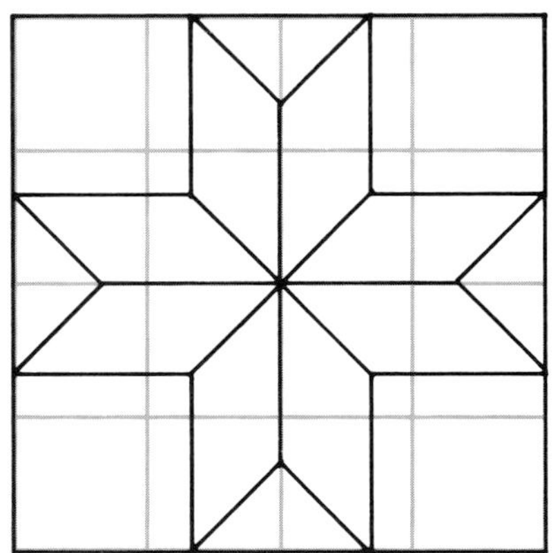

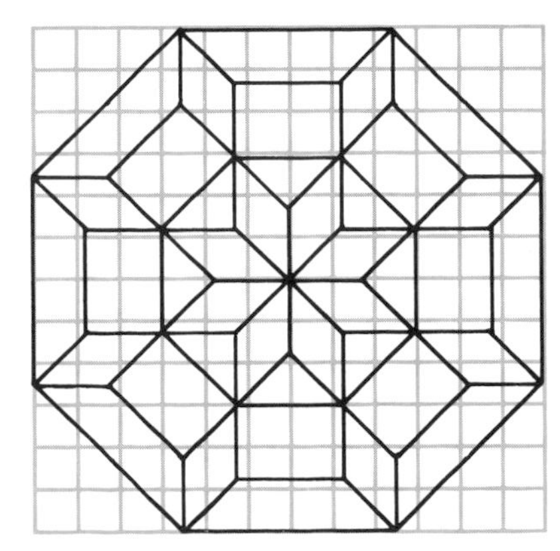

Wild Wings

Finished Quilt Size
88″ x 105″

Number of Blocks and Finished Size
14 blocks—12″ x 12″

Finished Widths for Outside Borders—2½″, ¾″, and 2″, respectively.

Setting Diagram

Each square equals 1".

Dove in Window

Goose in the Pond

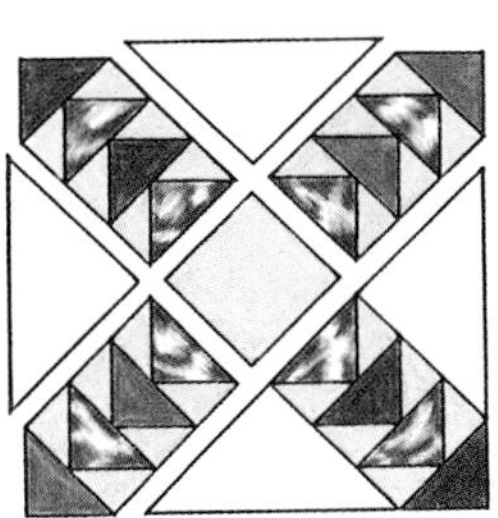

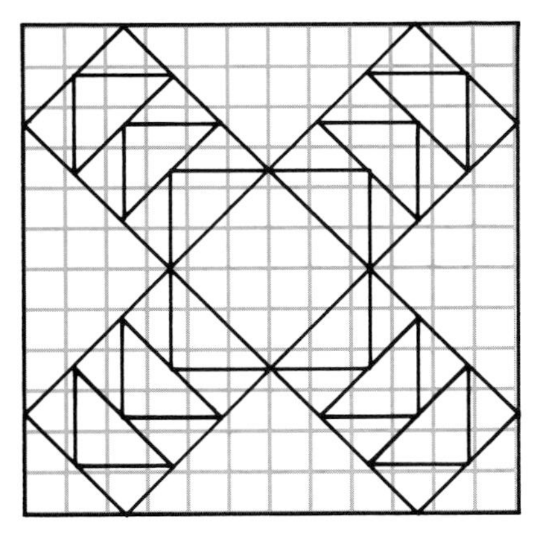

Birds in Air

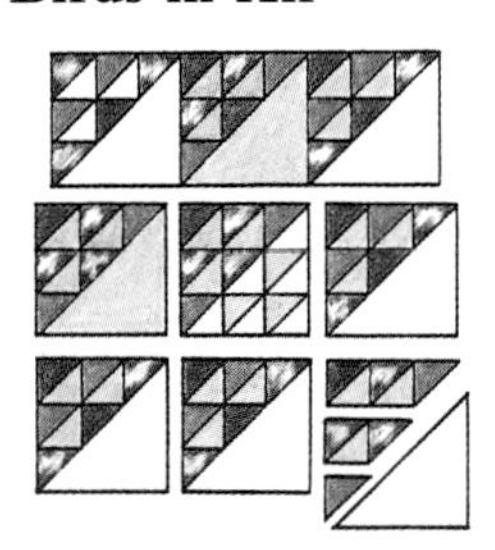

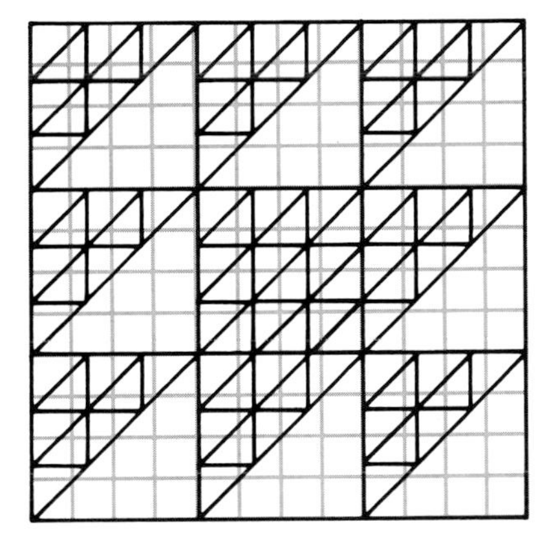

Fish Block

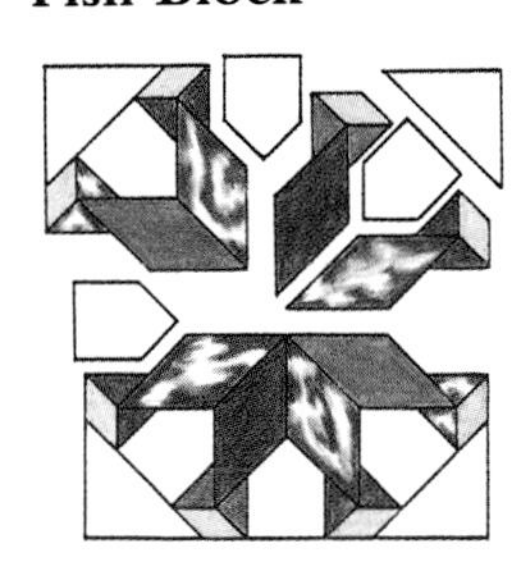

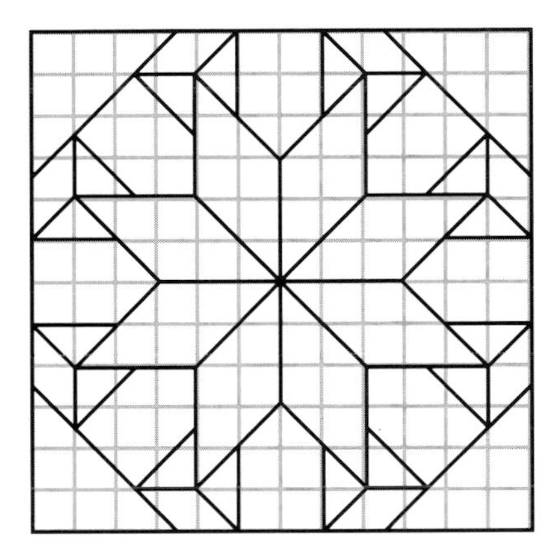

Ducks and Ducklings

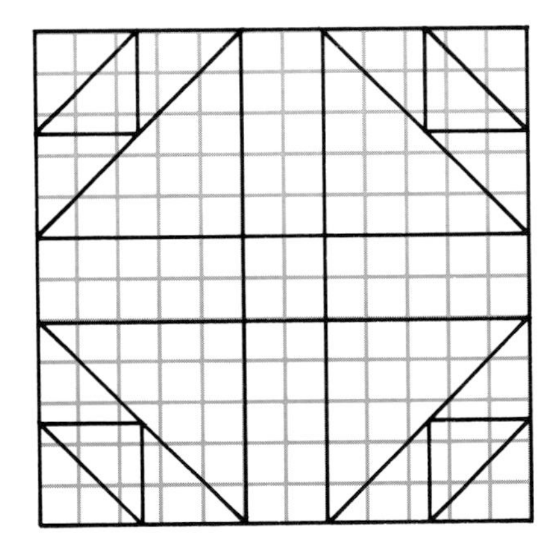

Wild Goose Chase

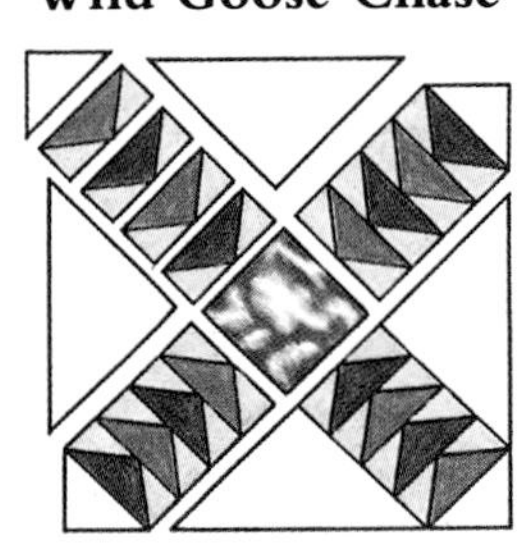

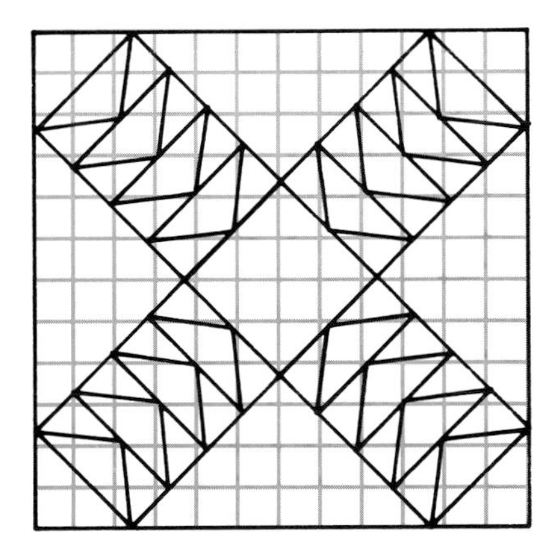

Chimney Swifts

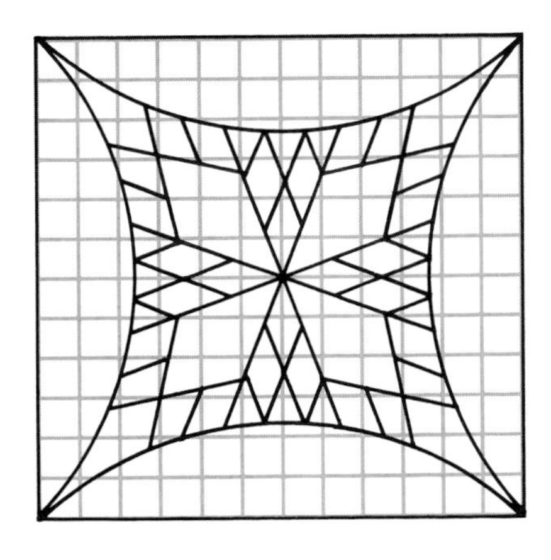

Goose Tracks

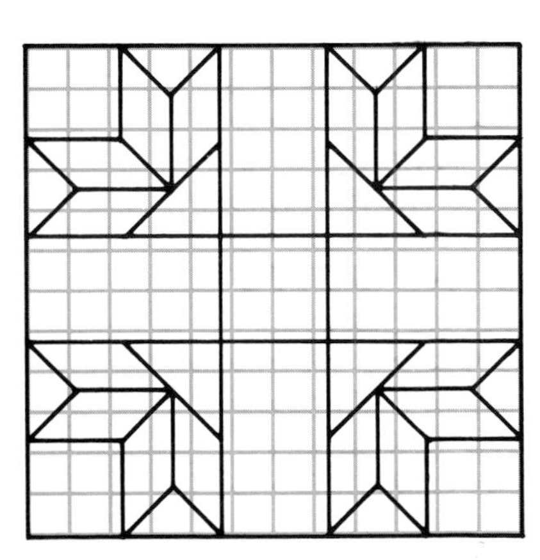

continued

Each square equals 1″.

Bird's Nest

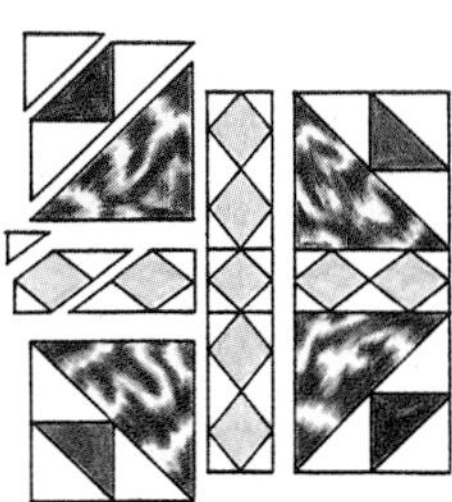

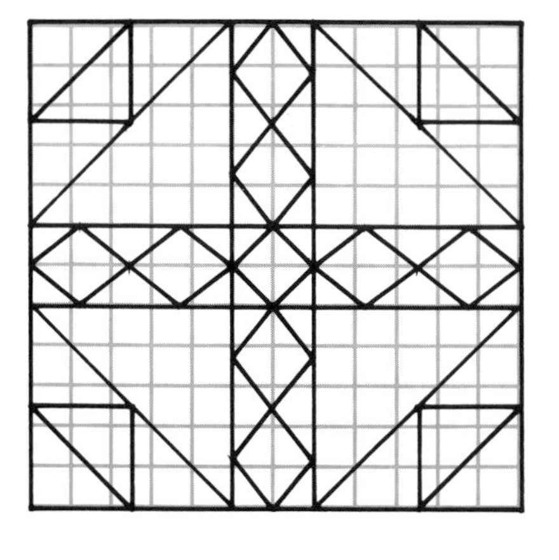

Hummingbird

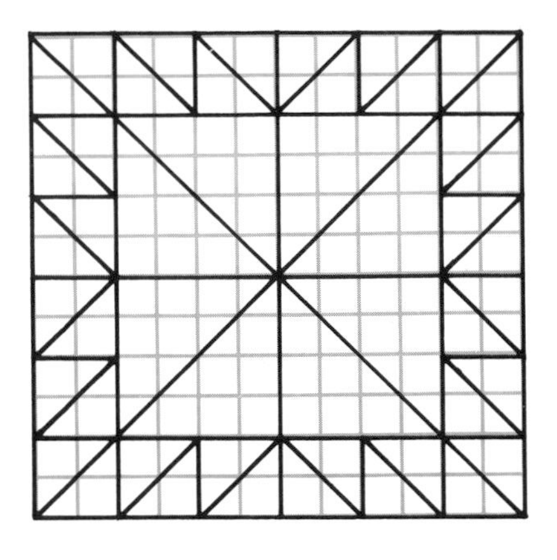

Goose Chase

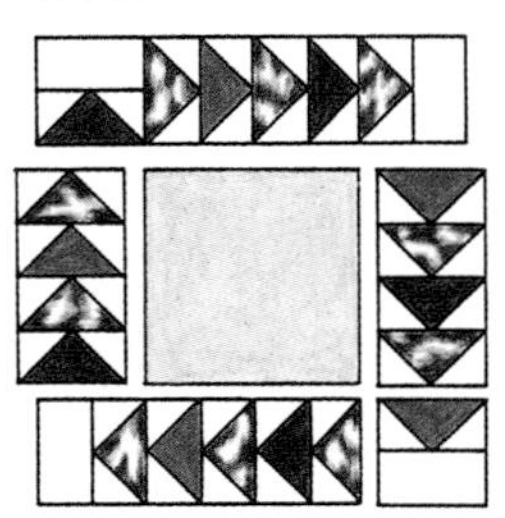

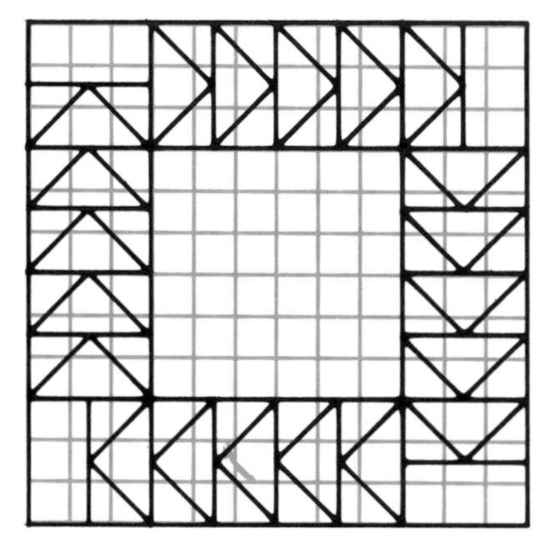

Crow's Foot

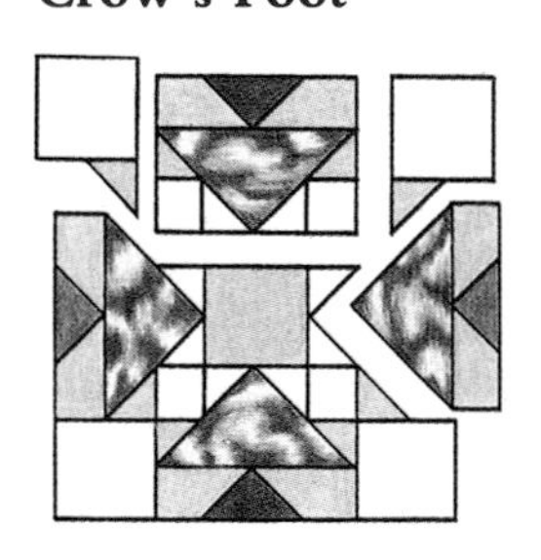

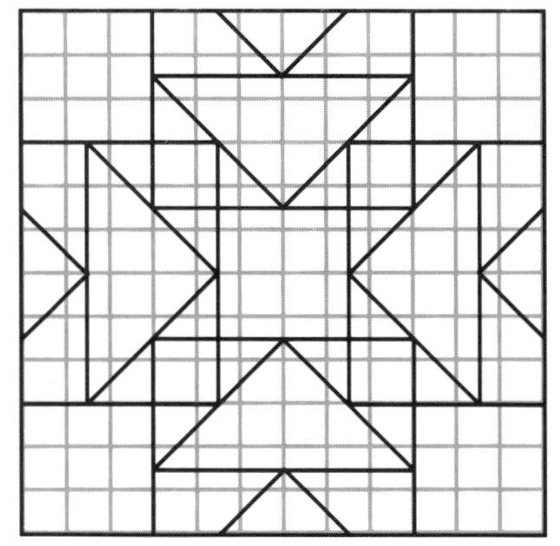

Flying Swallows

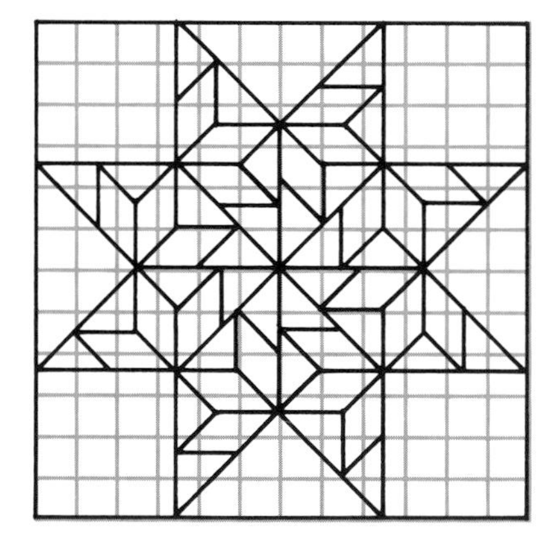

Duck's Foot in the Mud

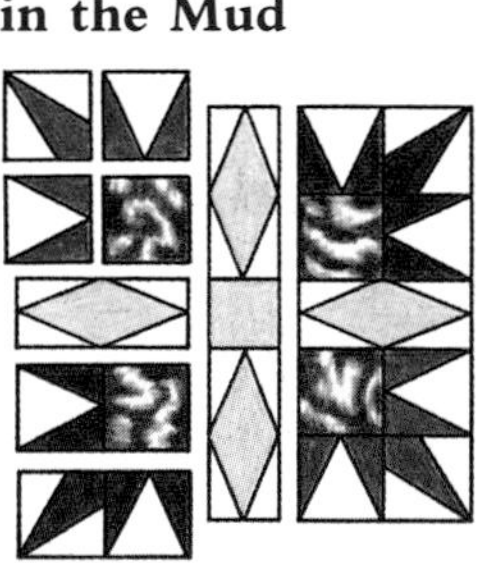

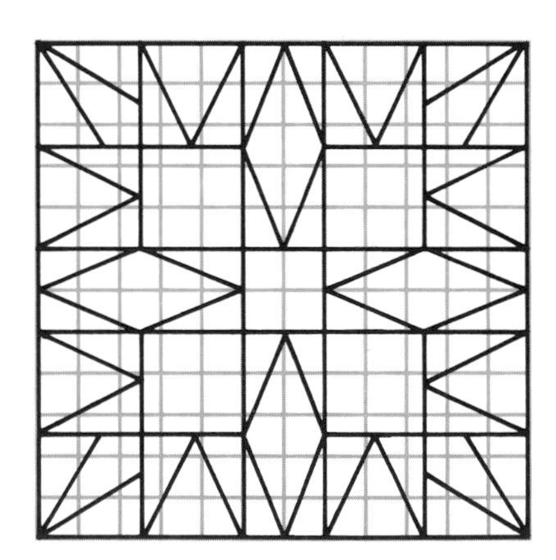

Ruby's Sampler

Finished Quilt Size
80″ x 100″ plus a 5″-wide ruffle on three sides

Number of Blocks and Finished Size
12 blocks—16″ x 16″

Finished Width of Sashing—4″

Finished Width of First Border—2½″

Finished Width of Second Border—5¼″

Setting Diagram

continued

Autumn Leaves

Each square equals 1".

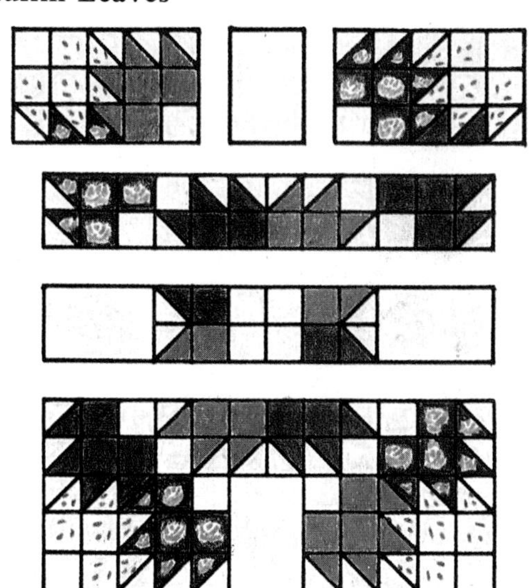

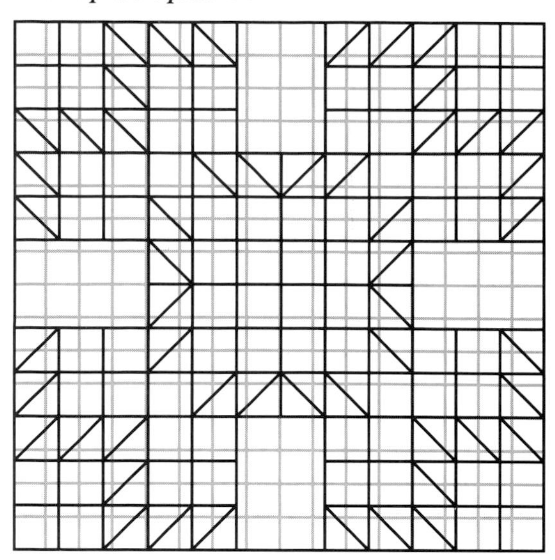

Honey Bee Variation

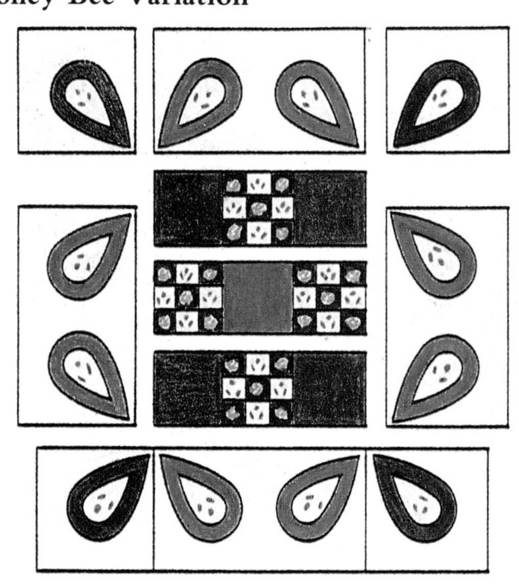

Dutch Rose Variation

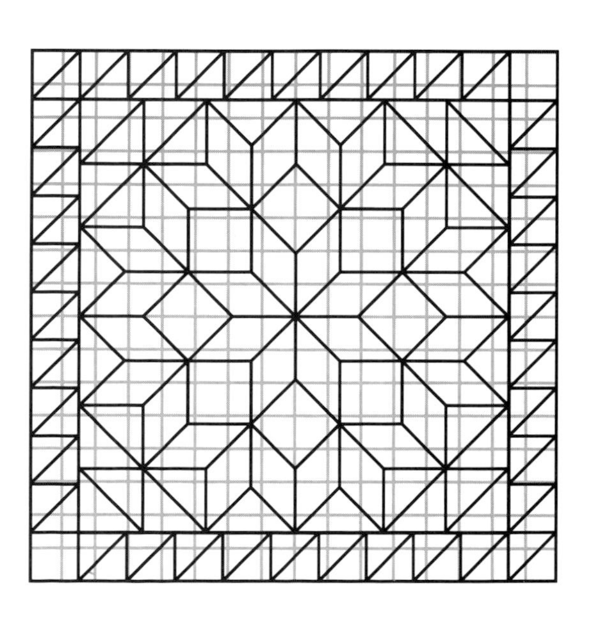

Dresden Plate Variation

Each square equals 1".

Join pieces and then appliqué to background block.

Ruby's Little Country Church

Join pieces and then appliqué to background block.

Goose in the Pond Variation

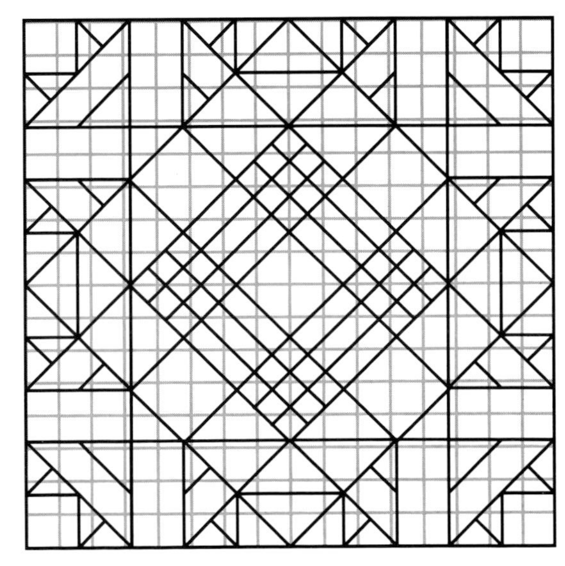

continued

Partridge in a Pear Tree

Each square equals 1".

Appliqué pieces to background block.

Ruby's Leaves and Tulips

Laurel Wreath

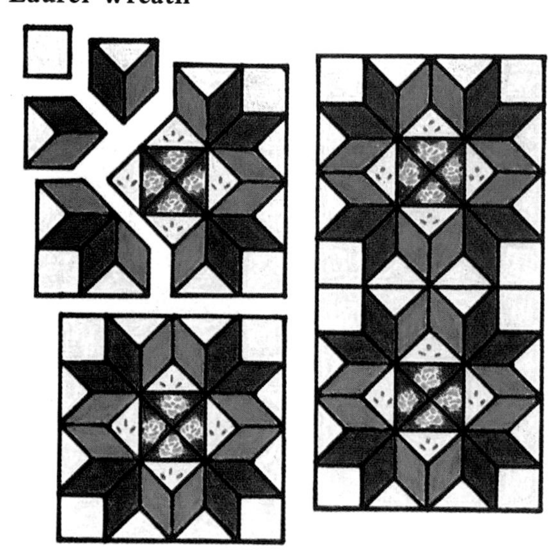

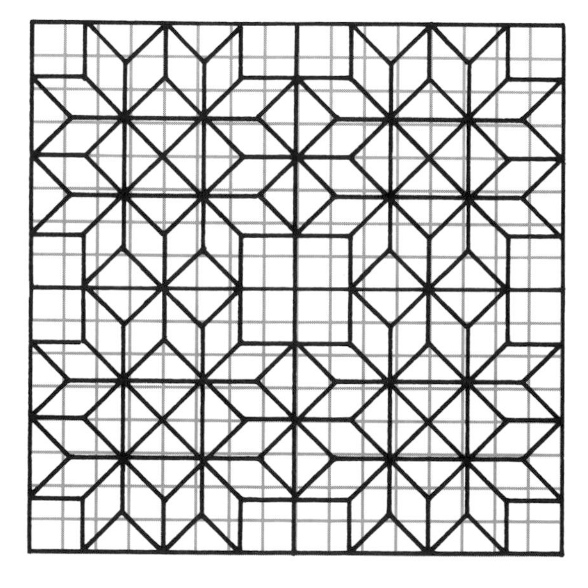

Hexagon Wreath with Variations

Each square equals 1".

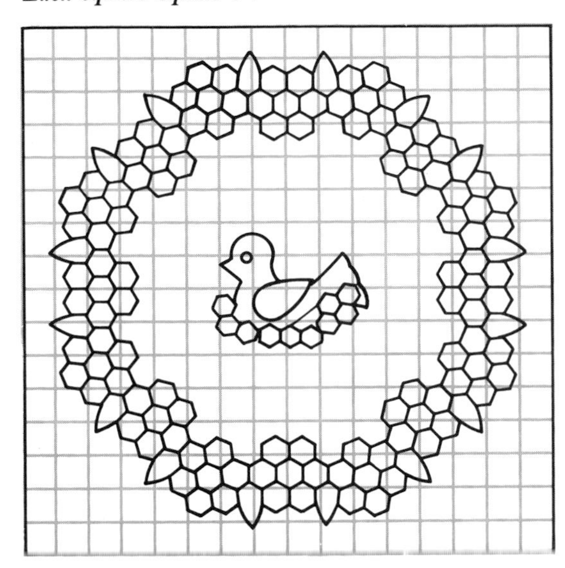

Join pieces and then appliqué to background block.

Pinecone Variation

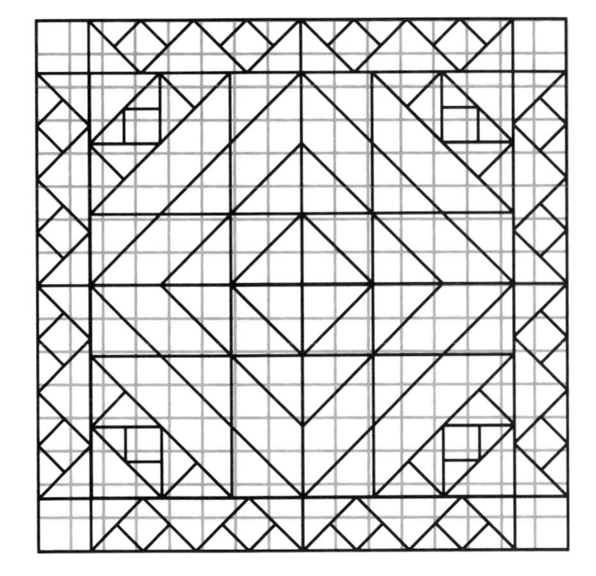

Grandmother's Flower Garden

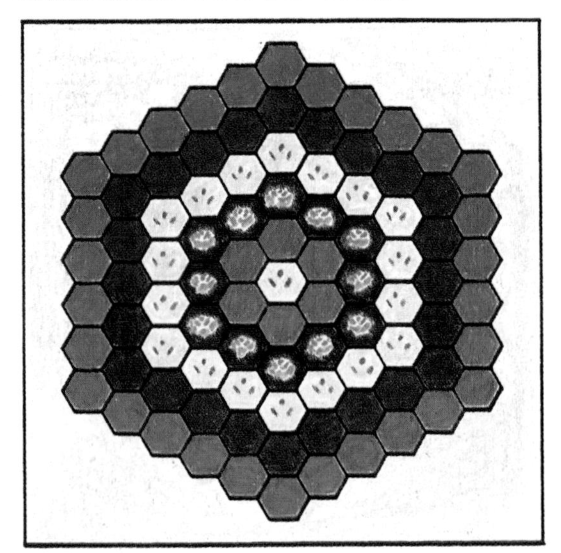

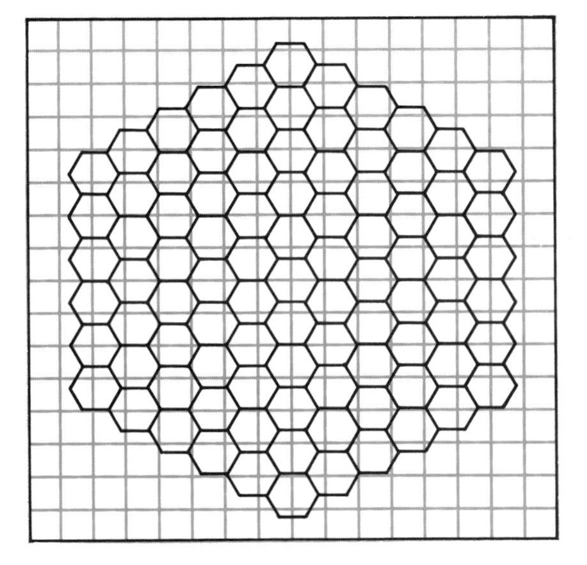

Join pieces and then appliqué to background block.

QUILTS ACROSS AMERICA

There's an arsenal of quilters
across this land so wide,
Connecting prairies and valleys with threads
that through their fingers glide.

Practiced by countless artisans from every
station of life,
Quilting continues on today—thanks to their
labor and strife.

The quilters' devotion to this craft
will forever bloom.
The wedding of their skills and senses
creates that special heirloom.

June Wolpert

Nashville, Indiana

In the short span of two years, June has progressed from a beginning quilter to a professional quilter, lecturer, and teacher. "My hobby has turned into a business," says June. June loves to teach and has taught classes on miniature quilts, quilted Christmas stockings, Mariner's Compass, feathered star, and stained-glass quiltmaking techniques.

Her quilting efforts have been rewarded with two Best of Show ribbons, three Grand Champion ribbons, several blue ribbons, and a Viewer's Choice. "Quilting has given me many happy hours," says June. "It is a wonderful hobby and occupation with unlimited possibilities."

Take a few minutes and admire June's wonderful sampler quilt, *Most Beautiful Star*, in our "All Sorts of Samplers" chapter.

Amish Goose
1983
Fabric in motion is *Amish Goose*. June's fabric placement and selection transform the image of a traditional block, Friendly Goose, into the style and image of a contemporary one. By mixing prints with solids and contrasting pinks with dark-colored fabrics, June caused swirling pinwheels to burst into view. But don't be intimidated—June's clever fabric manipulation makes this quilt look much more complicated than it is.

Amish Goose

Finished Quilt Size
75″ x 75″

Number of Blocks and Finished Size
25 blocks—12″ x 12″

Fabric Requirements

Black	—2¼ yd.
Maroon	—2 yd.
Teal blue	— ⅓ yd.
Teal blue print	—2 yd.
Dk. pink print	— ⅝ yd.
Lt. pink print	— ⅓ yd.
Green print I	—1 yd.
Green print II	— ¼ yd.
Purple print	— ¼ yd.
Dk. blue/green	— ½ yd.
Brown/blue print	— ⅞ yd.
Black for bias binding	—1 yd.
Backing	—5 yd.

Number to Cut

Template A	—25 maroon
Template B	—72 black
	32 maroon
	24 dk. pink print
	16 lt. pink print
	52 green print I
	4 brown/blue print
Template C	—8 black
	80 dk. pink print
	24 lt. pink print
	170 green print I
	64 dk. blue/green
	154 brown/blue print
Template D	—50 black
	50 maroon
	46 teal blue
	46 green print II
	8 purple print

Quilt Top Assembly

1. Referring to Block Piecing Diagram and colored block drawings, join square (A), triangles (B, C), and parallelograms (D), as shown.

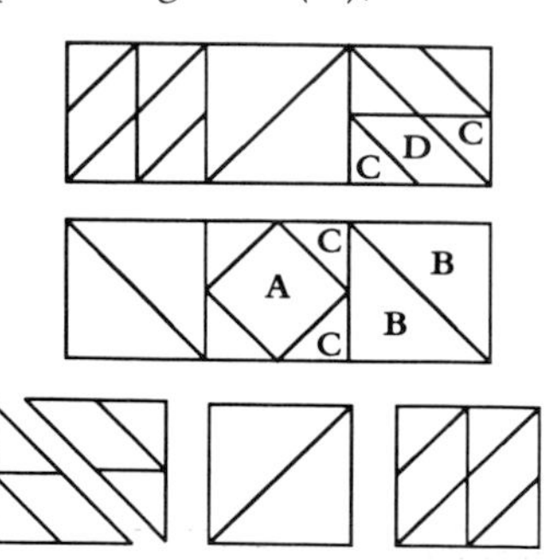

Block Piecing Diagram

Make number of blocks indicated in colored block drawings.

2. Arrange blocks, as shown in Block Setting Diagram. Arrows inside blocks indicate the top of each block. Join blocks at sides and make 5 rows. Join rows.

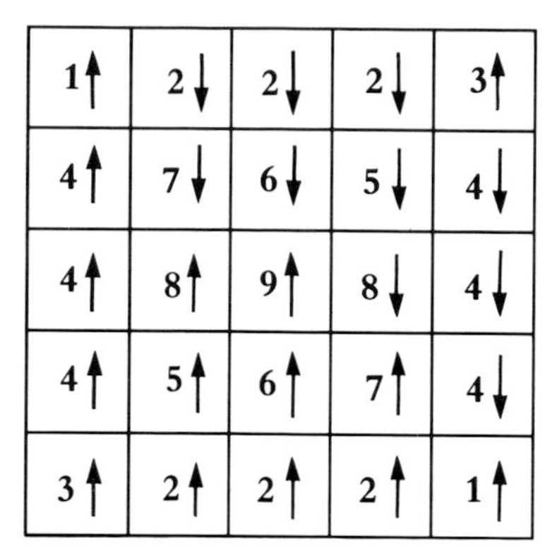

1↑	2↓	2↓	2↓	3↑
4↑	7↓	6↓	5↓	4↓
4↑	8↑	9↑	8↓	4↓
4↑	5↑	6↑	7↑	4↓
3↑	2↑	2↑	2↑	1↑

Block Setting Diagram

3. Cut 4 border strips, 1¾″ wide, from maroon. Join to quilt and miter corners.

4. Cut 4 border strips, 2¼″ wide, from teal blue print. Join to quilt and miter corners.

5. Cut 4 borders, 5″ wide, from black. Join to quilt and miter corners.

Block 4
Make 6.

Block 5
Make 2.

Block 6
Make 2.

Block 1
Make 2.

Block 7
Make 2.

Block 2
Make 6.

Block 8
Make 2.

Block 3
Make 2.

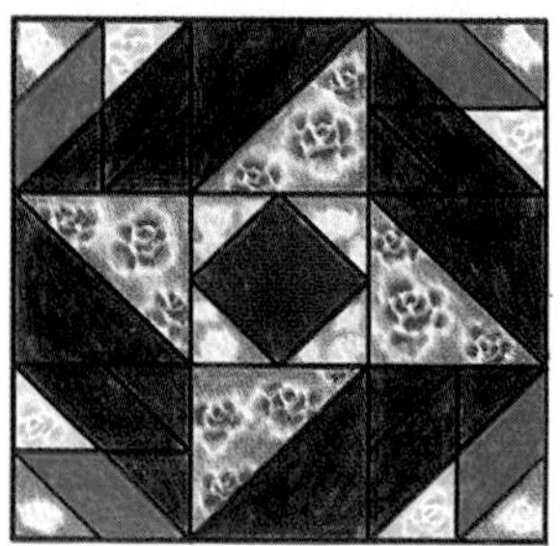

Block 9
Make 1.

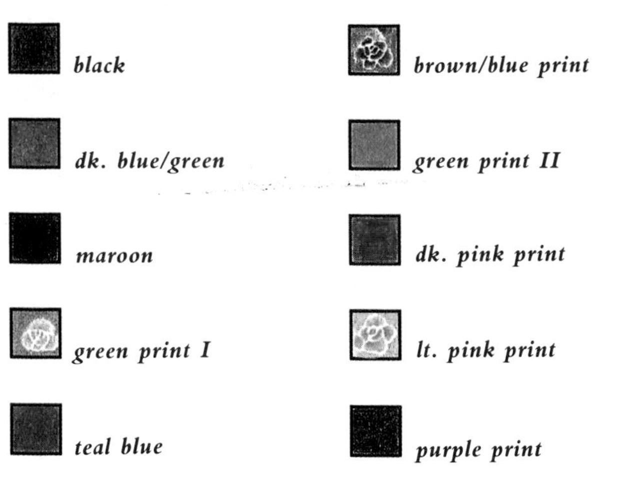

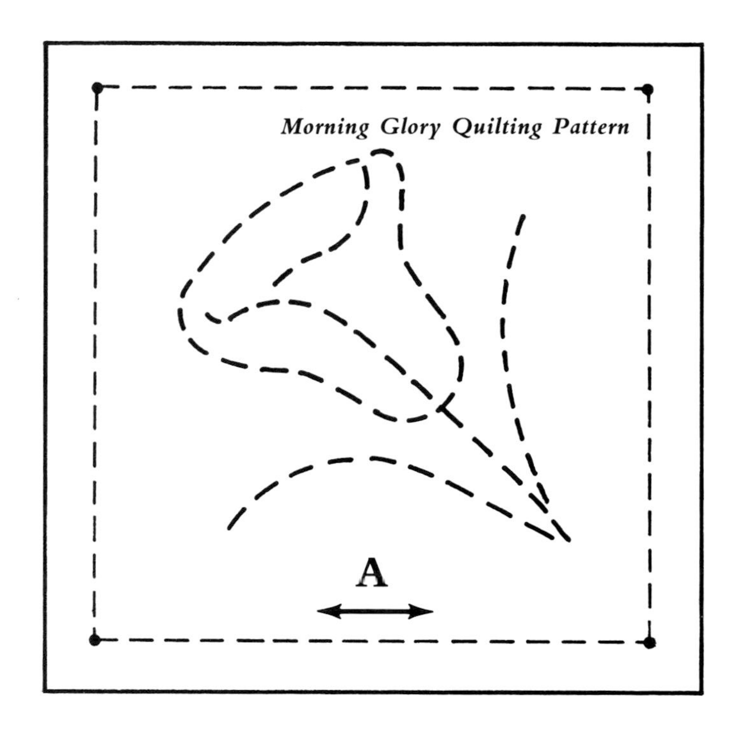

Quilting
Outline-quilt ¼″ inside seam line of each block piece. Quilt June's morning glory in the center of square A. June quilted her border with stacked parallelograms the size of piece D.

Finished Edges
Bind with black fabric.

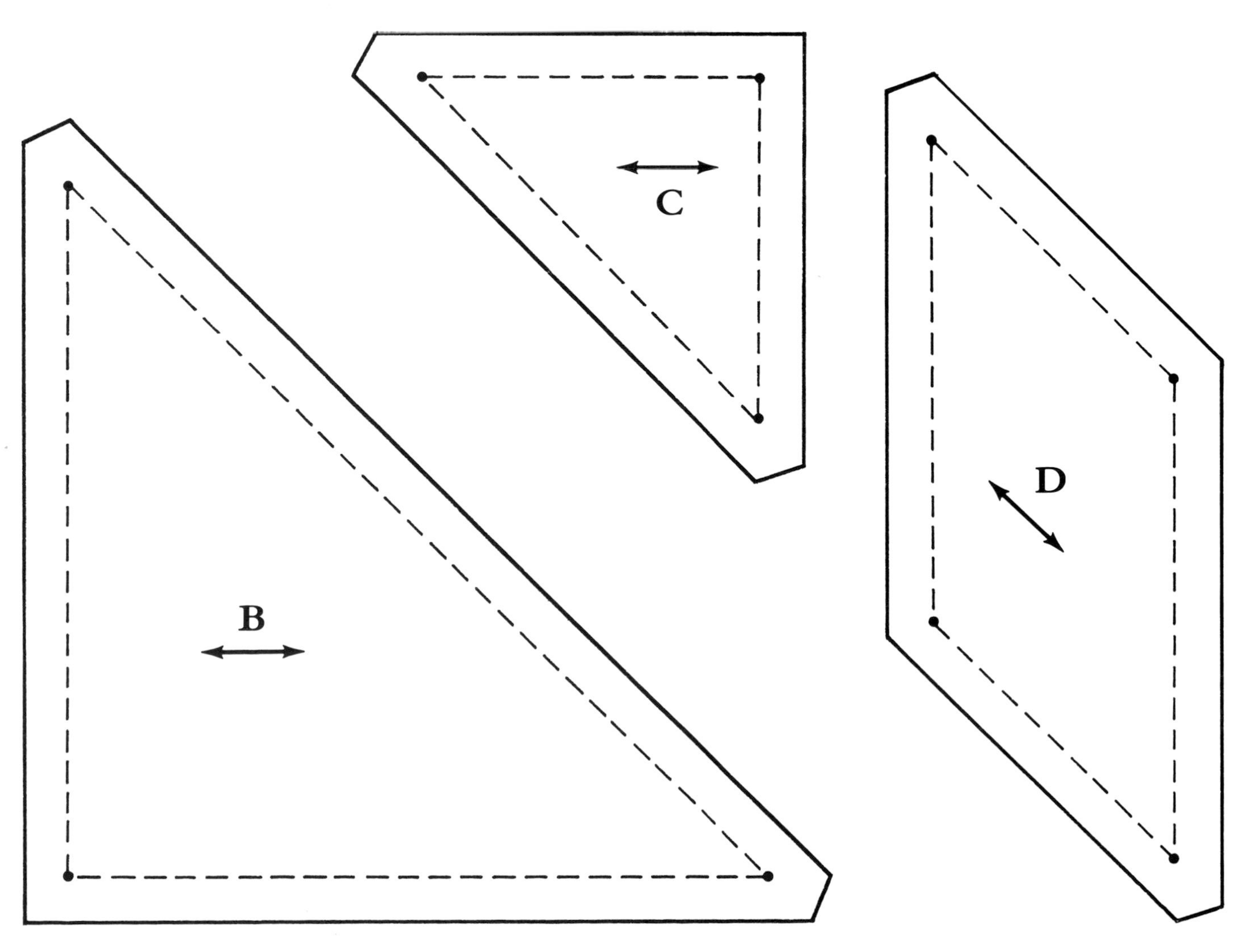

Ann A. Shibut

Richmond, Virginia

Do you have a "wreck" room? That's Ann's term for her quiltmaking room. "It is an unfinished room that I share with the freezer and the kitty-litter pans!" says Ann. But with a little ingenuity, Ann lined the walls with scores of cabinets and chests for fabrics, patterns, and equipment to make it a functional "wreck" room.

Her quiltmaking endeavors have prompted her to learn new business skills, sewing skills, and teaching skills. Says Ann, "Quilting has led me to new friends, to interesting places, and to personal satisfaction. It has brought me drawers overflowing with fabric, shelves drooping with books and magazines, corners filled with projects underway, and a mind busy with plans for the next project. It has filled my life in a very happy way. I am always busy and never bored!"

Her quilts have been exhibited at several local shows, and she has served as the director of the Richmond Quilters' Guild. She is presently treasurer of the Virginia Consortium of Quilters, a statewide quilting organization.

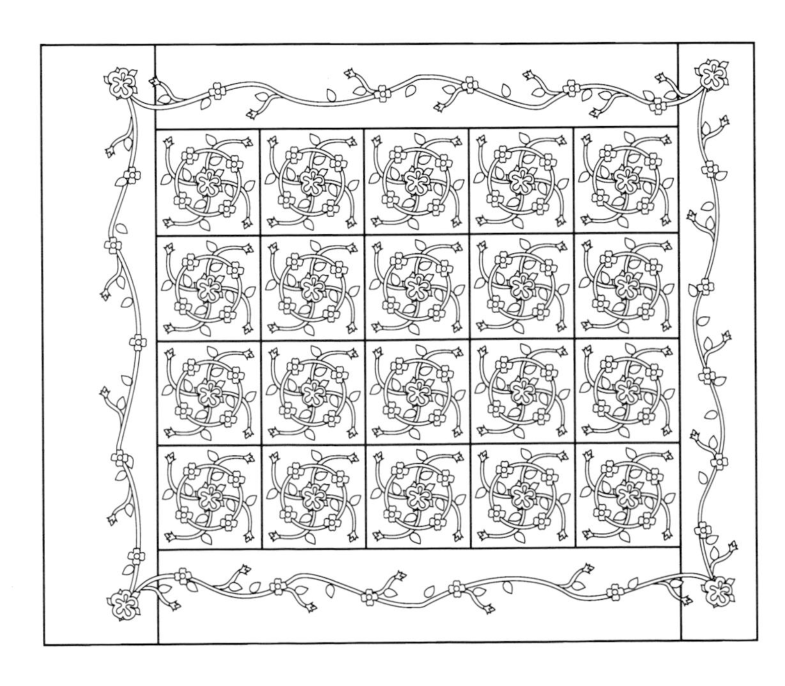

Dogwood and Hibiscus Wedding Quilt

1983

Ann designed and made this quilt as a wedding gift for her oldest son, Macon. "The groom was born in Hawaii and the bride, in Virginia," says Ann, "so I chose the state flower of each and included a wedding ring as a symbol of unending love."

The selection of colors, the placement of the flowers and vines, and rows of background quilting combine to make this one-of-a-kind quilt resemble the patterns of many traditional ones.

Dogwood and Hibiscus Wedding Quilt

Finished Quilt Size
88″ x 102″

Number of Blocks and Finished Size
20 blocks—15½″ x 15½″

Fabric Requirements

Dusty rose	— ¾ yd.
Dk. rose	— ½ yd.
White	— 1 yd.
Floral print	— ¼ yd.
Yellow ocher	— 1¼ yd.
Green	— 3 yd.
Rose print	— 8 yd.
Rose print for bias binding	— 1 yd.
Backing	— 8¾ yd.

Other Materials
Embroidery floss — dk. rose, yellow, brown

Number to Cut

Template A	— 24 dusty rose
Template B	— 103 dusty rose
Template C	— 24 dk. rose
Template D	— 100 white
Template E	— 100 floral print
Template F	— 103 green
Template G	— 210 green
Template H	— 120 green

Quilt Top Assembly

1. Cut twenty 16″ squares from rose print. Finger-crease each square in half twice to find the center. Referring to Appliqué Diagram I, appliqué ¼″-wide (finished width) green bias stems, leaves (G, H), and buds (B, F) on each square, as shown. Layer-appliqué ¼″-wide

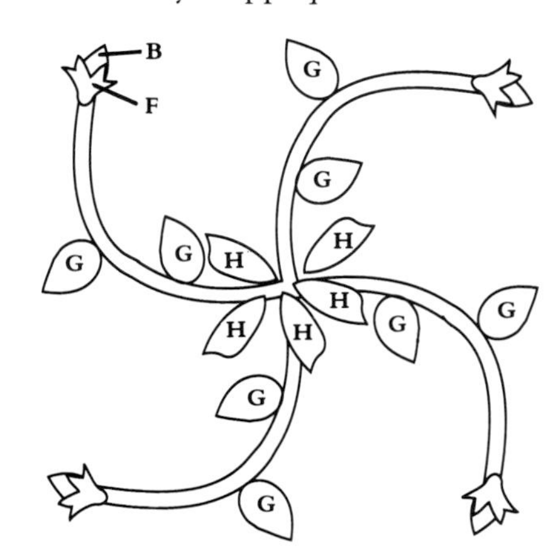

Appliqué Diagram I

Appliqué Diagram II

(finished width) yellow ocher bias ring, dogwood blossoms (D, E), and hibiscus (A, C), as shown in Appliqué Diagram II.

2. With embroidery floss, embroider hibiscus and dogwood flowers, as shown in Embroidery Diagrams. Small dots represent yellow French knots. Large dots represent dark rose French knots. The center of the hibiscus is satin-stitched with dark rose. Dogwood petals are accented with brown, as shown.

3. Join 4 blocks at sides to form a row. Make 5 rows. Join rows. (See quilt drawing.)

4. Cut 2 borders, 13½″ wide, from rose print for sides of quilt. Referring to Border Placement Diagram for Sides and quilt drawing, pin vines, flowers, and leaves in place and appliqué. Notice that each vine extends beyond the edge of the strip so that it can be appliquéd to top and bottom borders.

Cut 1 border, 10½″ wide, from rose print for top of quilt. Referring to Border Placement Diagram for Top Border and quilt drawing, pin vine, flowers, and leaves in place and appliqué, except for corner hibiscuses.

Cut 1 border, 15″ wide, from rose print for bottom of quilt. Referring to Border Placement Diagram for Bottom Border and quilt drawing, pin pieces and appliqué, except for corner hibiscuses.

5. Join side borders to sides of quilt. Join top and bottom borders to quilt. Appliqué vines and corner hibiscuses.

Embroidery Diagrams

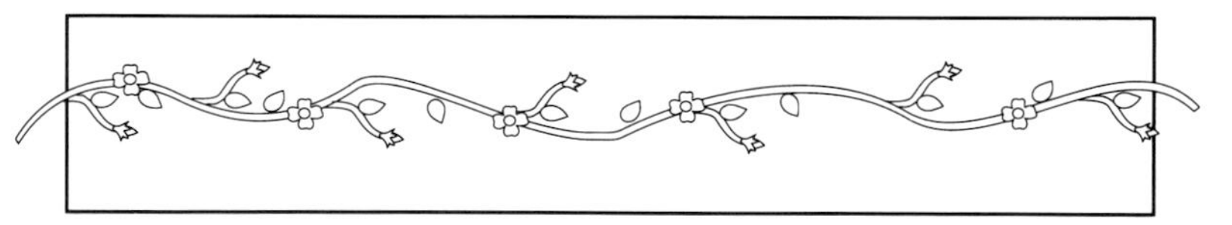

Border Placement Diagram for Sides

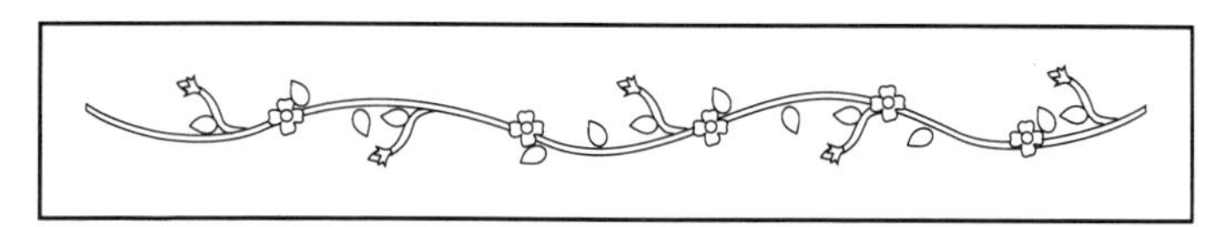

Border Placement Diagram for Top Border

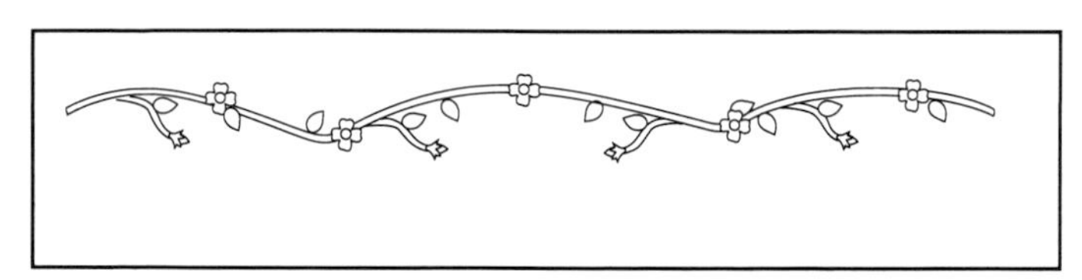

Border Placement Diagram for Bottom Border

Quilting
Outline-quilt outside seam lines of all appliquéd pieces. Ann mimicked the curves of the stems inside the yellow ring with curves of quilting. The remainder of the quilt is quilted with 1″ cross-hatching.

Finished Edges
Bind with rose print fabric.

Peony and Logs Medallion
1981

A bouquet of peonies bursts out of a contrasting hedge of Log Cabin blocks in Sue Ann's *Peony and Logs Medallion*. It is a very special quilt to Sue Ann for two reasons. First, it is the first quilt in which she used her own ideas to change a traditional design into one she could call her own. And second, it is the quilt that started her quilt business. "When people saw it hanging in the local bank," recalls Sue Ann, "orders came in for a similar one. Since then, quiltmaking has grown into a full-time business for me."

Peony and Logs Medallion won first prize at A Gathering of Quilts Show in Saltspringville, New York, in 1982. Sue Ann used Mountain Mist's Bed of Peonies classic pattern for her Peony block (see "Resources") and smartly adapted it to complement her vine border.

Many years of sewing for herself and attending art classes were logged by Sue Ann before she discovered quilting. "I never connected sewing and art until I began quilting," says Sue Ann. "There are so many possibilities in quilting. The combination of graphic design, color, and texture, both from the fabric and the quilting, is what makes quiltmaking a challenge for me."

The most delightful discovery for Sue Ann in quiltmaking has been the union she now feels with the rest of the world. For instance: "Every quilter has a memory or a story about a certain quilt pattern or a certain fabric from his or her past that one can relate to," says Sue Ann.

Sue Ann Jenkins

Cooperstown, New York

Peony and Logs Medallion

Finished Quilt Size
52″ x 52″

Number of Blocks and Finished Size
4 Peony blocks—12″ x 12″
4 Cornerstone Log Cabin blocks—8¾″ x 8¾″

Fabric Requirements

Red print	— ½ yd.
Green print	— 1½ yd.
Purple print	— 1¼ yd.
Brown prints	— 1¼ yd. total
Muslin	— 1⅜ yd.
Purple print for bias binding	— 1 yd.
Backing	— 3 yd.

Number to Cut

Template A	— 96 red print 32 green print
Template B	— 64 muslin 4 brown print
Template C	— 94 purple print 64 muslin 118 brown print
Template D	— 4 muslin
Template E	— 24 green print
Template F	— 16 green print 124 purple print 64 brown print

Quilt Top Assembly

1. Join 6 red print diamonds (A) and 2 green print diamonds (A) at sides, as shown in Peony Piecing Diagram. Set muslin squares (B) and muslin triangles (C) between diamonds, as shown in Peony Block Piecing Diagram. Stitch one side of square (B) or triangle (C) to one side of diamond (A). Begin stitching from the outside edge and stitch up to the seam line. Stop and backstitch 1 or 2 stitches. Remove fabric from the machine. Align the remaining sides and stitch from the center to the outside edge, backstitching 1 or 2 stitches at the start. Make 3 peony squares for each Peony block and 1 for each corner for a total of 16 peony squares. (See quilt photograph and Peony Block Piecing Diagram.)

Peony Piecing Diagram

2. Join 3 brown print triangles (C) to 1 purple print triangle (C), as shown in Peony Block Piecing Diagram. Join pieced triangle to muslin piece (D). Join pieced square to 3 peony squares, as shown in Peony Block Piecing Diagram. Make 4 Peony blocks.

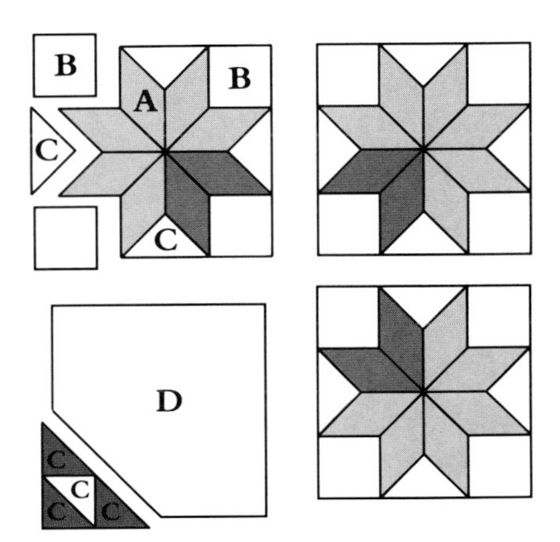

Peony Block Piecing Diagram

3. Using ½″-wide (finished width) bias strips from green print for stems, appliqué stems and leaves (E) to each Peony block, as shown in Peony Block Appliqué Diagram.

Peony Block Appliqué Diagram

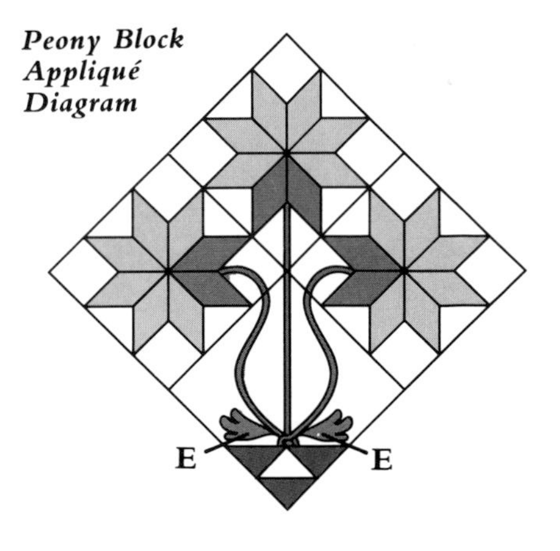

4. Join Peony blocks to form a square. (See Setting Diagram I.)
5. Join purple print triangles (F) to brown print triangles (F) at sides to form 4 strips. Adjust to fit quilt dimensions and join to quilt so that triangles meet in corners. (See quilt photograph.)

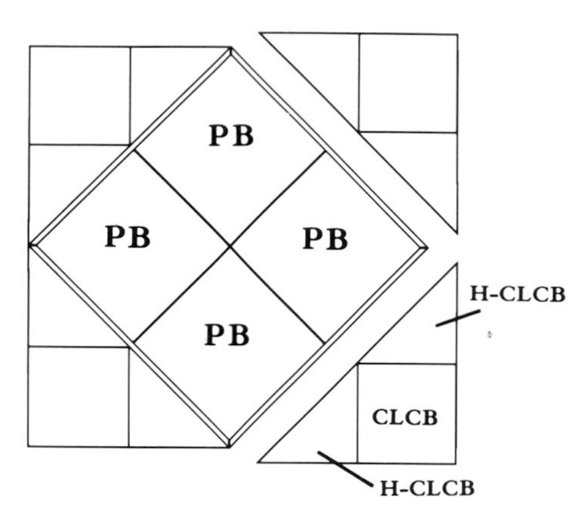

Setting Diagram I

PB = Peony Block
CLCB = Cornerstone Log Cabin Block
H-CLCB = Half-Cornerstone Log Cabin Block

6. Begin with a 1¾" purple print square (measurement includes seam allowance) and make 4 Cornerstone Log Cabin blocks, as shown in Cornerstone Log Cabin Block Piecing Diagram.

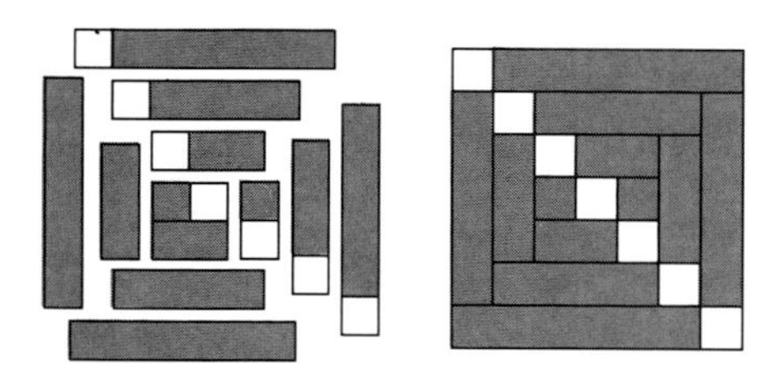

Cornerstone Log Cabin Block Piecing Diagram

7. Begin with a 1¾" brown print square and make 8 Half-Cornerstone Log Cabin blocks, as shown in Half-Cornerstone Log Cabin Block Piecing Diagram.
8. Join Cornerstone Log Cabin blocks, half and whole, as shown in Setting Diagram I. Join to quilt.

Half-Cornerstone Log Cabin Block Piecing Diagram

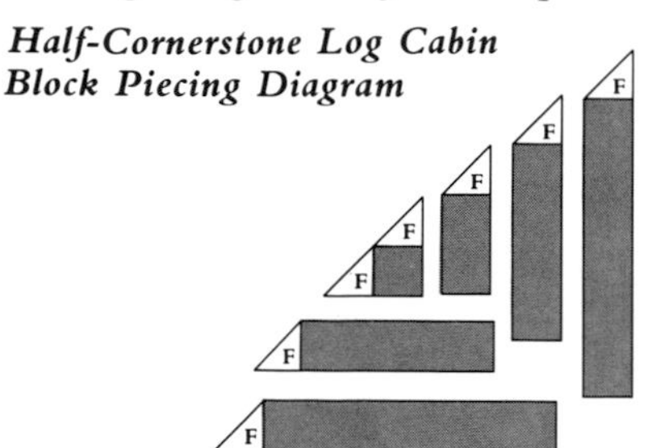

9. Cut 8 border strips, 1¾" wide, from purple print. Add a brown print triangle (F) to one end of each strip, as shown in Border Strip Piecing Diagram. Join strips at triangle ends to make 4 strips. Join strips to top and bottom of quilt.

Cut 4 squares, 1¾" on each side, from purple print and join to each end of remaining 2 strips. Join strips to sides of quilt.
10. Cut 4 borders, 6½" wide, from muslin. Join a peony square to the ends of 2 borders.

Make a square within a square by joining a brown print square (B) with purple print triangles (F), brown print triangles (C), and green print triangles (F), as shown in Square within a Square Piecing Diagram. Make 4.

Appliqué square within a square and peony vine to borders, as shown in quilt photograph. Use ½"-wide (finished width) bias strips from green print for vine. On borders without peony squares, leave the portion of the vine that will extend to meet the peony squares unappliquéd, until borders are attached to quilt.

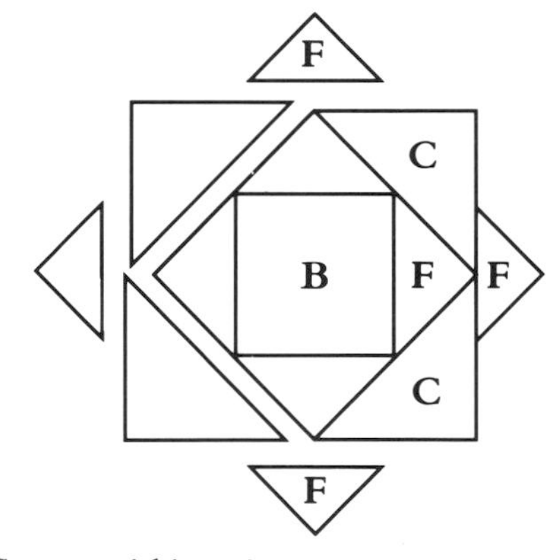

Square within a Square Piecing Diagram

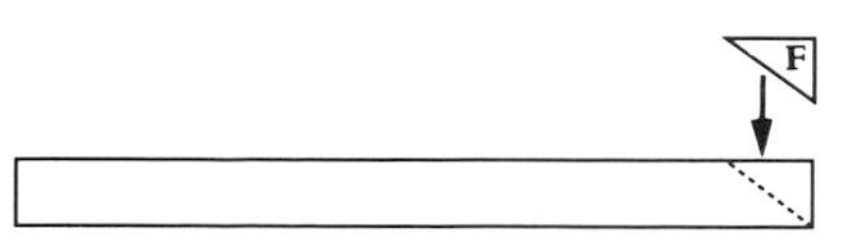

Border Strip Piecing Diagram
Lay triangle (F) over strip end and stitch, as shown. Trim away excess fabric.

11. Join appliquéd borders without peony squares to sides of quilt. Join remaining appliquéd borders to top and bottom. Finish appliquéing vines.

12. Join purple print triangles (C) to brown print triangles (C) to make border strips. Adjust to fit quilt dimensions. (See quilt photograph for proper placement.) Join strips to quilt. As you join strips, trim away any excess fabric even with quilt. (See Setting Diagram II and quilt photograph.) Join a brown print triangle (C) to each corner.

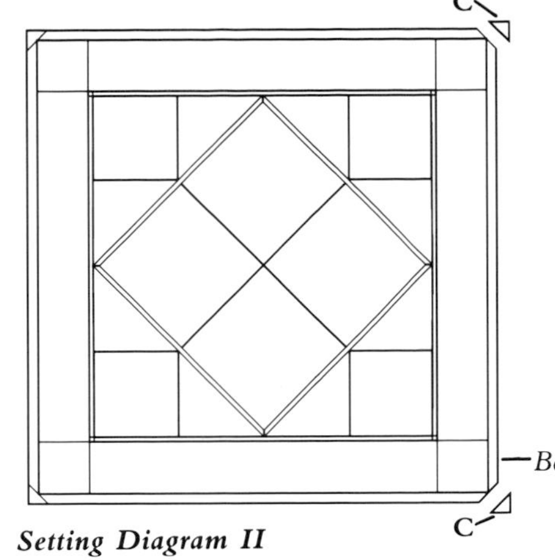

Setting Diagram II

Quilting

Outline-quilt around all appliqué pieces. Quilt remaining muslin background areas with parallel lines, ½″ apart. Outline-quilt ⅛″ inside seam line of peony diamonds (A), log cabin pieces, and purple print triangles in border strips.

Finished Edges

Bind with purple print fabric.

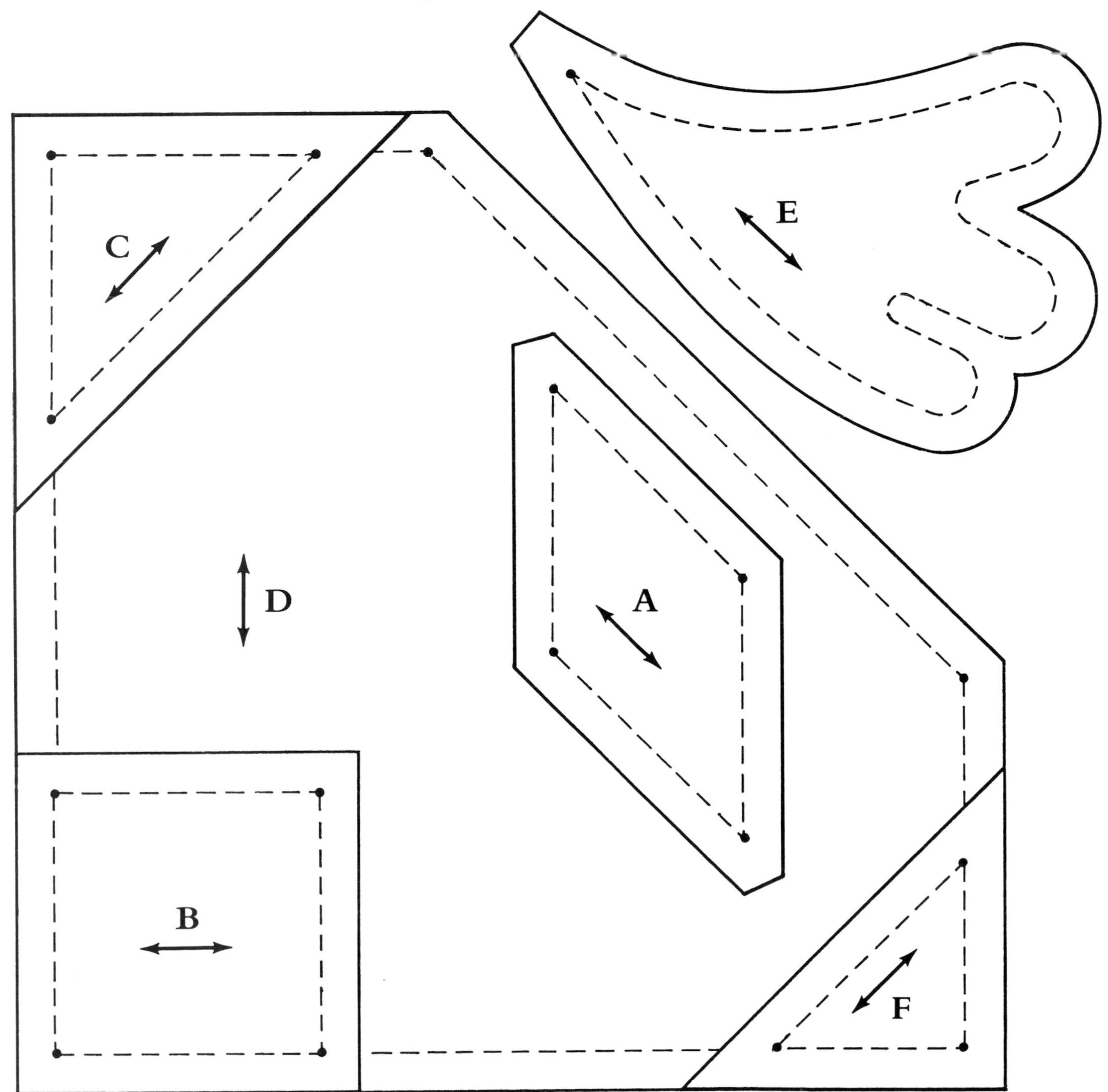

Lois L. Minyard

Baldwyn, Mississippi

"I love to make quilts and see the material come to life," says Lois. She has been quilting for most of her life and says she couldn't count all of the quilts she has made. When Lois first began making quilts, it was because she and her husband needed them for their home. Now she quilts for pleasure and for others, and chuckles, "I can't keep them on hand long enough to display before they're gone."

For Lois, quilting is a great joy and fulfillment. "It makes me happy to see what can be done with scissors, thread, and needle," says Lois.

Tulip Quilt
1985

Placed like vanes of a windmill, Lois's multicolored tulips are ready to catch the first breeze of early spring. After seeing fields and fields of tulips on a recent trip to Holland, Lois was inspired to design this quilt.

Her tulips are machine-appliquéd, but patterns are given with seam allowances for those of you who prefer hand-appliqué.

Tulip Quilt

Finished Quilt Size
81″ x 102″

Number of Blocks and Finished Size
20 blocks—18″ x 18″

Fabric Requirements

Lt. blue	—5½ yd.
Tulip solids	—3½ yd. total
Green	—1 yd.
Navy	—4¼ yd.
Navy for bias binding	—1¼ yd.
Backing	—6 yd.

Other Materials

Lightweight fusible interfacing	—4½ yd.
Fabric-compatible glue stick	

Number to Cut

Template A	—80 tulip solids
Template A*	—80 tulip solids
Template B	—80 tulip solids
Template C	—80 green
Template D	—80 green

* — Flip or turn over template if fabric is one-sided.

Quilt Top Assembly
1. Cut twenty 18½″ squares from light blue. Finger-crease each square on the diagonal; then finger-crease again on the opposite diagonal for placement lines. Place a tulip with stem and leaf in each corner of square, as shown in Placement Diagram. Notice that Lois placed tulips of the same color opposite each other.

Placement Diagram

If you are machine-appliquéing tulips as Lois did, apply lightweight fusible interfacing to tulip and stem pieces. Trim excess fabric outside seam line. Anchor each piece to block, using a glue stick. Satin-stitch over raw edges, using thread the same color as the piece. Appliqué 20 tulip blocks.
2. Cut 15 sashing strips, 3½″ x 18½″, from navy. Arrange tulip blocks in desired color arrangement. Alternate 4 tulip blocks with 3 sashing strips and join, at sides, beginning with a tulip block to form a row. Make 5 rows.
3. Cut 4 sashing strips, 3½″ wide, from navy to place between rows. Alternate tulip rows with sashing strips and join, beginning with a tulip row. (See quilt photograph.)

Quilting
Lois quilted parallel lines, 2″ apart, across each tulip block. Outline-quilt inside seam line of sashing strips.

Finished Edges
Bind with navy fabric.

Petal Placement Line
B
Place on the fold.
Petal Placement Line
Petal Placement Line
C
Stem Placement Line
Stem Placement Line
Petal Placement Line
A
Tulip Placement Lines
D
Leaf Placement Line
Leaf Placement Line

Kim could easily title her first exposure to quilting as "My Adventures with Quilting." "I loved an old log cabin quilt made by my great-grandmother," says Kim, "and at the age of 15, I decided to teach myself to quilt." As Kim remembers, "I didn't realize that the fabric pieces were usually stitched together in blocks. So, I cut my scraps into odd shapes and just started piecing them together at one corner." She continues, "I ended up stitching curved seams and setting in corners, doing everything the hard way. The result was a very crazy quilt!" Kim kept plugging away, and it seems that her fortitude and determination won out. Her second quilt was a beautiful Lone Star. Before she graduated from high school, she had completed four quilts. Several years later, as a wife and a mother, Kim still finds quilting as rewarding and intriguing as she did then.

Kim A. Christensen-Kent

Racine, Wisconsin

Amish Homage
1984
The soft flannel backing and the bright, crisp colors of Kim's *Amish Homage* make this quilt irresistible to any infant. "I wanted to make a rainbow quilt for my baby," says Kim, "because bright colors are more stimulating to babies than pastels."

Quilters will recognize Kim's *Amish Homage* as a contemporary version of the traditional Amish Shadows or Roman Stripe pattern.

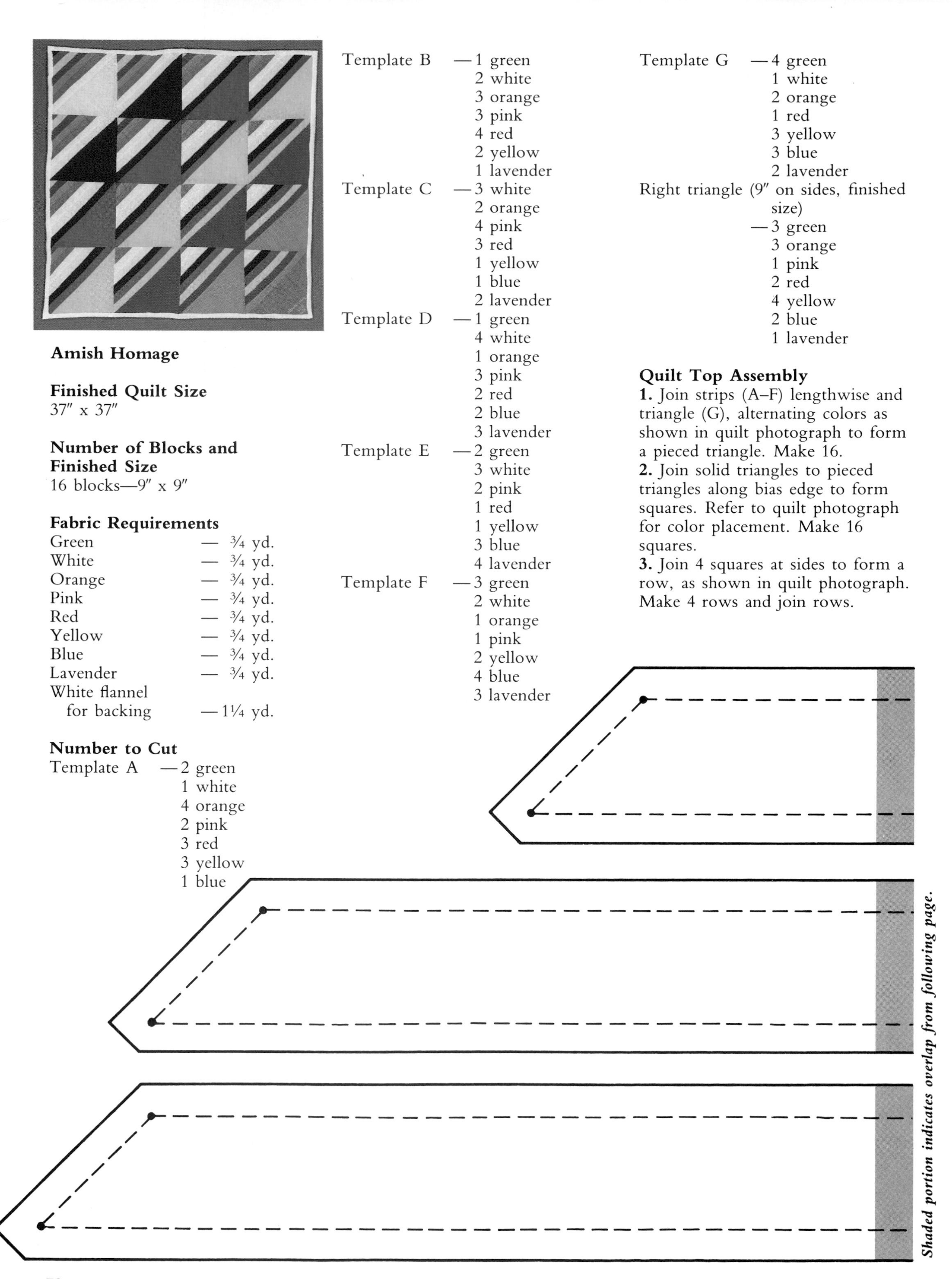

Amish Homage

Finished Quilt Size
37″ x 37″

Number of Blocks and Finished Size
16 blocks—9″ x 9″

Fabric Requirements

Green	— 3/4 yd.
White	— 3/4 yd.
Orange	— 3/4 yd.
Pink	— 3/4 yd.
Red	— 3/4 yd.
Yellow	— 3/4 yd.
Blue	— 3/4 yd.
Lavender	— 3/4 yd.
White flannel for backing	— 1 1/4 yd.

Number to Cut

Template A — 2 green, 1 white, 4 orange, 2 pink, 3 red, 3 yellow, 1 blue

Template B — 1 green, 2 white, 3 orange, 3 pink, 4 red, 2 yellow, 1 lavender

Template C — 3 white, 2 orange, 4 pink, 3 red, 1 yellow, 1 blue, 2 lavender

Template D — 1 green, 4 white, 1 orange, 3 pink, 2 red, 2 blue, 3 lavender

Template E — 2 green, 3 white, 2 pink, 1 red, 1 yellow, 3 blue, 4 lavender

Template F — 3 green, 2 white, 1 orange, 1 pink, 2 yellow, 4 blue, 3 lavender

Template G — 4 green, 1 white, 2 orange, 1 red, 3 yellow, 3 blue, 2 lavender

Right triangle (9″ on sides, finished size) — 3 green, 3 orange, 1 pink, 2 red, 4 yellow, 2 blue, 1 lavender

Quilt Top Assembly

1. Join strips (A–F) lengthwise and triangle (G), alternating colors as shown in quilt photograph to form a pieced triangle. Make 16.
2. Join solid triangles to pieced triangles along bias edge to form squares. Refer to quilt photograph for color placement. Make 16 squares.
3. Join 4 squares at sides to form a row, as shown in quilt photograph. Make 4 rows and join rows.

Quilting
Quilt diagonal lines the length of quilt, 1¼″ apart, in the direction opposite to the lengthwise seams of pieced triangles.

Finished Edges
Turn 1″ of flannel backing to front and miter corners. Turn raw edge under ¼″ and blindstitch to quilt.

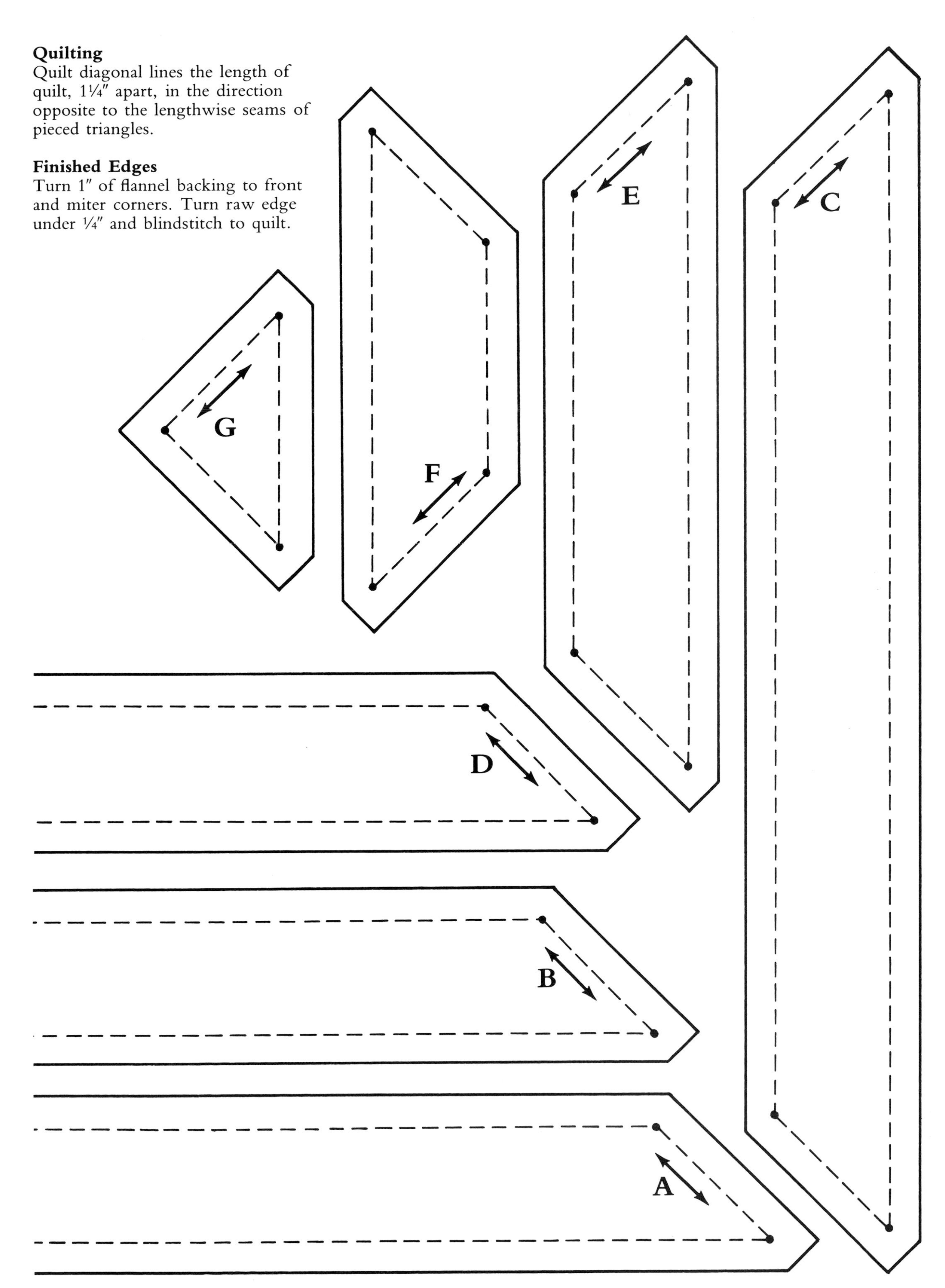

Judy Sogn

Seattle, Washington

Since learning to quilt four years ago, Judy says, quiltmaking has become the major focus of her life. "I have always enjoyed some form of needlework," says Judy, "but none is as rewarding to me as quilting." As Judy puts it, "There's a mystique surrounding quiltmaking. The excitement of designing our own work; the challenge of tackling a complicated pattern; the sense of accomplishment with each new finished project; the fellowship with other quilters; the fulfillment of sharing our techniques with others; the joy of seeing our work exhibited; and a link to the women of the past are just a few pleasures of quilting." She continues, "Quilting has meant all this and more to me, and I look forward to many more happy quilting years."

Christmas Tulips

1984

Smartly arranged scarlet tulips, found in Judy's quilted wall hanging, will gladden anyone's holiday mantel. Inspired by the Rosegay pattern, published in the Spring/Summer 1983 issue of *Quiltmaker* (see "Resources" for details), Judy made a few pattern adjustments, set the design on the diagonal, and suddenly roses became tulips. Its streamlined qualities make this quilt a geometric delight.

Christmas Tulips

Finished Quilt Size

37½" x 37½"

Fabric Requirements

Dark green	— ½ yd.
Dark green print	— 1¼ yd.
Red with white circles	— ⅜ yd.
Red floral print	— ⅛ yd.
Cream with red print	— ½ yd.
Muslin	— 1 yd.
Dark green for bias binding	— 1 yd.
Backing	— 1¼ yd.

Number to Cut

Template A	— 1 dk. green 4 red floral print
Template B	— 32 dk. green 16 red with white circles 4 cream with red print
Template C	— 8 dk. green
Template C★	— 8 dk. green
Template D	— 16 red with white circles
Template E	— 16 red with white circles
Template F	— 16 red floral print
Template G	— 8 cream with red print
Template G★	— 8 cream with red print
Template H	— 32 muslin
Template I	— 4 muslin
Template J	— 32 muslin
Template K	— 8 muslin
Template L	— 28 cream with red print 4 muslin

★ — Flip or turn over template if fabric is one-sided.

Quilt Top Assembly

1. Referring to Tulip Block Piecing Diagram, join pieces (A, B, D, E, F, J, H, and L) into 3 rows. Join rows to complete block.

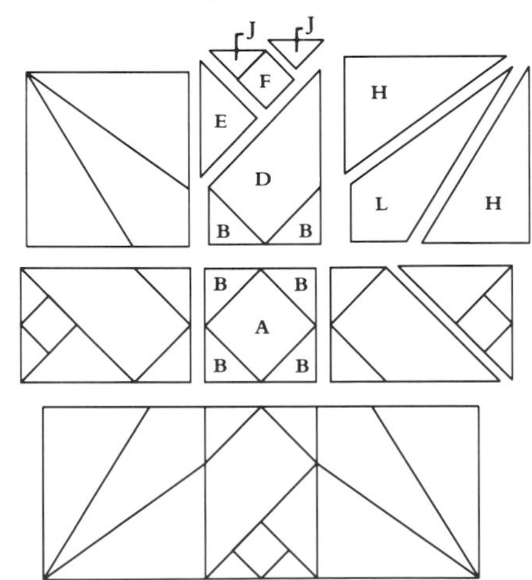

Tulip Block Piecing Diagram

2. Join triangles (C) to shapes (G), as shown in Tulip Strip Diagram. Join pieced shape to sides of piece (I). Begin stitching from the outside edge and stitch up to the seam line. Stop and backstitch 1 or 2 stitches. Remove fabric from the machine. Align the remaining sides and stitch from the center to the outside edge, backstitching 1 or 2 stitches at the start. Make 2 tulip strips with corner blocks, as shown in the Tulip Strip Diagram, and 2 without.

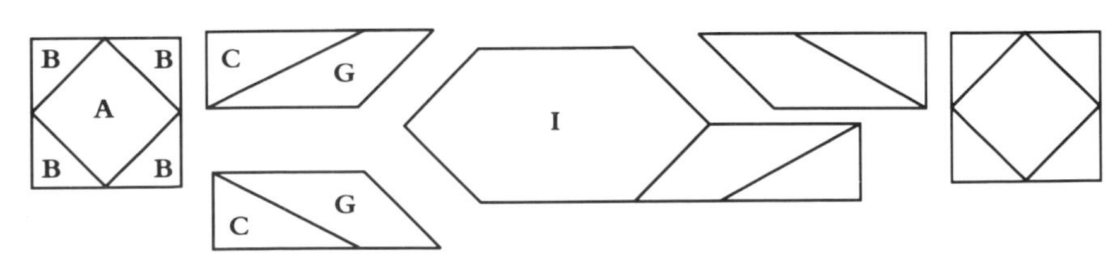

Tulip Strip Diagram

Join strips without corner blocks to opposite sides of tulip block. Join strips with corner blocks to the top and bottom.

3. Referring to quilt photograph, cut 4 right triangles from muslin to join to quilt. Join the bias edges of triangles to sides of quilt.

4. Cut 4 borders, 2½" wide, from dark green print. Join to quilt and miter corners.

5. Refer to the tulip portion of the Tulip Block Piecing Diagram and make 12 tulips, using pieces B, D, E, F, and J.

Join pieces (H, K, and L), as shown in Border Rectangle Piecing Diagram. Make 8 pieced rectangles.

Alternate 3 tulips with 2 pieced rectangles and join at sides, as shown in Tulip Border Piecing Diagram. Join pieces (H and L) to each end, as shown. Make 4 borders.

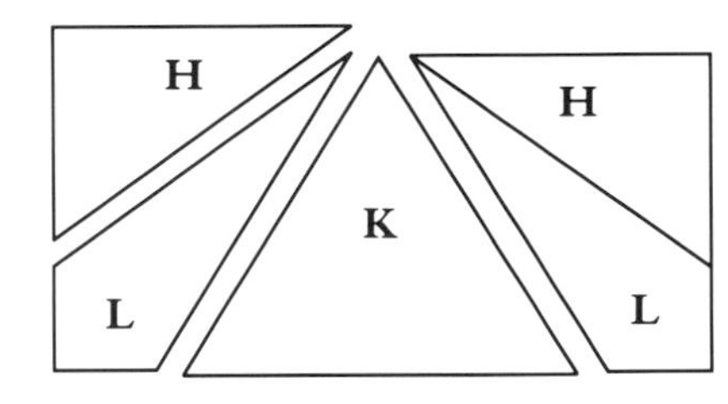

Border Rectangle Piecing Diagram

6. Join 2 borders to opposite sides of quilt. Begin and end stitching at seam line, backstitching 1 or 2 stitches at beginning and end. Join piece (L) to each end of remaining borders, as shown in Corner Piecing Diagram. Join borders to quilt in same manner as above. Join borders at corners.

7. Cut 4 borders, 3" wide, from dark green print. Join to quilt and miter corners.

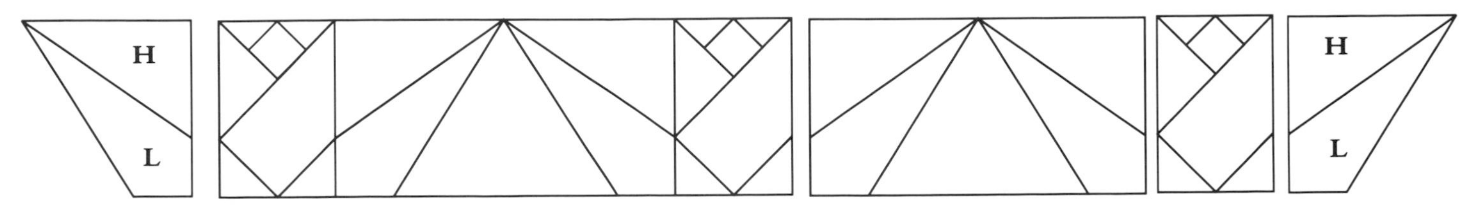

Tulip Border Piecing Diagram

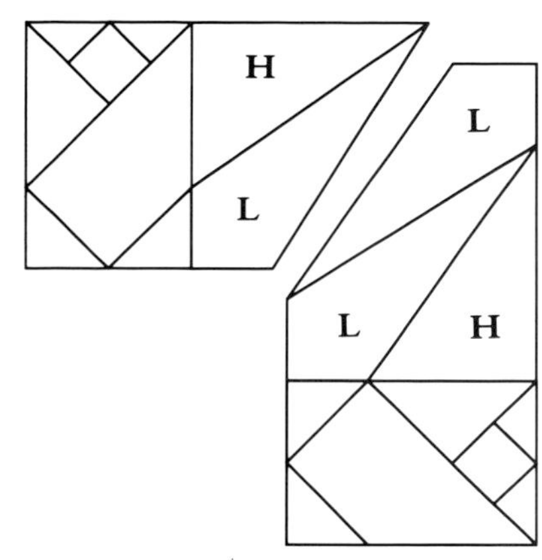

Corner Piecing Diagram

Quilting
Outline-quilt inside seam line of all tulips. Quilt lines from the seam junction of pieces H, L, and K, as shown in Quilting Diagram. Quilt feather pattern in corners of large triangles of center section. Quilt a ½″ cross-hatching pattern for the remainder of open areas of center section. Judy used an unbroken rope pattern for the dark green print border.

Finished Edges
Bind with dark green fabric.

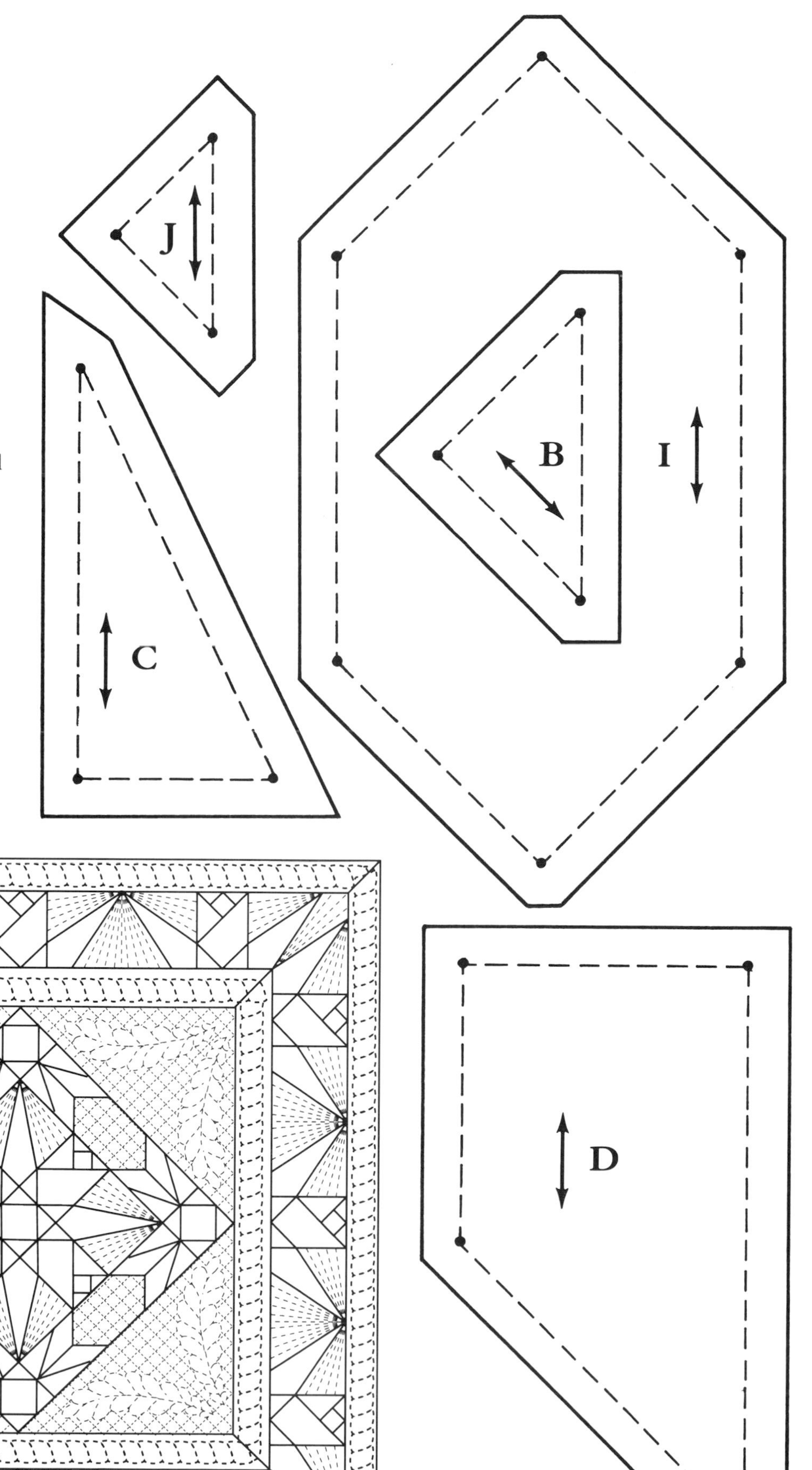

Quilting Diagram

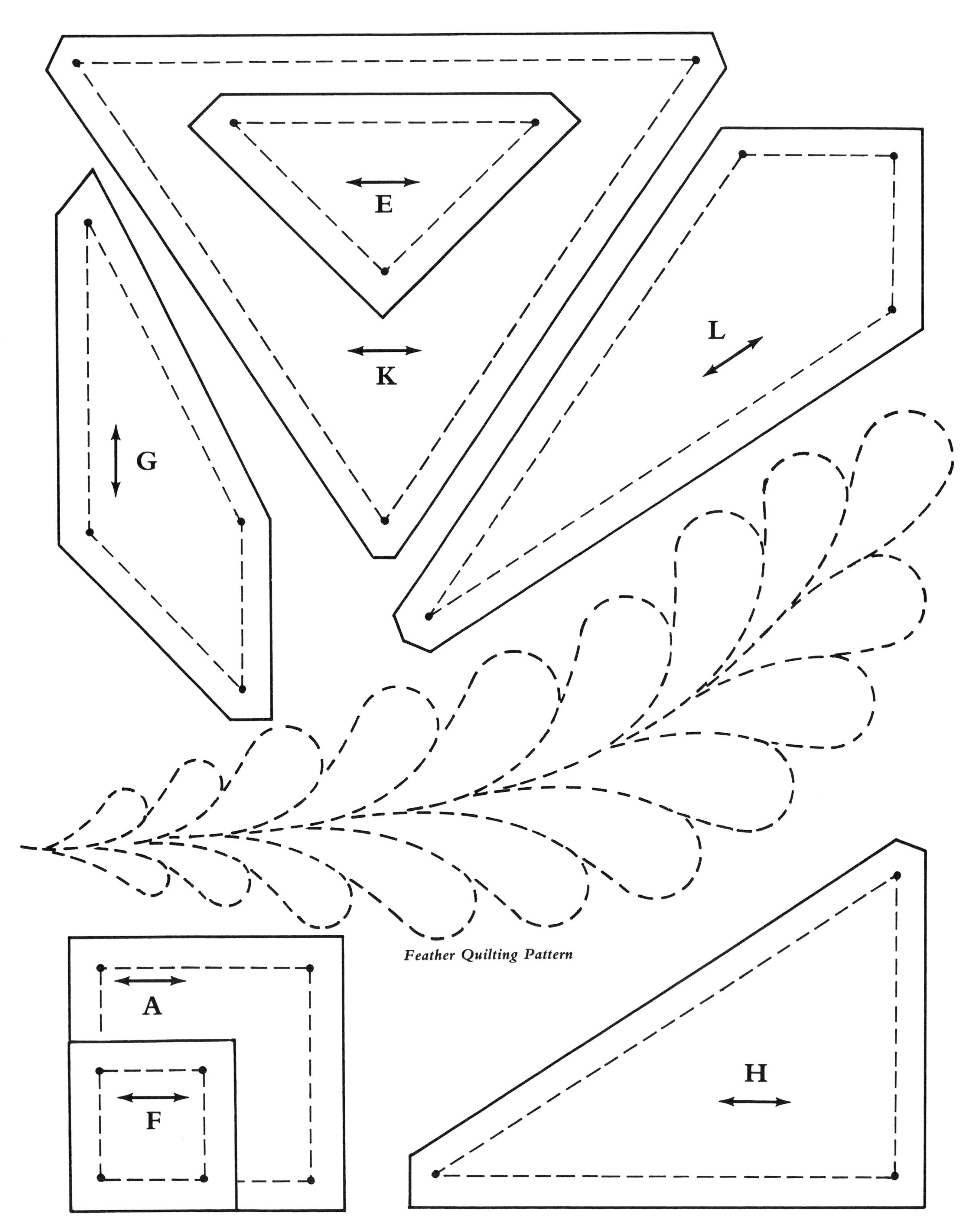

Feather Quilting Pattern

Roberta first became intrigued with papermaking after taking a workshop in 1979. She had been a quilter for several years, especially interested in pattern, color, and texture. Accordingly, her papermaking efforts served as the catalyst that sparked her creative intellect to combine the two crafts. "In addition, I regarded my paper palette as a resource for my quilts," says Roberta. "I think about real quilts when I'm working in paper."

As a serious and dedicated fiber artist, Roberta is anxious to share with quilters her method for duplicating fabric quilts as paper quilts. "My artistic concern is accessibility," says Roberta, "and that my concepts, formal expression, and techniques be understood and enjoyed by many."

Roberta Fountain

Chico, California

Log Cabin Paper Quilt

1986

Many of Roberta's earliest paper quilts incorporated simple traditional quilt patterns, such as Log Cabin. Roberta chose this piece as a starting point for quilters to make their first paper quilt, because of its simplicity and easy construction.

This paper quilt was displayed by Roberta in a solo show that she entitled "Home Is Where the Quilts Are." "This is my house built with many colors," says Roberta. "When I first created this quilt, I had this thought in mind:

Each log a concrete thing
we do, we say,
over time,
to build a structure,
the relationship,
a rainbow of feelings. ©1986

Since Roberta uses a piecework approach, quilters will find many similarities between fabric quiltmaking and construction of paper quilts. "One thing to consider when making fiber pulp," says Roberta, "is that you might call it a water sport—splashy and somewhat messy—so working outside is ideal. Also, be careful to keep excess water mopped up around the blender."

The technique for making fiber pulp is rather simple. The only major piece of equipment one needs is a blender. And best of all, with a paper quilt there are no seam allowances or grain lines to worry about!

Log Cabin Paper Quilt

Finished Size
31″ x 31″

Number of Blocks and Finished Size
9 Log Cabin blocks—8″ x 8″

Materials
Assorted paper★ — old letters, cards, announcements, envelopes, junk mail, construction paper
Assorted fabric★★ — cotton, silk, rayon, linen, or blends in the same rainbow colors as the papers
★Not suitable—glossy papers and newspaper.
★★Not suitable—knits and heavy upholstery fabric.

Tools
Blender with 2 speeds
9 plastic containers for storage, *optional* (1 for each color)
9 buckets (1 for each color)
10 nylon or brass mesh screens (rustproof) in sturdy frames†
Sponges
White glue or methyl cellulose (wallpaper paste)
Scissors
Ruler
Mat board
Scale for weighing paper and fabric

† — You will need 1 screen for each color. A 15″ x 15″ screen should be large enough for each color in this project. One large screen, at least 36″ x 36″, is needed for the backing. Or, fewer buckets and screens will be necessary if colored papers are made on consecutive days, peeled off when dry, and the screen reused for the next color.

Number to Cut
Red — 18 pieces—2½″ x 1″
Orange — 18 pieces—4″ x 1″
Dk. yellow — 18 pieces—5½″ x 1″
Lt. yellow — 18 pieces—7″ x 1″
Green — 18 pieces—7½″ x 1″
Med. blue — 18 pieces—6″ x 1″
Dk. blue — 18 pieces—4½″ x 1″
Blue-violet — 18 pieces—3″ x 1″
Red-violet — 9 pieces—1¾″ x 1¾″

Log Cabin Paper Quilt Assembly

1. Gather paper to recycle. Cut away cellophane and remove staples and tape. Sort paper collection into colors: red, orange, dark yellow, light yellow, green, medium blue, dark blue, blue-violet, red-violet. Select a color for the backing. This color will not be visible, but it needs to be one that will not run and stain the rest of the piece. (For example, if you choose light yellow, make a larger quantity of light yellow than the other colors. If you choose a color not listed above, you will need another plastic container and bucket.)

Tear or cut papers into pieces no larger than 1″ square.

2. Gather fabric to recycle. Cut away seams, buttons, all sewing details, and selvages. Cut fabrics into pieces no larger than ½″ square.

3. Weigh paper and fabric pieces. A combined weight of 4 pounds should yield a sufficient amount of material for this project.

4. Gather tools and prepare work space. Combine and mix equal amounts of cut paper and cut fabric of the same color group. A mix of more paper than fabric is okay. Cover the color groups with water in the bucket and soak the cut bits for at least 1 hour to soften. These may be stored in a plastic container in the refrigerator if they are to be held for 2 days or more before using.

5. To make paper pulp, put one handful (about ⅓ cup) of one color of soaked fabric/paper mixture into blender. Add water until the blender container is ¾ full. Start blending on slow speed and increase speed to high, blending approximately 20 seconds altogether. Listen to your machine for signals that it is working too hard. If you are blending a large amount, watch for a heated motor and give it a rest. Pour paper pulp in bucket.

Often threads from fabrics wrap around the blender's blades. These must be wiped away from the blade after each blender load. These threads stress the blender's ability and can overwork the machine.

Work in this manner for each color, storing each color in a separate bucket.

6. To make flat sheets of paper, pour pulp onto a raised screen to allow for dripping. Keep thickness of pulp even. (When it is dry, it will be much thinner than it is now.) Set aside screen (still raised) to allow pulp to dry. Pulp should dry in 2 days or less.

Make sheets of green, medium blue, and red-violet in a size sufficient for the number of pieces specified and reserve the remainder of the pulp for the borders.

7. When sheets of paper are dry, cut into measured pieces. Any left-over scraps can be blended again and poured to make a fresh sheet of paper.

8. Arrange blocks in log cabin pattern, as shown in photograph of Log Cabin block. Start with the center square and lay strips in a counterclockwise direction. Apply a ¼″ line of glue along one long edge of the back of each strip, overlap the previous strip, and press together. Make 9 Log Cabin blocks.

9. For a backing sheet, pulp and pour a sheet of paper large enough to hold all 9 blocks. (Use the largest screen to make this backing sheet, because you will be adding a pulp border to these blocks.) While the backing sheet is still wet, apply a thin layer of glue to the back of the dried blocks and quickly set them into the wet backing sheet, touching block edge to block edge. (See quilt photograph.) Press down firmly.

10. For the borders and edges, carefully pour the reserved green pulp between the Log Cabin blocks, masking where the blocks meet. Use your fingers to guide the flow of the pulp into the place you want it to go. Pour a thin green border around the outside of the assembled blocks. Next pour a blue border around the outside, and finally, a red-violet border.

11. Using a sponge, carefully press down across the whole face of the paper quilt, section by section, forcing the excess water to drain away. The paper quilt will take 2 to 4 days to dry. When dry, peel it carefully off the screen. Lightly spray paper quilt with a water mister and flatten it under plywood if the paper has curled. Back with mat board and frame.

Elaine describes herself as a normal wife and mother, but a craft nut. "I enjoy many crafts, but especially quilting because it is very relaxing and portable," says Elaine. "I can take it with me anywhere, as I do most of my quilting lap style."

Elaine learned to quilt as a child, while attending Vacation Bible School one summer. "Quilting is a great tradition, which I hope to perpetuate with my own children," says Elaine. Her *Hands Around Ozona* is testimony to her dedication to do just that.

Elaine R. Haggenbottom

Palm Harbor, Florida

Hands Around Ozona
1986

Changing schools—leaving friends to embark on a world of strange classrooms and fresh faces—can bring on a handful of tears from even the bravest. Elaine's son Andy encountered this situation when his third grade class was divided after having been together since kindergarten. Elaine decided his class would not be just another class forgotten. With some helpful advice from friends at a local shop, Rainbow's End, she concluded that handprints would be most representative of how each child was at that time, and of the love and friendship that had developed among them. In addition, getting the children involved in a farewell project made changing schools a special event and may have alleviated some of those "new school" fears.

Michelle Fascina, one of Elaine's friends, suggested using blue paint for boys and red paint for girls and alternating the colors on the quilt. *Hands Around Ozona* was presented to Ozona Elementary School on May 9, 1986, where it remains on display.

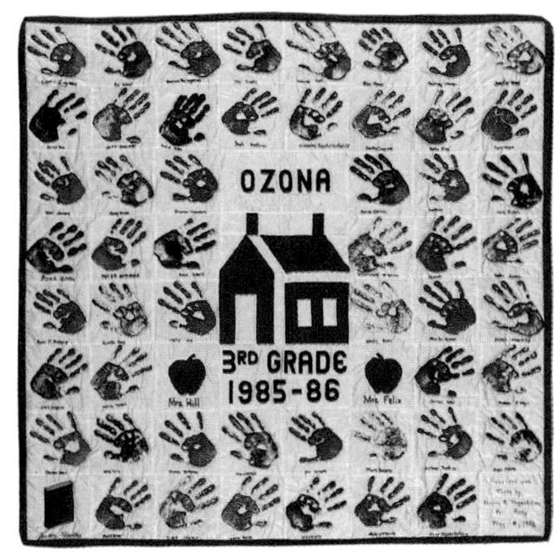

Hands Around Ozona

Finished Quilt Size
49" x 49"

Number of Blocks and Finished Size
1 Schoolhouse block—12" x 12"
52 Handprint blocks—6" x 6"
2 Teacher blocks—6" x 6"
1 Principal block—6" x 6"
1 Presentation block—6" x 6"

Fabric Requirements

White polished cotton	— 2½ yd.
Red polished cotton	— ½ yd.
Blue polished cotton (includes yardage for binding)	— 1 yd.
Backing	— 3 yd.

Other Materials

Acrylic paint	— 2 oz. bottle red
	— 2 oz. bottle blue
Permanent marker	— fine felt-tip red
	— fine felt-tip blue

2" alphabet templates
Lightweight fusible interfacing
Fabric-compatible glue stick
Plastic or aluminum pie plates
Pencils

Number to Cut

Template A	— 2 white
Template B	— 2 red
Template C	— 1 white 1 red
Template D	— 2 white
Template E	— 1 red
Template F	— 1 white
Template G	— 1 red
Template H	— 1 white
Template I	— 1 white
Template J	— 2 red
Template K	— 1 white
Template L	— 2 red
Template M	— 2 white
Template N	— 2 red
Template O	— 1 red
Template P	— 2 red*
Template Q	— 1 blue

* — Number will vary with the number of teachers you have. See Step 2.

Quilt Top Assembly

1. Cut fifty-six 6½" squares from white polished cotton. Set 4 squares aside for Teacher, Principal, and Presentation blocks. The remaining 52 will provide 26 blocks for girls and 26 blocks for boys. Of these 26, 12 will be left hands and 14 right hands.

Have children lightly print their names on blocks with pencils. Pour acrylic paint into plastic or aluminum pie plates. Dip hand into paint and press to fabric with a quick release. Have a wet towel available for cleaning hand, or better yet, do hand printing near a sink so children can immediately wash their hands. Acrylic paint will easily wash off with soap and water. Lay block aside and let dry thoroughly. When dry, print over penciled names with a permanent marker in matching red or blue.

2. Prepare Teacher and Principal blocks for appliqué by applying lightweight fusible interfacing to each apple and book. Trim excess fabric outside seam line. Anchor each to center of 6½" square, using a glue stick. Satin-stitch to cover raw edge of apple and book. Satin-stitch along contour lines marked on patterns. Print teacher's and principal's names at the bottom of their blocks with permanent marker.

3. Print information on Presentation block with permanent marker.

4. Cut 2 rectangles, 12½" x 6½", from white polished cotton. Using alphabet templates, pencil school name on one and grade with years on the other. Color letters and numbers with acrylic paint.

5. Join pieces A through O, as shown in Schoolhouse Block Piecing Diagrams.

6. Referring to quilt photograph and Setting Diagram, arrange blocks. Assemble quilt into sections, as shown in Setting Diagram, and prepare quilt for lap quilting.

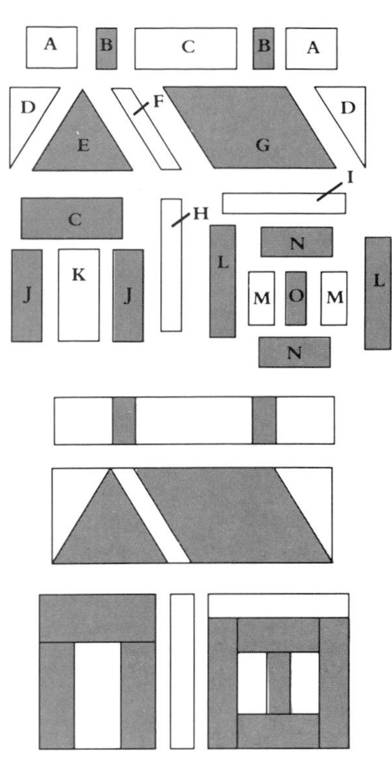

Schoolhouse Block Piecing Diagrams

If you prefer to quilt one large quilt top, join Handprint block sections to form 2 columns, each 3 blocks wide and 8 blocks long. (See Setting Diagram.) Join columns to sides of Schoolhouse block section.

Quilting
Outline-quilt around each handprint in thread color to match the handprint. Using white thread, outline-quilt ⅛" outside seam line of red pieces of Schoolhouse block, appliquéd apples, and book. Outline-quilt ¼" inside 12" seam lines of rectangles.

Finished Edges
If sections were lap-quilted, join as described in the second paragraph of Step 6.

Bind with blue polished cotton.

Setting Diagram

Schoolhouse Block Section
Schoolhouse Block
Handprint Block Section
Principal
Teacher
PB

LH = Left Hand RH = Right Hand
PB = Presentation Block

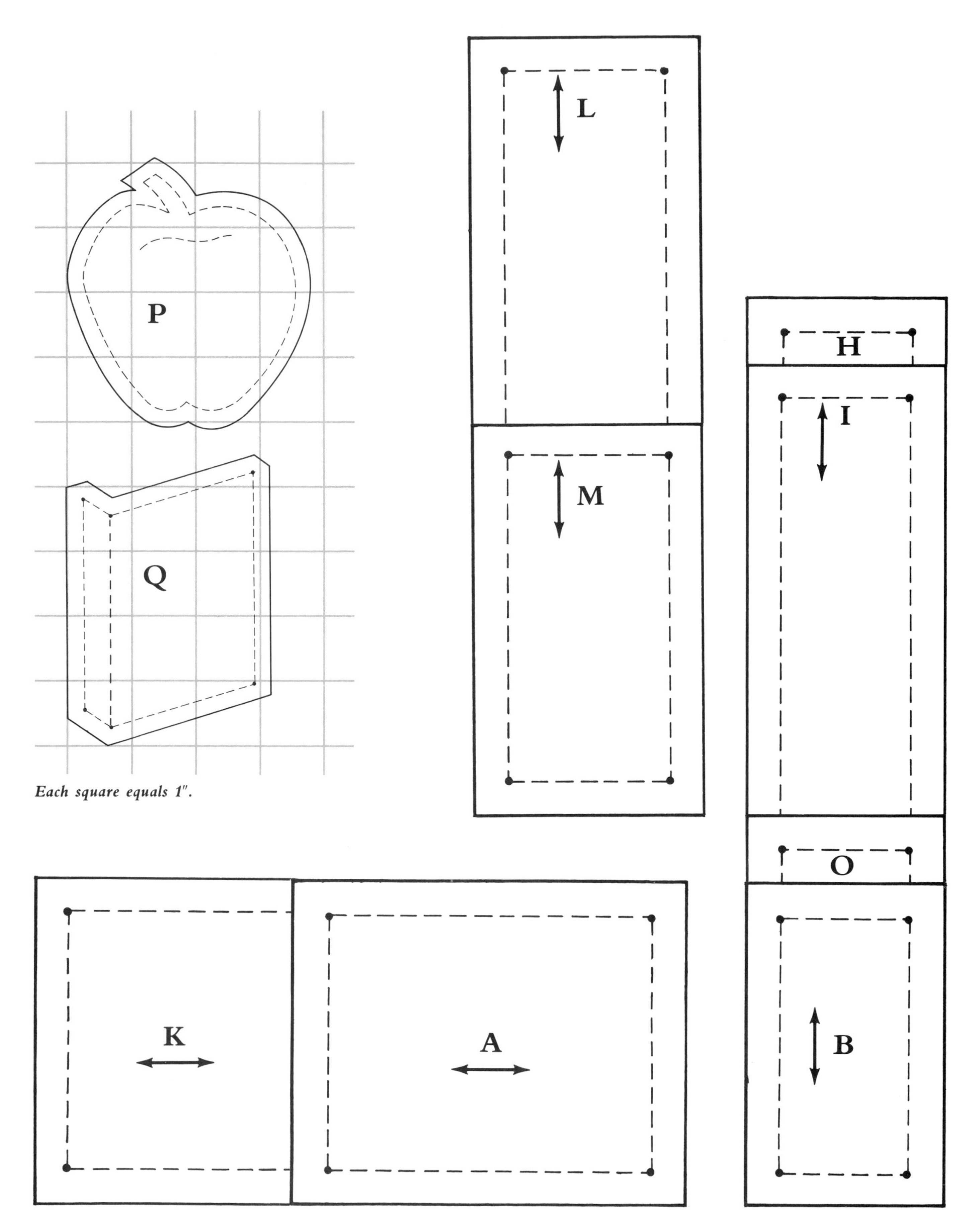

Each square equals 1″.

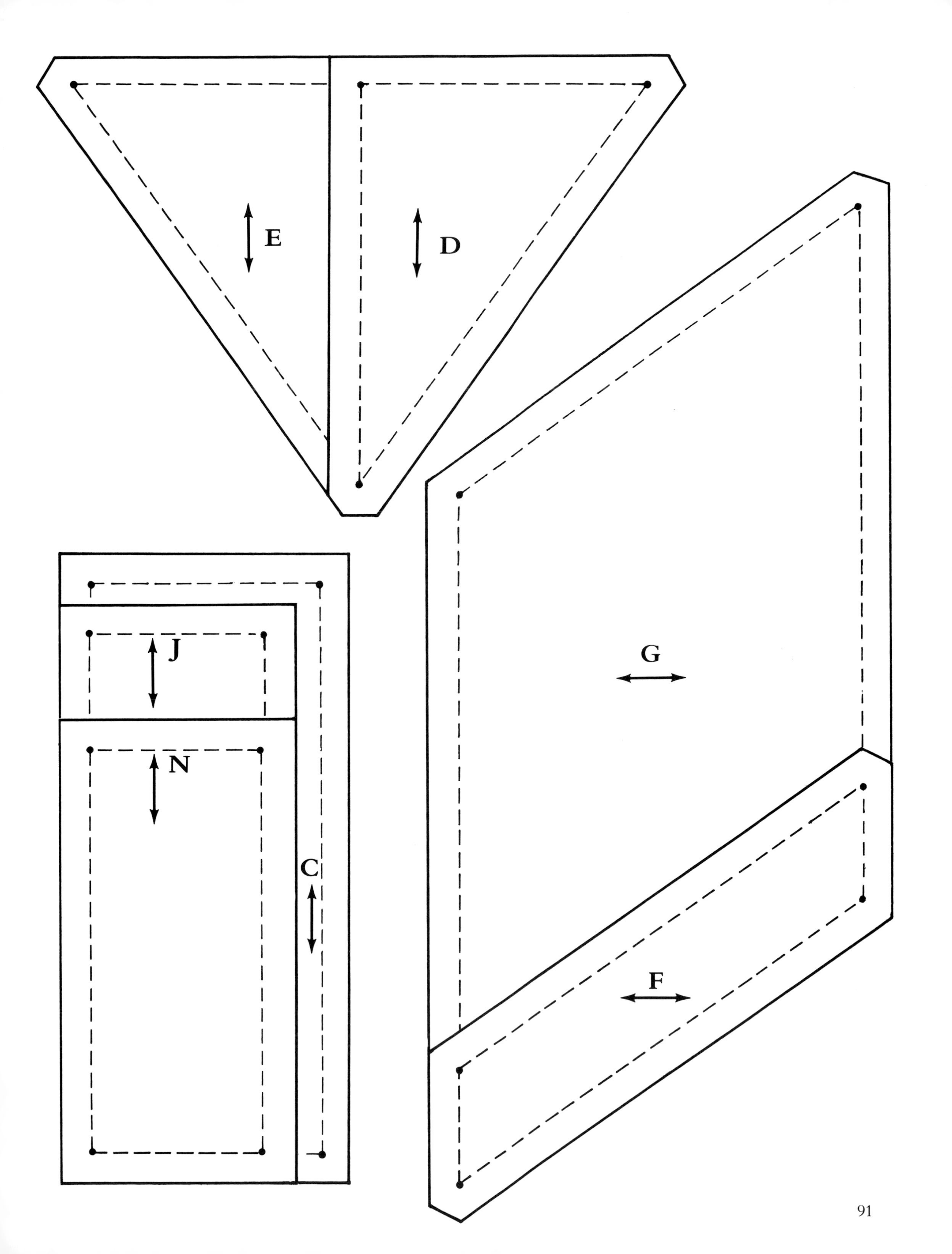
E
D
G
J
N
C
F

Linae Frei

Northbrook, Illinois

"To me quilting is painting with fabrics," says this professional painter and fine arts major. Linae first explored quiltmaking while recuperating from surgery some 14 years ago. Without any previous experience in quiltmaking, Linae tackled a box of fabrics left to her by a friend and produced her first quilt.

Today, 21 quilts later, Linae especially enjoys designing quilts. "Ideas come from everywhere," she exclaims. Trying new things and then facing the challenge of making them work are the facets of quiltmaking most appealing to Linae. "I continue to paint and exhibit my work," says Linae, "but I have not been able to stop quilting! Quilting and painting are very important to me; they fill my life."

Draw Me

1976

Remember those dot-to-dot drawings you did as a child? Here's your chance to do one again, this time with fabric, yarn, and buttons! With dozens of buttons, playing the role of dots, and yards of yarn, playing the role of pencil marks, Linae had a grand time making caricature drawings of animals. A smiling turtle follows a curly-tailed pig. A handsome buffalo faces a flying eagle. And a hopping kangaroo poses next to a princely cat.

Linae confesses, "I hate sewing a missing button on a garment, but sewing these on was a delight." *Draw Me* won the New York State Award for the National Quilt Competition sponsored by the United States Historical Society and the Museum of American Folk Art in 1975. The quilt has also appeared in several national publications. (See "Resources.")

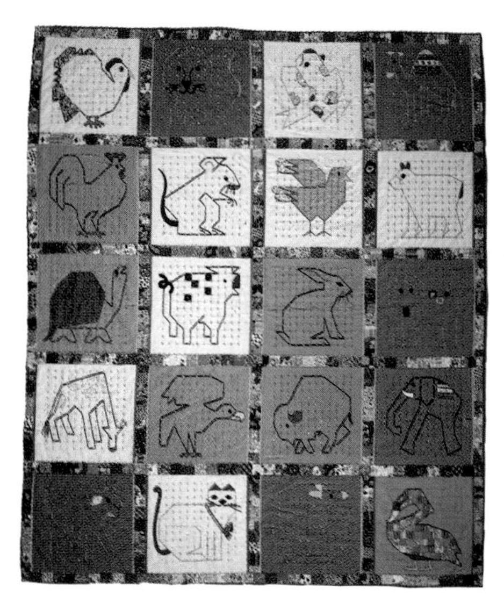

Draw Me

Finished Quilt Size
101″ x 126″

Number of Blocks and Finished Size
20 blocks—21½″ x 21½″

Fabric Requirements

Heavy cotton or kettle cloth:	
Blue	—2 yd.
White	—2½ yd.
Brown	—2 yd.
Scrap fabrics	—4 yd. total
Blue for bias strips	—1 yd.★
Beige for bias strips	—1¼ yd.★
Red for bias binding	—1¼ yd.
Backing	—11 yd.

★ — Yardage is for make-your-own bias strips.

Other Materials
Cording,
¼″ diameter — 13½ yd.
Shirt buttons, small, white, 2-holed—2,736
Tapestry needle
Assorted medium-weight yarns
Scrap fabrics
Assorted buttons for animal eyes

Number to Cut
Sashing square— 465 to 485 scrap fabrics (See Step 7.)

Quilt Top Assembly
1. Cut six 22″ squares from blue heavy cotton or kettle cloth, eight from white, and six from brown, respectively, for a total of 20 animal blocks.
2. Cut twenty 23″ squares of batting.
3. With marking pencil, center and draw a grid, 16½″ x 16½″, of 1½″ squares on each block. Center batting squares under blocks and carefully machine-quilt the grid.
4. Refer to block diagrams and make a string outline of each animal, using a needle and basting thread. Insert the needle and thread through the material only where the direction changes.

Using a tapestry needle and yarn, follow the string outline with a stemstitch, inserting the needle and yarn through the fabric and batting.
5. Appliqué blocks with fabric, as shown in block diagrams and photographs. Sew on buttons for animal eyes and embroider, as shown.
6. Frame each animal block on vertical sides with ¾″-wide (measurement includes seam allowance) bias strips. Use blue for white blocks and beige for blue blocks and brown blocks, except use blue for the goose block. (See quilt and block photographs.)
7. Cut 3½″ sashing squares (measurement includes seam allowance). Join 9 sashing squares at sides to form strips for sides of each block. Strips will be longer than the sides of blocks. Make 25 sashing strips. Alternate 5 sashing strips with 4 animal blocks, as shown in Setting Diagram. Join at sides to form a row. For variety, shift placement of strips along the sides. After joining, trim away any excess fabric even with block. Make 5 rows.
8. Join remaining number of sashing squares at sides to form sashing rows. Make 6 sashing rows. Alternate sashing rows with animal block rows, as shown in Setting Diagram and quilt photograph. Vary sashing row placement in same manner as in Step 7. Join rows. Trim away any excess fabric of sashing rows even with block rows. For accent, Linae couched a single thread of yarn along seam lines of sashing rows. (See quilt photograph.)

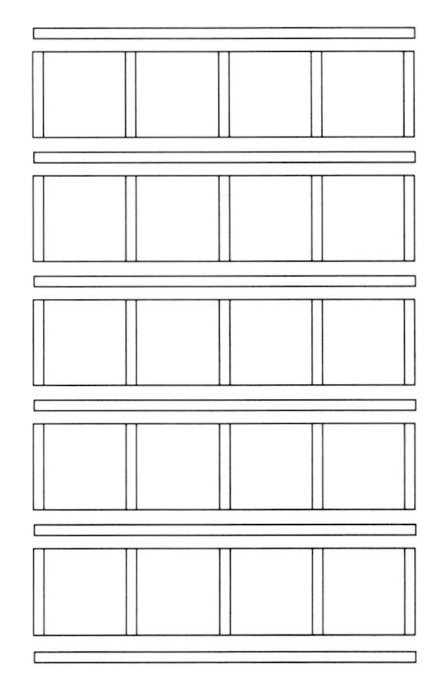

Setting Diagram

9. Turn top over. Cover area behind sashing strips with batting. Place backing on quilt and baste.
10. Sew shirt buttons to front at grid intersections, stitching through all layers. This reinforces the quilt and helps hold back to top. (Notice, the goose block has only one button—for his eye.)

Finished Edges
Cover cording with a continuous bias strip of red. Sew covered cording to quilt front. Turn under edge of backing and blindstitch to covered cording.

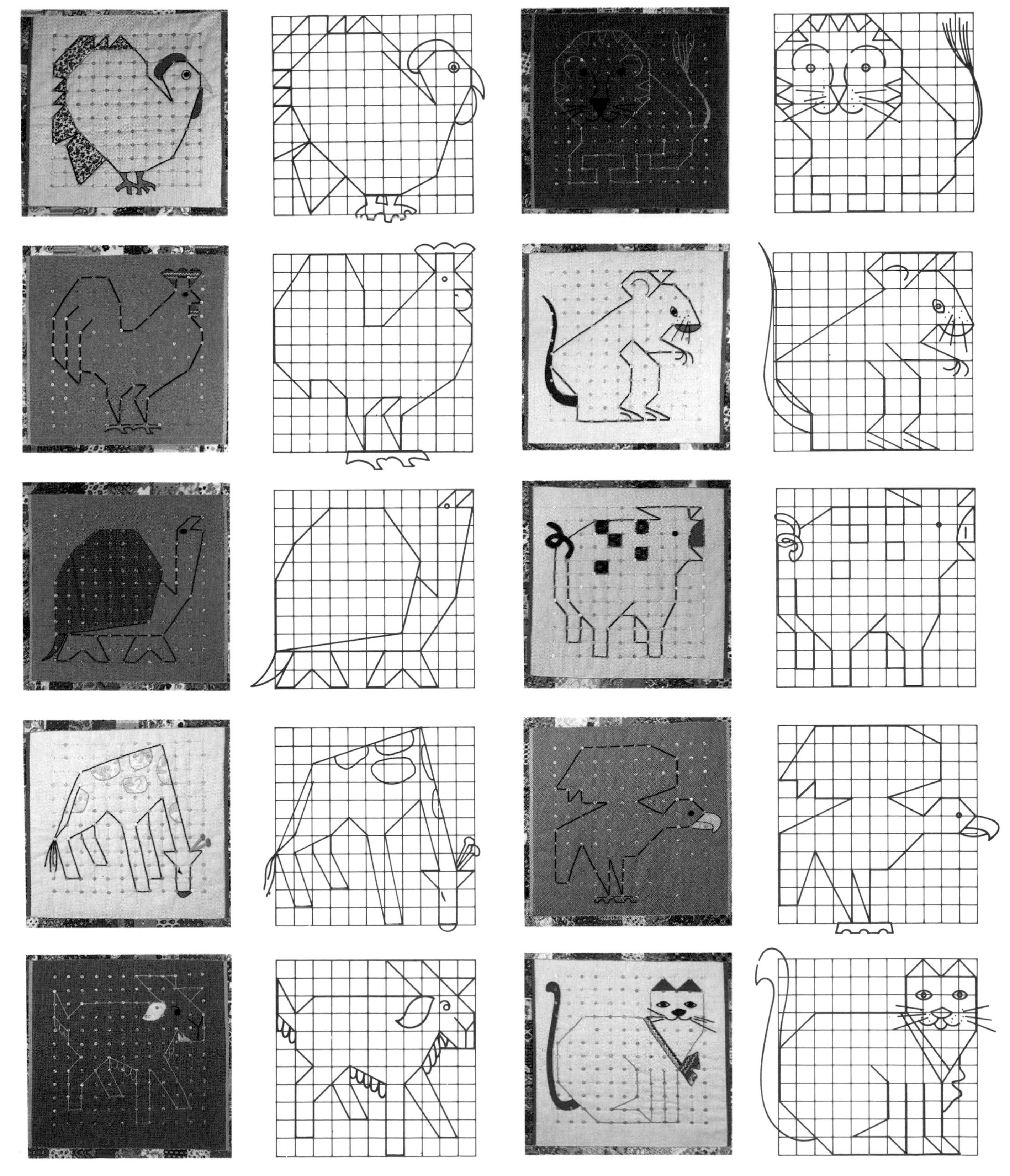

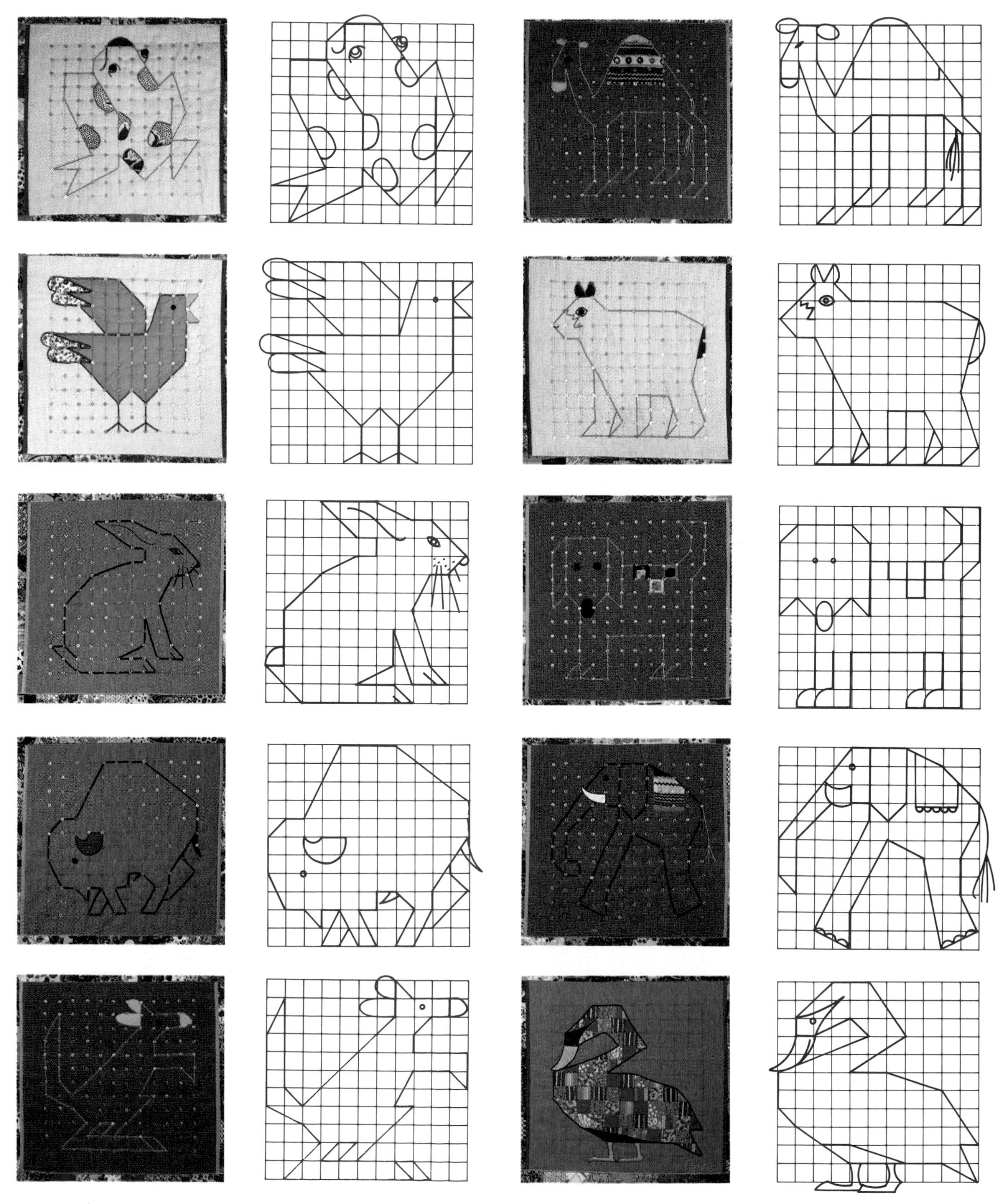

Karen majored in mathematics and elementary education in college and was an elementary schoolteacher for six years. "I ended that career to pursue my interest in teaching quilting to adults," says Karen. With dedication, she painstakingly tries every new technique that comes along before teaching it to her students. "I have found it sheer joy to pass on a craft that I love," continues Karen. "It hardly seems like work at all!"

Quilting has allowed Karen to combine her four greatest loves in one endeavor: sewing, working with fabric, mathematics, and teaching. Be sure and turn to our "All Sorts of Samplers" chapter and partake of Karen's enchantment with star patterns as seen in her *Star Crazy* sampler.

Karen Bowdren LaDuca

Pittsford, New York

Periwinkle Pinwheels
1982

Imagine legions of slender pinwheels turning in obedience to a gentle breeze. Then emblazon that image on a meadow of periwinkles, their heads tilting in response to the same gentle breeze. With its cool and refreshing hues and its flow of movement, Karen's *Periwinkle Pinwheels* takes an imagined vision and makes it reality.

Karen designed and made *Periwinkle Pinwheels* for her nephew, Camden Chase Bowdren. "Cam's quilt is well loved," says Karen. "He must have it to take his nap, and it even travels with him to nursery school!" Because of his attachment to the quilt, Karen made a duplicate of *Periwinkle Pinwheels* to use in teaching and exhibitions.

Periwinkle Pinwheels won first place in the Crib Quilt Category at the 17th Annual National Quilting Association Show in July 1986.

Periwinkle Pinwheels

Finished Quilt Size
45″ x 52″

Fabric Requirements

Purple with white pindots★	— 1½ yd.
Periwinkle print	— 1 yd.
Muslin, unbleached	— 1¼ yd.
Periwinkle print for bias binding	— 1 yd.
Backing	— 2½ yd.

★ — Throughout the directions, purple with white pindots will be designated as purple.

Number to Cut

Template A	— 96 purple
Template B	— 96 periwinkle print
Template C	— 34 muslin
Template D	— 31 muslin

Quilt Top Assembly

1. Join all purple triangles (A) to all periwinkle triangles (B) at longest sides. Join 4 to make a pinwheel, as shown in Pinwheel Assembly Diagram. Make 24 pinwheels. Set 4 pinwheels aside for corner blocks.

2. Alternate 3 parallelograms (D) with 4 pinwheels, as shown in Row Assembly Diagram, and join to form a row. Join triangle (C) to each end to complete row. Make 5 rows.

3. Join rows with parallelograms (D) between the rows, as shown in Row Assembly Diagram. Join triangles (C) to top and bottom rows, as shown.

4. Cut 4 border strips, 2″ wide, from muslin. Join to quilt and miter corners.

5. Join 4 triangles (C) to sides of pinwheel for corner Pinwheel block, as shown in Corner Pinwheel Block Piecing Diagram. Make 4.

6. Cut 2 borders, 7½″ wide, from purple for sides of quilt and join to quilt.

7. Cut 2 borders, 7½″ wide, from purple for top and bottom of quilt. Join a corner Pinwheel block to each end. Join to quilt.

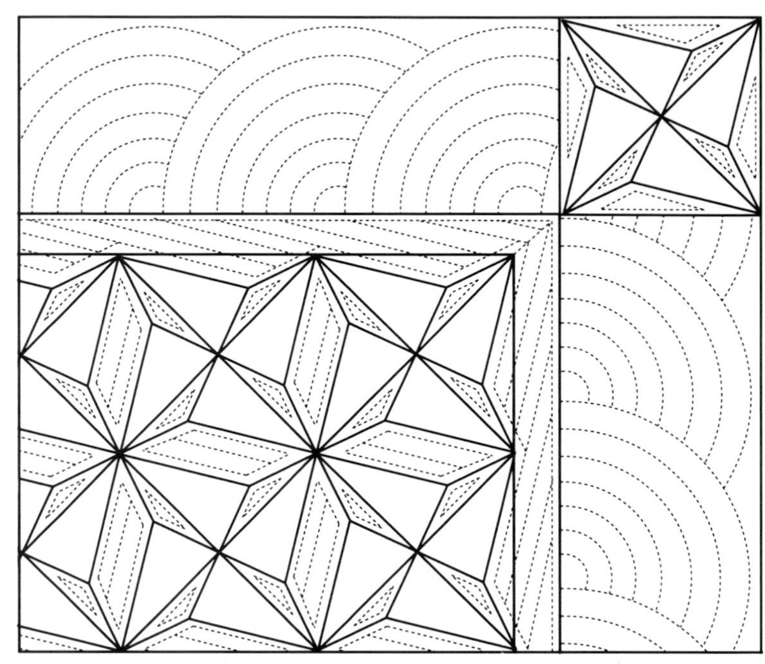

Quilting Diagram for a Quarter of Quilt

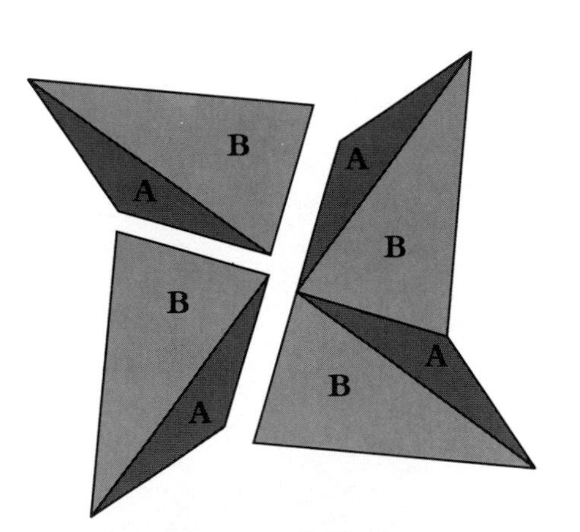

Pinwheel Assembly Diagram

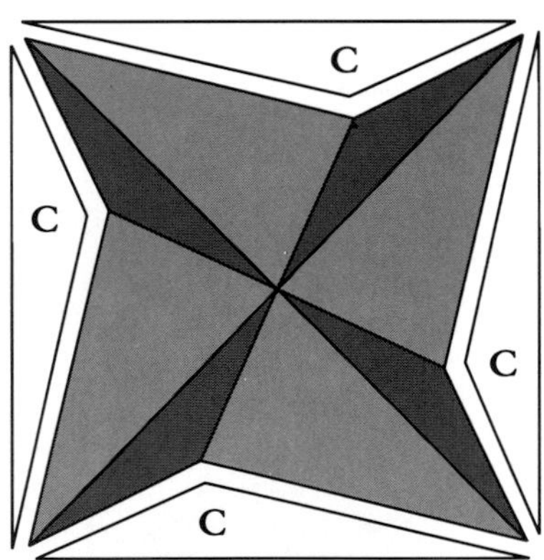

Corner Pinwheel Block Piecing Diagram

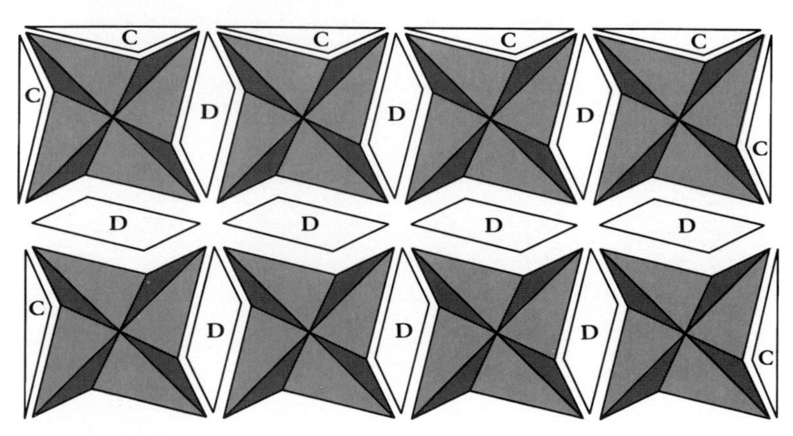

Row Assembly Diagram

Quilting

Outline-quilt ¼″ inside seam lines of triangles (A) and parallelograms (D). Quilt in-the-ditch along long sides of triangles (B). (See Quilting Diagram for Quarter of Quilt.) Parallel lines on muslin strips are ½″ apart. Karen quilted a fan pattern on the purple border. Quilting lines forming fan pattern are 1″ apart.

Finished Edges

Bind with periwinkle print fabric.

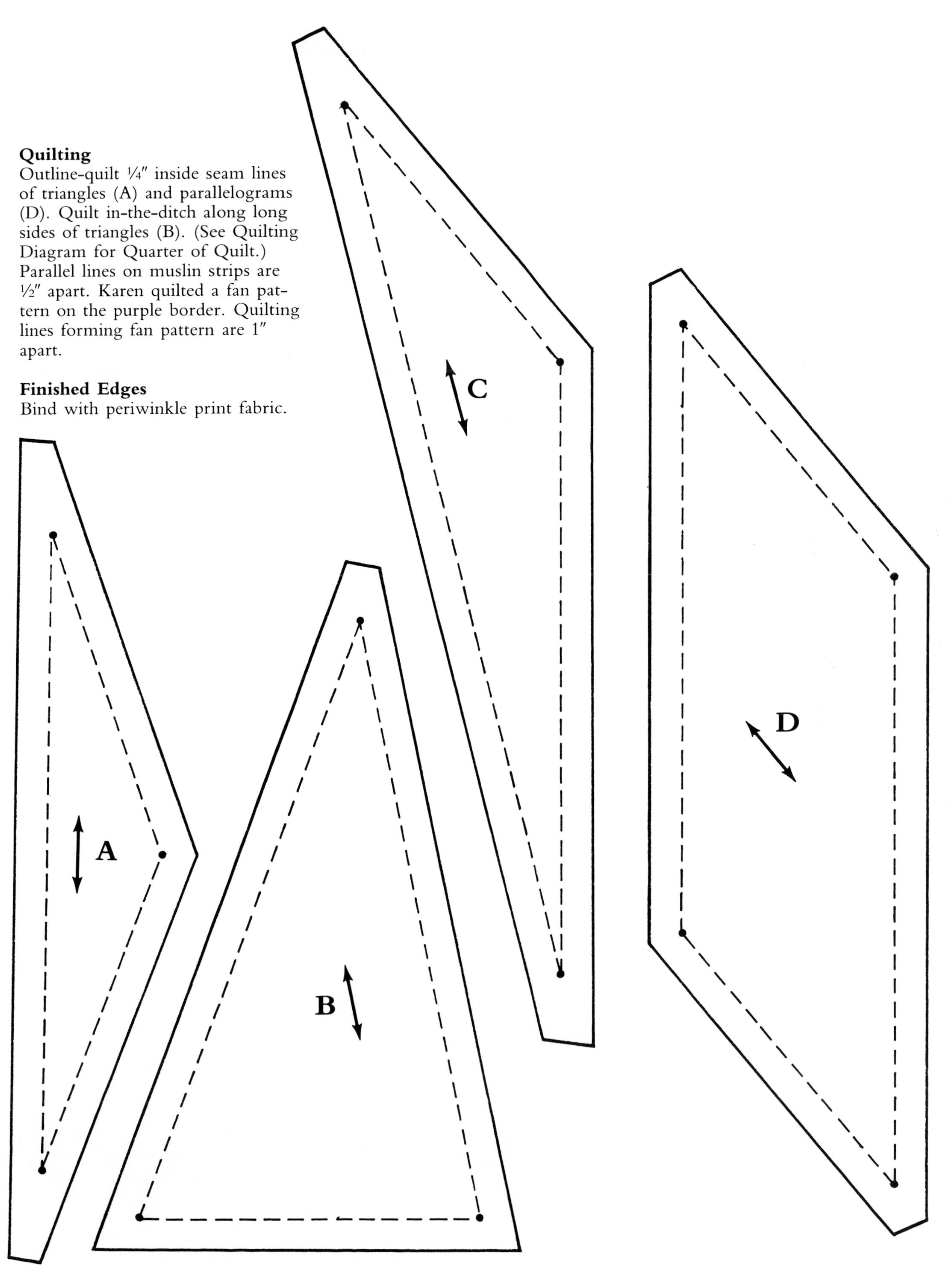

TRADITIONS IN QUILTING

I have a quilt that granny made,
my friends might like to see.
With patience and generosity
she made this quilt for me.

Now I, much like my granny,
have stitched a quilt or two.
She never told me I'd like to quilt,
but honey, I just do.

So, it's my turn to pass the thread
to others down the line.
It's my way of remembering her and
keeping this art alive.

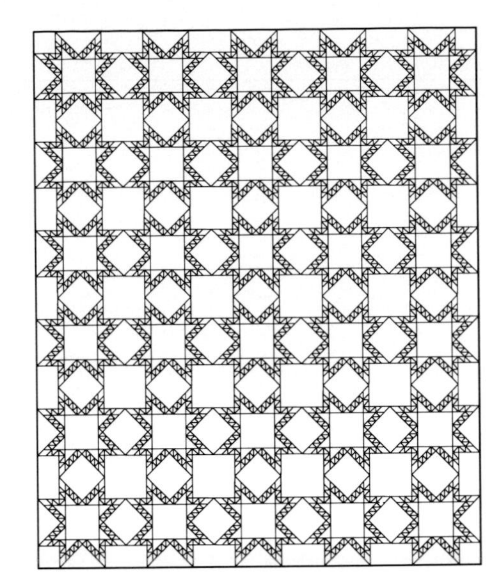

Mary Ellis Barnes

White House, Tennessee

Mary Barnes was Nadine Milam's grandmother, a lady who quilted most of her life and remained an enthusiastic quilter even after her 80th birthday. She made numerous quilts, but *Feathered Star* was one that happened to land in the hands of Nadine. The quilt was given to Nadine's uncle as a wedding gift. After he died, it was given to Nadine by his wife. "We cherish it," says Nadine, "because it is a part of our family's history."

Quilters can be found everywhere in Nadine's family tree. Nadine's mother, Cora Barnes, was a quilter, as was her husband's mother, Elizabeth Covington. "Each one always had a quilt up," remembers Nadine.

As for Nadine, she says, "When my mother let me help her, I liked the hand piecing."

Nadine B. Milam
Gardendale, Alabama

Feathered Star

1900s

It's hard to walk past *Feathered Star* and not stop. Its brightly colored stars catch your eye, and then its excellent condition beckons you to take a second look.

Like most feathered star quilts pieced in the 1900s, this one was constructed as a bar quilt. Stars were made first and were connected with squares to form rows. This method was preferred by quilters long ago because the connecting squares provided large unseamed areas to display flourishes of their finest quilting.

Feathered Star

Finished Quilt Size
64″ x 77″

Number of Feathered Stars—30

Fabric Requirements

Yellow-orange	—3 yd.
Muslin	—4¼ yd.
Yellow-orange for bias binding	—1 yd.
Backing	—4½ yd.

Number to Cut

Template A	—30 yellow-orange 49 muslin
Template B	—240 yellow-orange
Template C	—1200 yellow-orange 1560 muslin
Template D	—240 yellow-orange
Template E	—22 muslin
Template F	—20 muslin
Template G	—18 muslin
Template H	—4 muslin

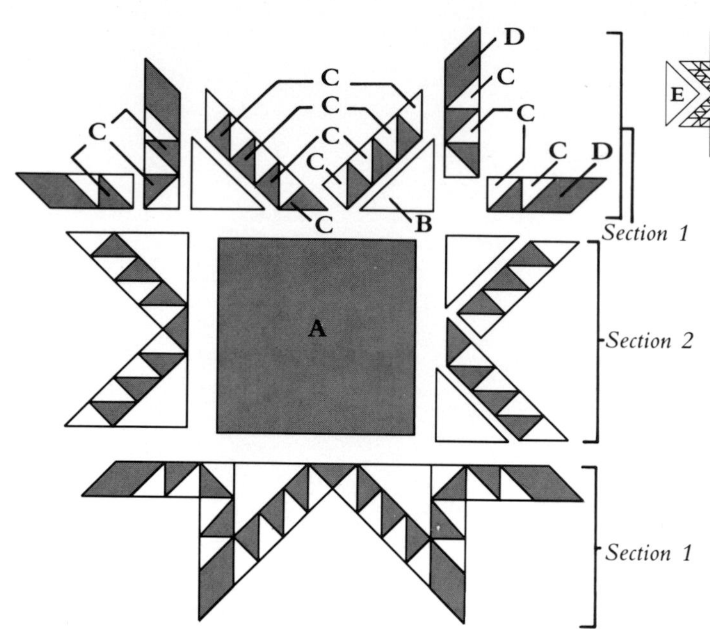

Feathered Star Piecing Diagram

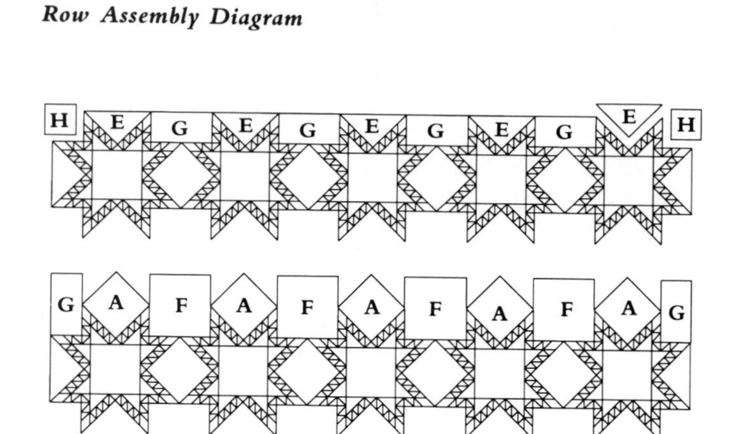

Row Assembly Diagram

Setting Diagram

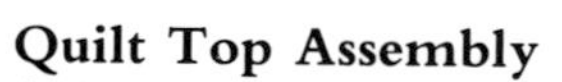

Quilt Top Assembly

1. Join triangles (B, C) and diamonds (D) to form sections, as shown in Feathered Star Piecing Diagram. Join section 2s to square (A), as shown. Join section 1s to square (A) to complete star. Make 30 feathered stars.

2. Arrange triangles (E) and squares (A) between stars, as shown in Row Assembly Diagram. Join to form a row. Make 6 rows.

To sew these triangles and squares between the star points, begin stitching from *seam line* of outside edge to *seam line* of inside edge. Stop and backstitch 1 or 2 stitches. Remove fabric from machine. Align the remaining sides and stitch from the center to the *seam line* of outside edge, backstitching 1 or 2 stitches at the start.

3. Join rows by setting in rectangles and squares (G, A, and F), as shown in Setting Diagram. Set in corner squares (H), triangles (E), and rectangles (G) at top and bottom of quilt.

Quilting

Nadine's grandmother outline-quilted ⅛" inside every seam line of Feathered Star. She quilted her original floral motif inside squares and diamonds.

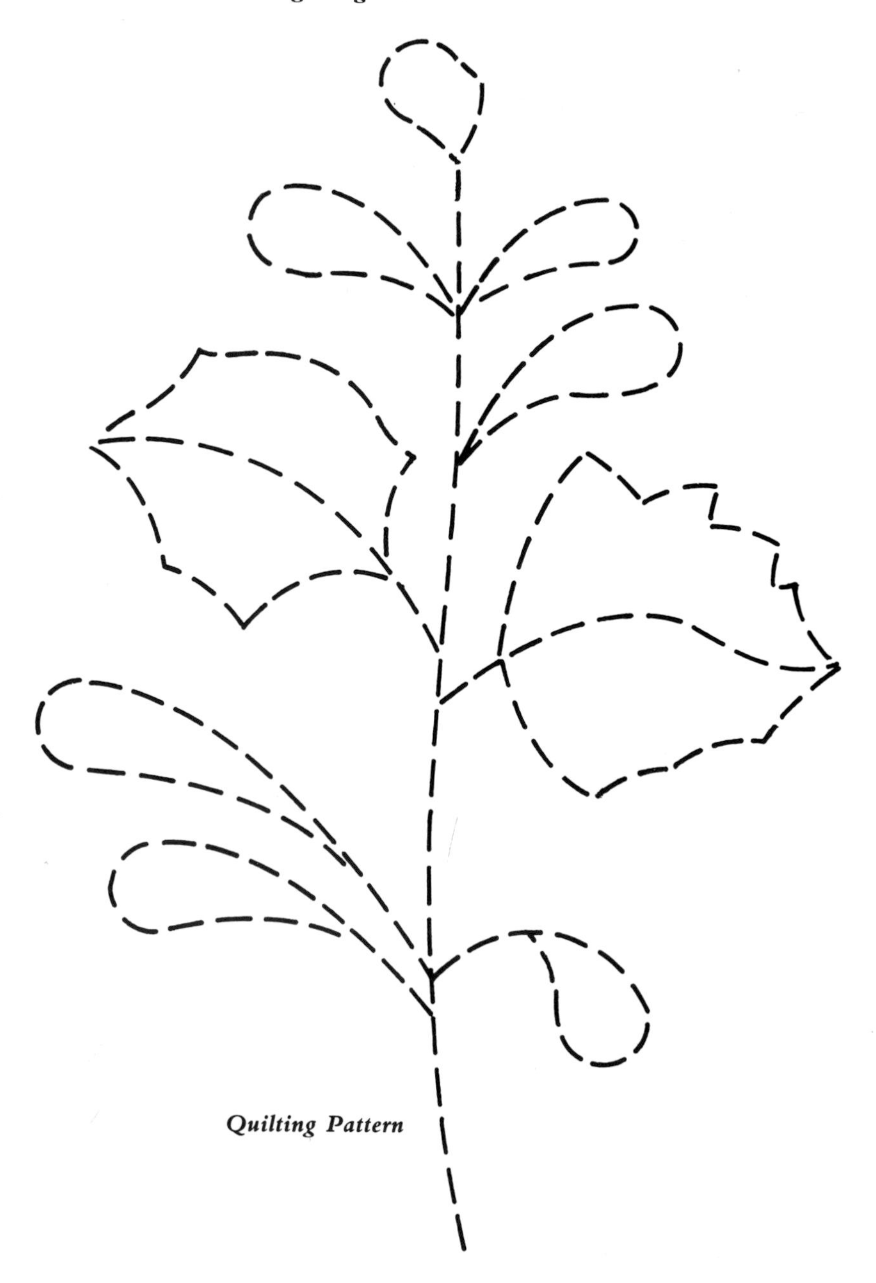
Quilting Pattern

Finished Edges

Bind with yellow-orange fabric.

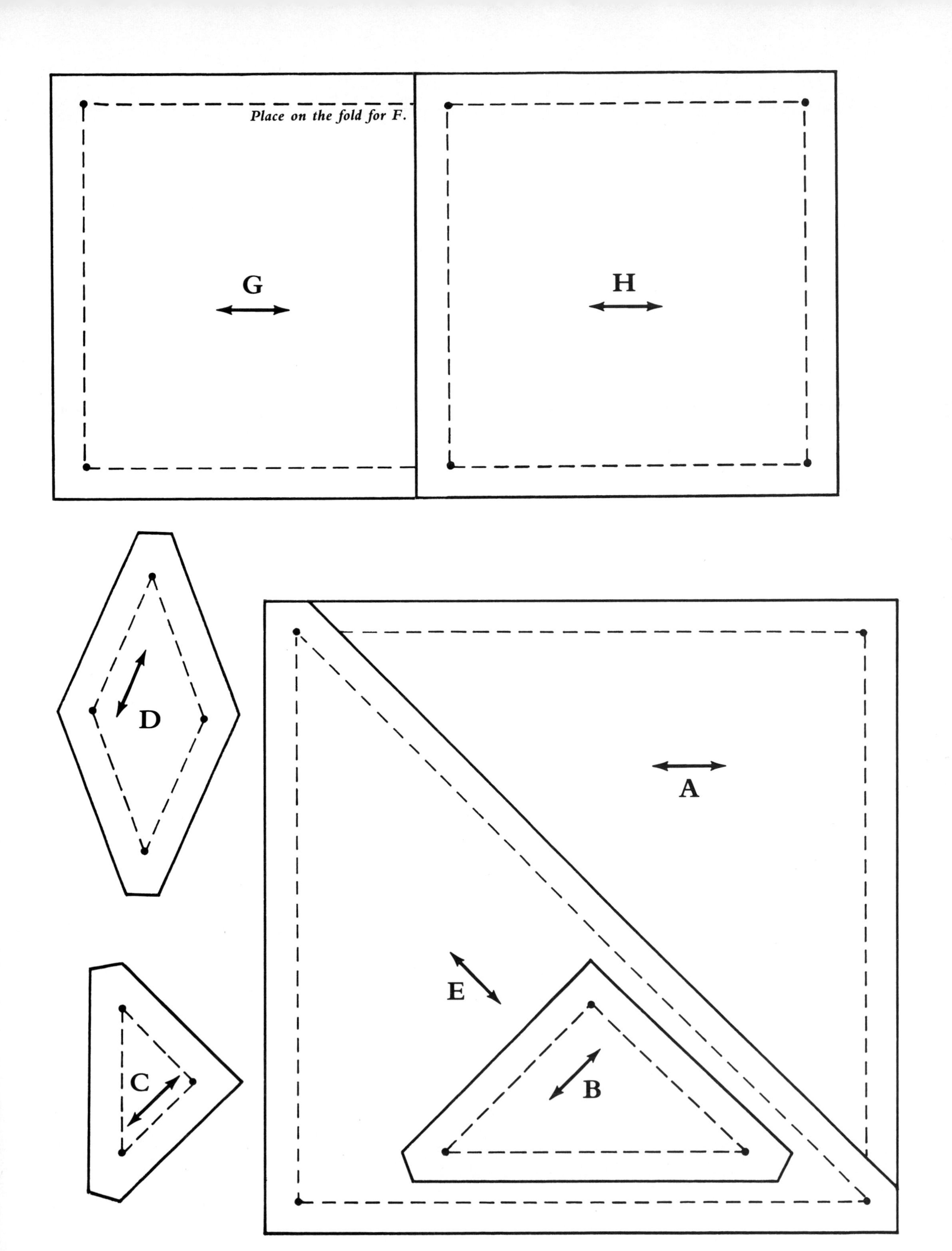
Place on the fold for F.
G
H
D
A
E
C
B

Blocks
1986

Just a glimpse of frilly dolls and building blocks can evoke all kinds of childhood memories and thoughts of that time when life was simple and an hour seemed to last forever. In those carefree days our hands were kept busy carefully placing block upon block to build our latest sky-reaching tower, while our imaginations would soar into realms kept secret from all adults.

In that same simple way, Darlene placed block upon block to make her *Blocks* quilt and precisely lined them up along the border. The simplicity of design and style is appealing and leaves large areas for imaginations to fill with loads of quilting. Quilters will find that the pattern is very similar to the Card Trick and many friendship album blocks.

Darlene Watson

Cookeville, Tennessee

One day, while thumbing through a book of patchwork patterns, Darlene remembered a score of pleasant childhood experiences associated with quilting. "While my mother quilted, I would play under the quilt when it was hung in a frame," says Darlene. "And when I wasn't playing under the quilt, my mother showed me how to push the needle in and out of the material."

Quilting bees were a lot of fun for the kids in the community (including Darlene) but maybe not so much fun for the quilters. "We would chase each other around, bumping into each other and sometimes the quilting frame," recalls Darlene. "This would cause the quilters to stick their fingers, and we would all be promptly scolded for being so rowdy."

The memory of those happy days and the appeal of all the beautiful patchwork patterns caused Darlene to decide to piece her first quilt top. "Not only did I want to create something special that I could leave to my children and grandchildren, but I wanted to surround them with that same warm feeling that I experienced as a child," says Darlene.

Blocks

Finished Quilt Size
Approximately 94″ x 106″

Number of Blocks and Finished Size
12 blocks—approximately 16″ x 16″

Fabric Requirements

Pink print	—3 yd.
Purple print	—3 yd.
Muslin	—5¾ yd.
Muslin for bias binding	—1 yd.
Backing	—8½ yd.

Number to Cut

Template A	—98 pink print 98 purple print
Template B	—156 muslin
Template C	—48 muslin

Quilting Diagram for a Quarter of Quilt

Quilt Top Assembly

1. Refer to Block Piecing Diagram and join purple and pink print squares (A) with muslin triangles (B and C), as shown. Make 12 blocks.

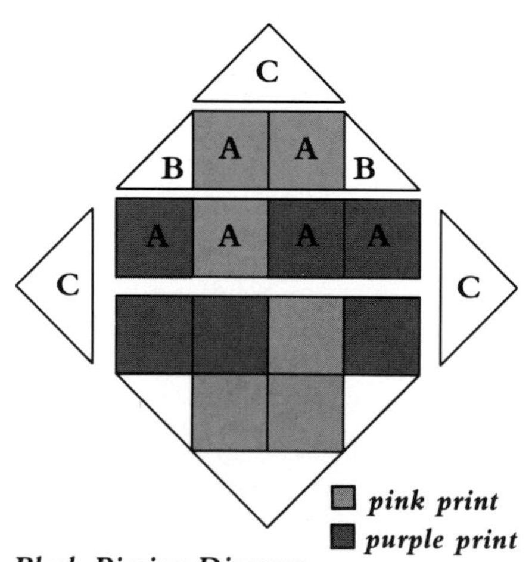

Block Piecing Diagram

2. Cut 6 muslin squares, 10 large muslin triangles, and 4 muslin corner triangles and set with pieced blocks, as shown in Setting Diagram. Join in 4 diagonal rows, as shown. Join rows.

Setting Diagram

B = Pieced Block
M = Muslin

3. Cut 2 border strips, 4¼" wide, from muslin and join to sides of quilt. Cut 1 border strip, 4¼" wide, and join to bottom of quilt.

4. Make pieced borders by alternating purple and pink print squares (A) and joining with muslin triangles (B). (See Border Piecing Diagram and quilt photograph.) Make borders for the sides and bottom of quilt. Join border to sides. Trim any excess fabric even with quilt. Join remaining border to bottom of quilt and trim.

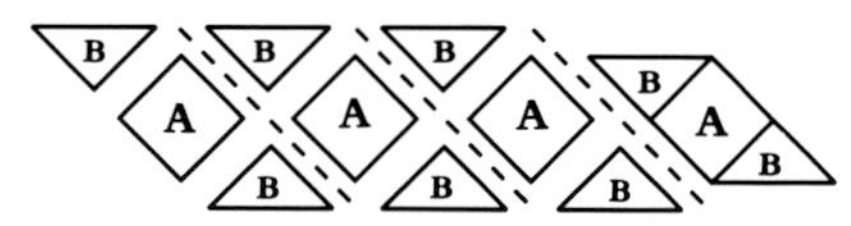

Border Piecing Diagram

5. Cut 2 border strips, 2¼" wide, from pink print and join to sides of quilt. Cut 1 border strip, 2¼" wide, from pink print and join to bottom of quilt.

6. Cut 2 border strips, 2¼" wide, from purple print and join to sides of quilt. Cut 1 border strip, 2¼" wide, from purple print and join to bottom of quilt.

7. Cut 1 border strip, 3¾" wide, from muslin and join to top of quilt.

Quilting
Darlene quilted parallel lines, 1¼″ apart, following the shapes of the pieced blocks. (See Quilting Diagram for a Quarter of Quilt.) She designed a floral vine wreath for each muslin square.

Finished Edges
Darlene rolled her backing to the front for her finished edge. (You may prefer to join a separate binding of muslin.)

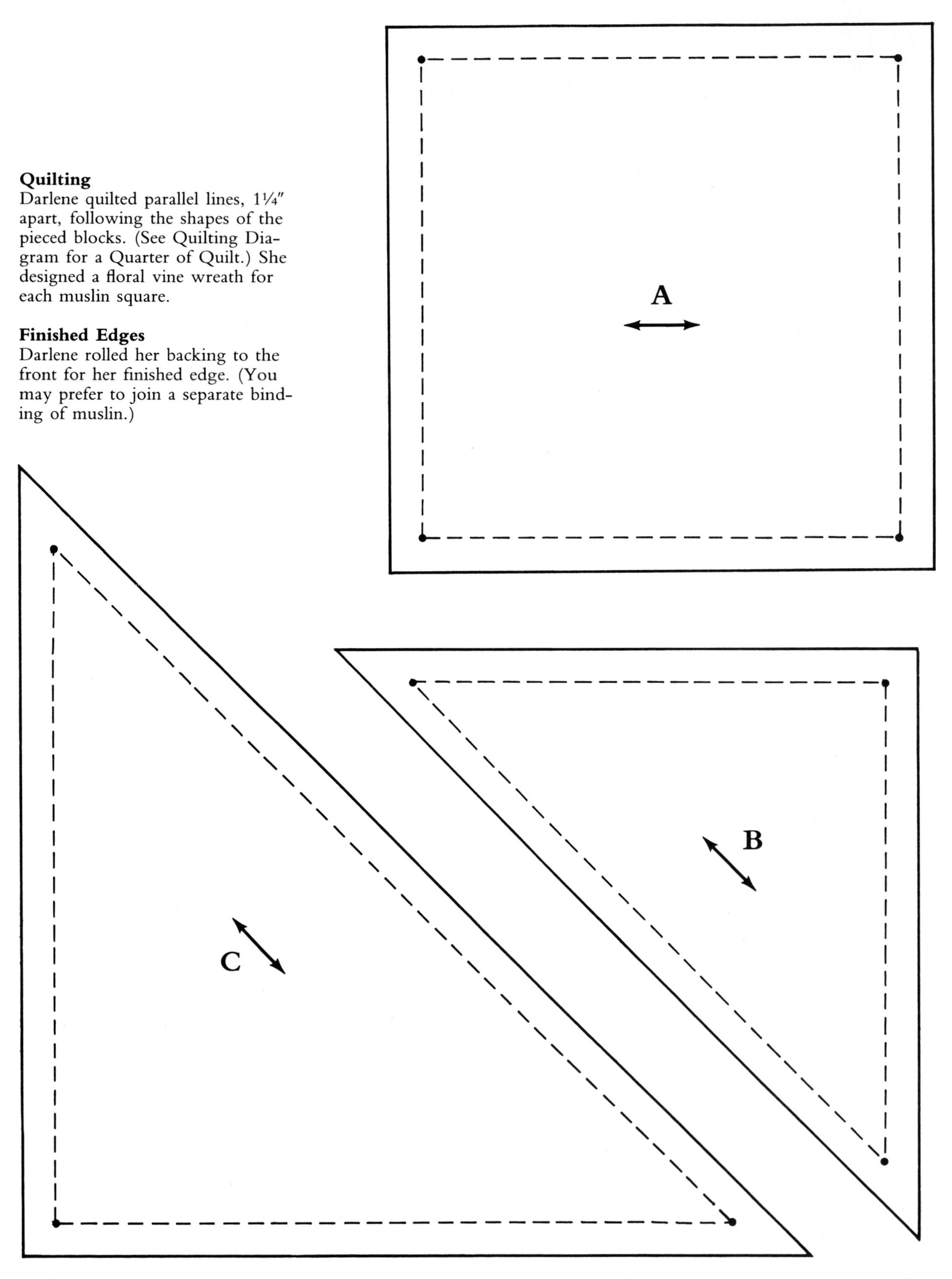

Elsie Meeks Halladay Simkins

Circleville, Utah

Widowed at the age of 44 and left with four children to raise, Elsie Meeks Halladay Simkins turned to the one thing she knew and loved the best, quilting. Along with taking in laundry, quiltmaking provided a source of income for Elsie and her family. Those were the days just prior to and during the Depression, and the going price for a quilt was $25 to $30. Needless to say, Elsie made hundreds of quilts. Every chance she had, she clipped and saved patterns from newspapers, designed numerous pattern variations, and made quilts, using scraps of fabric. She especially prided herself on her even and durable quilting and would faithfully save her money just to buy enough fabric for a proper whole-cloth, one-color backing. She served as the quilt chairman for her church, and designed and made many quilts for church bazaars.

Elsie's great-niece Janine Rees has very faint memories of her great-aunt but is proud of Aunt Elsie's quilting reputation and the interest they share in quilting. When Janine was ready to learn to quilt, she said, "I'd already decided that a whole quilt was way too complicated a project for me to even think about, especially since I didn't even know how to hold a needle." But Mrs. Arthella Taylor, a good friend and neighbor, changed all that. With her gentle nudging and encouragement, Janine started from the beginning, step-by-step, on one of Mrs. Taylor's quilts. And as time passed, "I really learned how to quilt! I'm so glad Mrs. Taylor insisted I learn to quilt on the real thing," says Janine. "Having her show me made the art of quilting come to life for me."

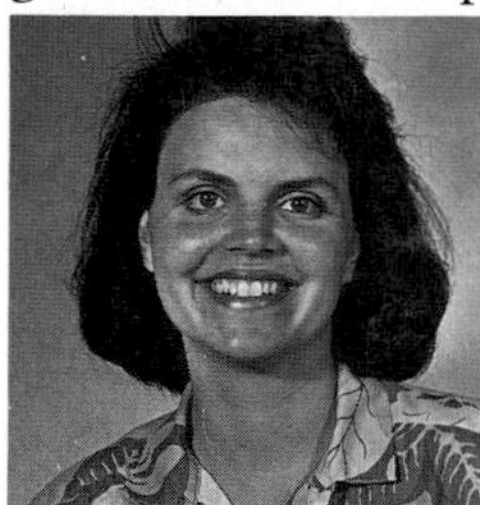

Janine Rees
Roosevelt, Utah

Today, Janine considers herself a novice and has completed one quilt. With toddlers around the house, time isn't readily available. But much like her Aunt Elsie, Janine regularly clips and saves quilt patterns for the day when she does have the time.

Aunt Elsie's Quilt
1941

Vibrant lavender and peach blossoms, accented with black blanket stitching, give a pristine image to this 48-year-old quilt. The quilt was made by Janine Rees's great-aunt Elsie Meeks Halladay Simkins as a gift for her sister, Janine's grandmother. The quilt now belongs to Janine's mother, but it was Janine's idea to share it with the readers of *Great American Quilts*.

"The quilt was only used for company," says Janine, "and therefore, is in excellent condition." The pattern is believed to have been designed by Aunt Elsie, but it may remind some of you of the Rose Cross pattern. Or can you think of another?

Aunt Elsie's Quilt

Finished Quilt Size
86½" x 94"

Number of Blocks and Finished Size
9 blocks—23½" x 26"

Fabric Requirements

Green	— ½ yd.
Purple	— ¾ yd.
Peach	—3 yd.
Muslin	—6½ yd.
Purple for bias binding	—1 yd.
Backing	—5½ yd.

Other Materials
Embroidery floss — black

Number to Cut
Template A — 36 green
Template B — 36 purple
Template C — 9 peach
Template D — 36 peach
Template E — 16 purple

Quilt Top Assembly
1. Cut 9 blocks, 24" x 26½", from muslin. Finger-crease each block on the diagonal; then finger-crease again on the opposite diagonal to find the center. Use diagonal creases as guidelines for placement of appliqué pieces. Pin or baste appliqué pieces in place, as shown in Placement Diagram, and appliqué. Using black embroidery floss, blanket or buttonhole-stitch around each piece for a decorative finish and stemstitch along creases.

Placement Diagram

2. Cut 12 sashing strips, 4½" x 26½", from peach. Alternate 4 sashing strips with 3 blocks and join at the sides to form a row, as shown in Setting Diagram. Make 3 rows.
3. Cut 12 sashing strips, 4½" x 24", from peach. Alternate 4 purple accent squares (E) with 3 sashing strips to form a row. (See Setting Diagram.) Make 4 rows.
4. Alternate sashing rows with block rows, beginning with a sashing row, and join.

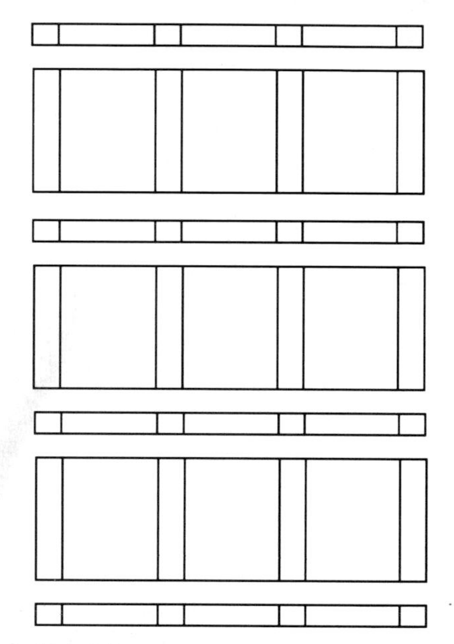

Setting Diagram

Quilting
Janine's great-aunt outline-quilted outside blanket-stitched edges and stemstitching. Four groups of five concentric circles were quilted in the non-appliquéd areas. (See quilt photograph.) To make concentric circles, quilt a small circle in the center of each of the 4 accent squares surrounding the center block. Quilt the next circle 2" from this circle and continue until you have completed five circles. For the sides and corners, quilt a half or quarter circle, respectively, beginning outside the seam line of each accent square. Add concentric circles, as before. Arcs were quilted in the area between the groups of concentric circles to join them together. (See quilt photograph.)

Finished Edges
Bind with purple fabric.

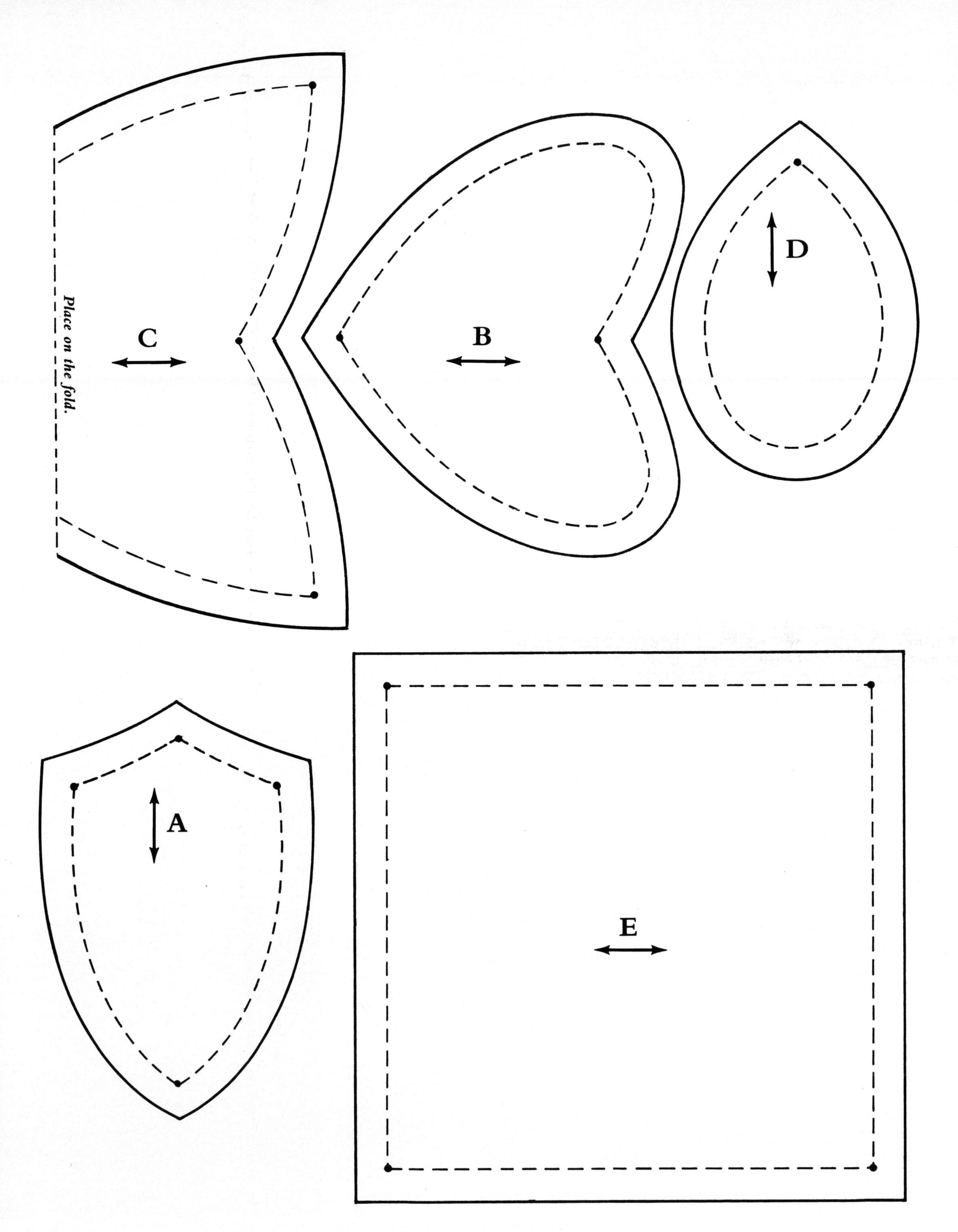
Place on the fold.
C
B
D
A
E

LaMena Nichols Browning

Montgomery, Alabama

"Twenty years of devoted labor" is what LaMena calls the time she spent making a series of nine quilts as wedding gifts for her grandchildren. "My mother set the example," says LaMena. "She made quilts for each of her eight grandchildren, long before quilting became headlines in the craft world."

LaMena's nine quilts are styled and color coordinated according to whether they are for a granddaughter or grandson. The granddaughters' quilts are traditional patterns and are made with cotton. The grandsons' quilts are made entirely of bright, new swatches of wool and can be used either as wool coverlets or wall hangings. "I chose wool," says LaMena, "so as to incorporate the family heritage, in that their great-grandfather was the founder of the Women's Division of Pendleton Woolen Mills."

This retired schoolteacher and wife of a minister has been fond of fabrics and threads since she was a very young girl. "I especially enjoy utilizing old things—adapting and preserving the customs and styles of the past," says LaMena. "I made my sons' overcoats and caps, and used men's suits to make women's clothing, curtains, and rugs." One highlight of her needlework accomplishments was the display of all nine quilts at a solo exhibit in Montgomery last spring.

Rising Sun
1988
Prismatic arms of color radiating from LaMena's mellow sunrise bring the cheerful message that a new day is emerging. The crow of the rooster and the chirping of birds can almost be heard. It's LaMena's scrap-quilt version of the traditional Sunrise block, dressed up with a 3″ white eyelet binding.
As the note embroidered in the corner indicates, this quilt will be a gift to granddaughter "Lisa Nichole from Grand-Mother."

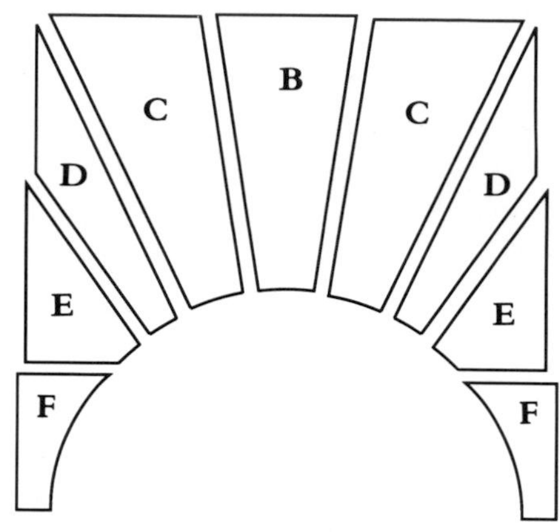

Block Piecing Diagram I

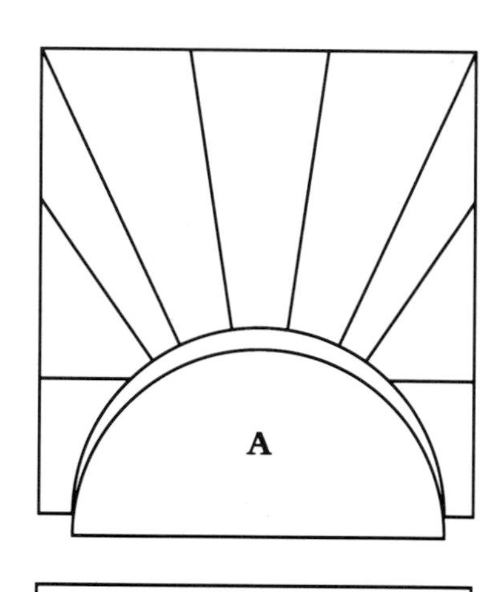

Block Piecing Diagram II

Rising Sun

Finished Quilt Size
88″ x 95″

Number of Blocks and Finished Size
24 Rising Sun blocks—11″ x 14″

Fabric Requirements

Scrap fabrics	—6 yd. total
Yellow	—5 yd.
White for bias binding	—1 yd.
Backing	—8½ yd.

Other Materials

White eyelet edging, 3″ wide	—8¼ yd.

Number to Cut

Template A	—28 yellow
Template B	—28 scraps
Template C	—28 scraps
Template C★	—28 scraps
Template D	—28 scraps
Template D★	—28 scraps
Template E	—28 scraps
Template E★	—28 scraps
Template F	—28 scraps
Template F★	—28 scraps
Template G	—24 scraps
	—24 yellow

★ — Flip or turn over template if fabric is one-sided.

Quilt Top Assembly

1. Join pieces B through F, as shown in Block Piecing Diagram I. Join to yellow sun (A). Join solid yellow rectangle (G) to the bottom, as shown in Block Piecing Diagram II, to complete Rising Sun block. Make 24 blocks with piece G and 4 blocks without piece G.

2. Cut 28 blocks, 11½″ x 11″, from yellow. Join scrap rectangle (G) to the bottom of *24* blocks.

3. Alternate 4 blocks, made in step 2, with 4 Rising Sun blocks (RS) to form a row, as shown in Setting Diagram. The bottom row is made from the blocks made without piece G. Join blocks at sides to make 7 rows. Join rows.

Quilting

Outline-quilt outside seam lines of Rising Sun block pieces. Quilt Rising Sun design on solid yellow blocks. (See quilt photograph.)

Finished Edges

With right sides facing, align and layer edge of quilt, white eyelet edging, and binding in that order on sides and bottom of quilt. (The top edge is bound without edging.) Stitch edging and binding to quilt. Turn binding and blindstitch to back of quilt.

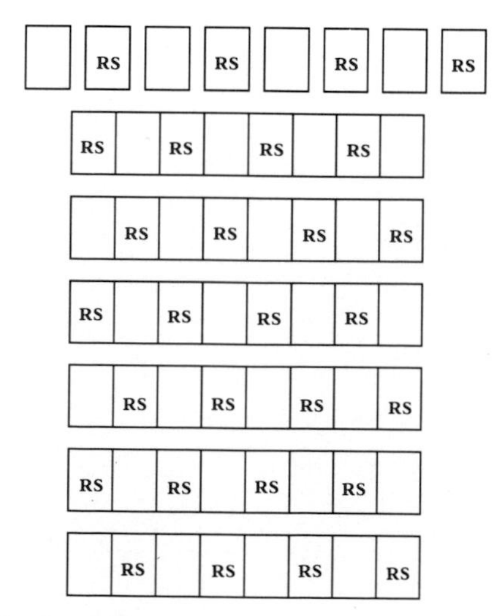

Setting Diagram
RS = Rising Sun Block

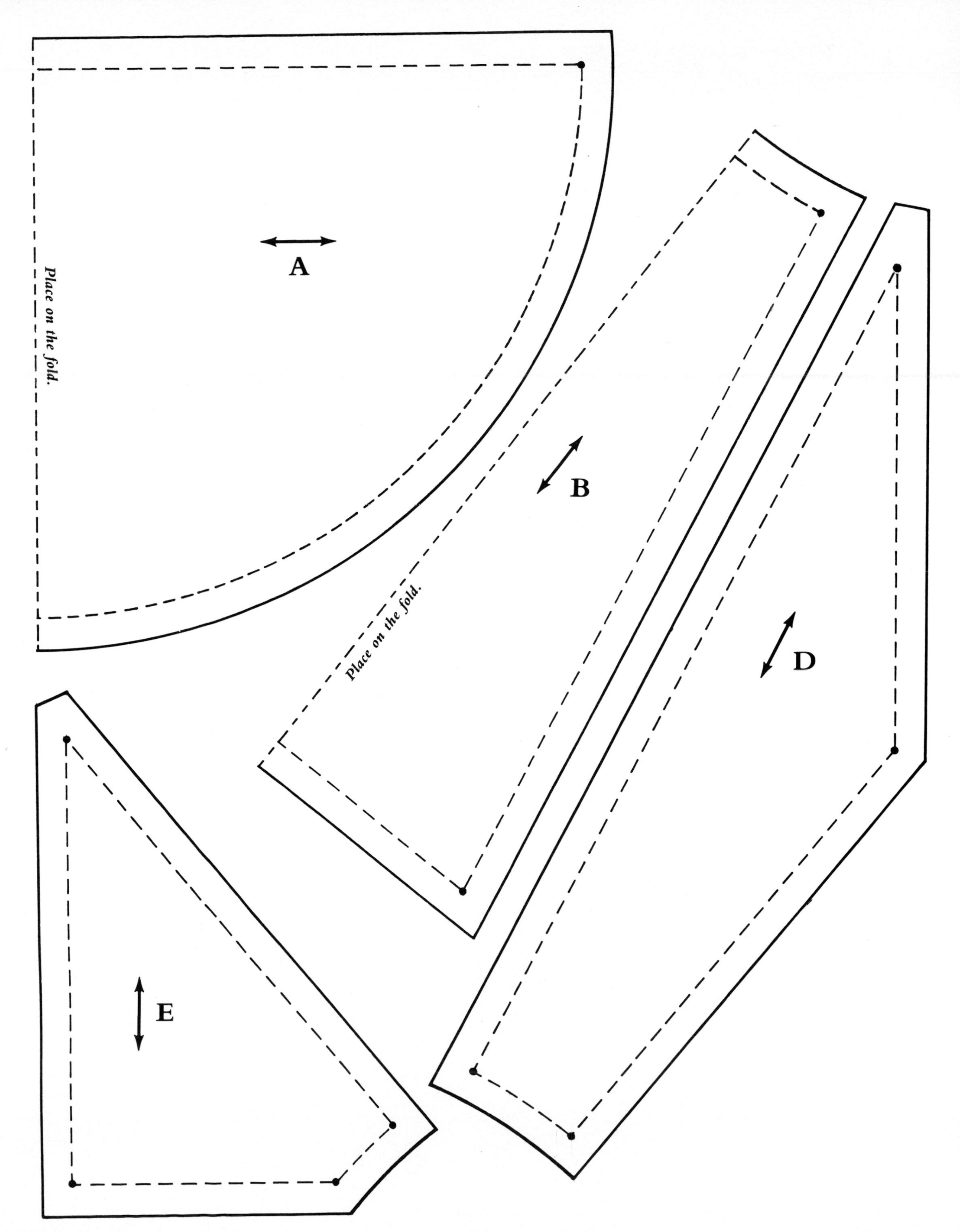
A
Place on the fold.
B
Place on the fold.
D
E

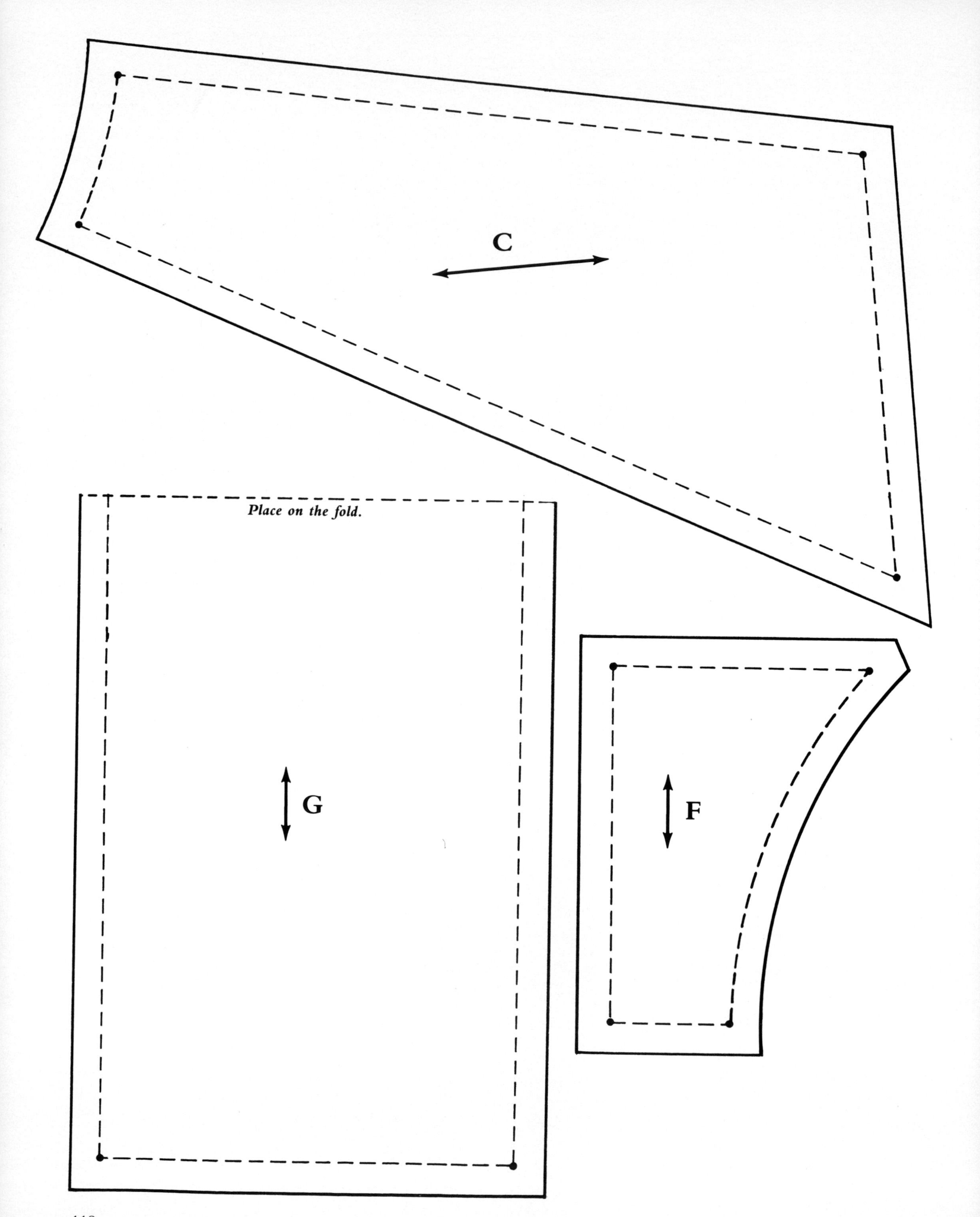
C
Place on the fold.
G
F

Turkey Tracks
1988

While watching a dear friend making a quilt, LaMena was reminded of her mother and the hours she spent making quilts. LaMena so admired the pattern her friend was piecing that she asked for the pattern and asked her friend to help her get started on a quilt of her own. That was 1970, many years before her granddaughter Emily was born. But this Turkey Tracks quilt will be for Emily (who is now 10 years old) on her wedding day.

When using gingham, it is best to purchase fabric whose threads are woven straight and avoid those fabrics where the pattern is only printed on the top. If the gingham is not woven straight, be sure to cut the fabric, rather than tear it.

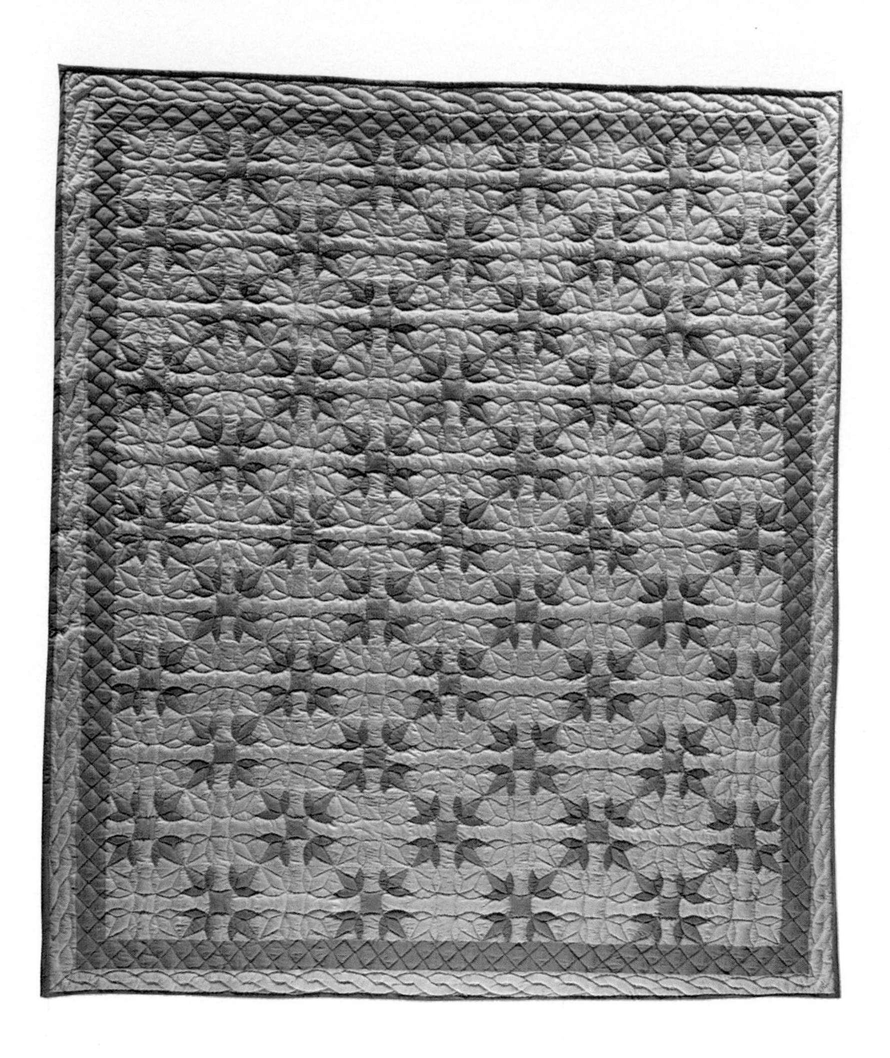

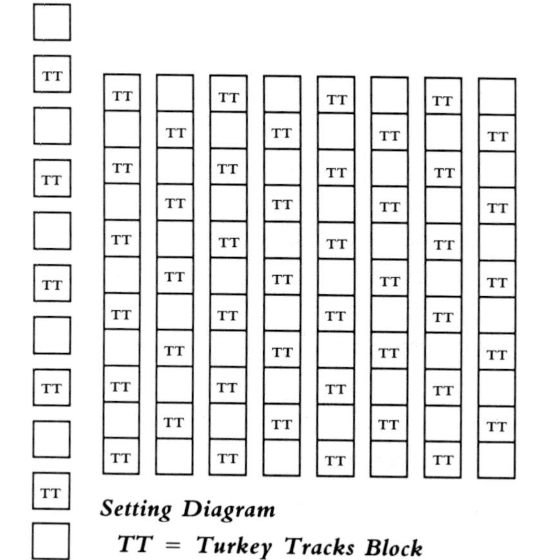

Setting Diagram
TT = Turkey Tracks Block

Turkey Tracks

Finished Quilt Size
84″ x 100″

Number of Blocks and Finished Size
49 Turkey Tracks blocks—8″ x 8″

Fabric Requirements
Blue/white gingham—2⅞ yd.
Blue —1⅛ yd.
White —8 yd.
Blue for bias binding —1¼ yd.
Backing —8½ yd.
* — Throughout the directions, blue/white gingham will be designated as gingham.

Number to Cut
Template A —49 gingham
Template B —196 gingham
Template C —392 blue
Template D —392 white
Template E —196 white

Quilt Top Assembly
1. Referring to Block Piecing Diagram, join pieces (E) to center piece (A), as shown.
Join pieces (B, C, and D), as shown. Make 4 and join to each corner to complete the block. Make 49 Turkey Tracks blocks.

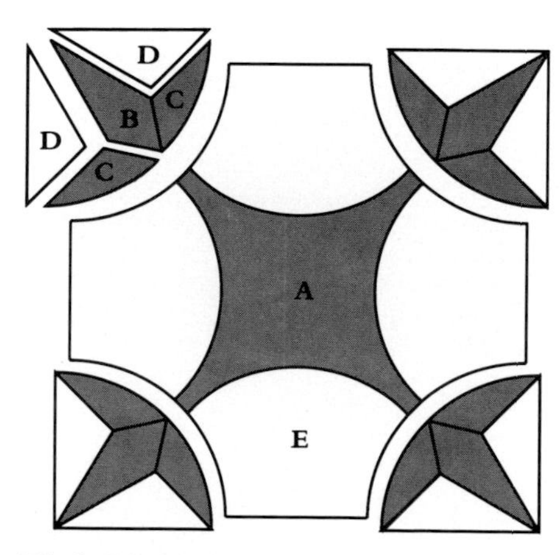

Block Piecing Diagram

2. Cut fifty 8½″ squares from white. Alternate Turkey Tracks blocks (TT) with white squares, as shown in Setting Diagram. Join blocks and white squares at tops and bottoms to form rows. Join rows.
3. Cut 4 border strips, 3½″ wide, from gingham. Join to quilt and miter corners.
4. Cut 4 border strips, 3½″ wide, from white. Join to quilt and miter corners.

Quilting
Outline-quilt outside seam line of blue and gingham pieces of the Turkey Tracks blocks. Quilt Turkey Tracks design in the solid white blocks. A diamond pattern was quilted on the gingham borders and an unbroken rope pattern on the white borders.

Finished Edges
Bind with blue fabric.

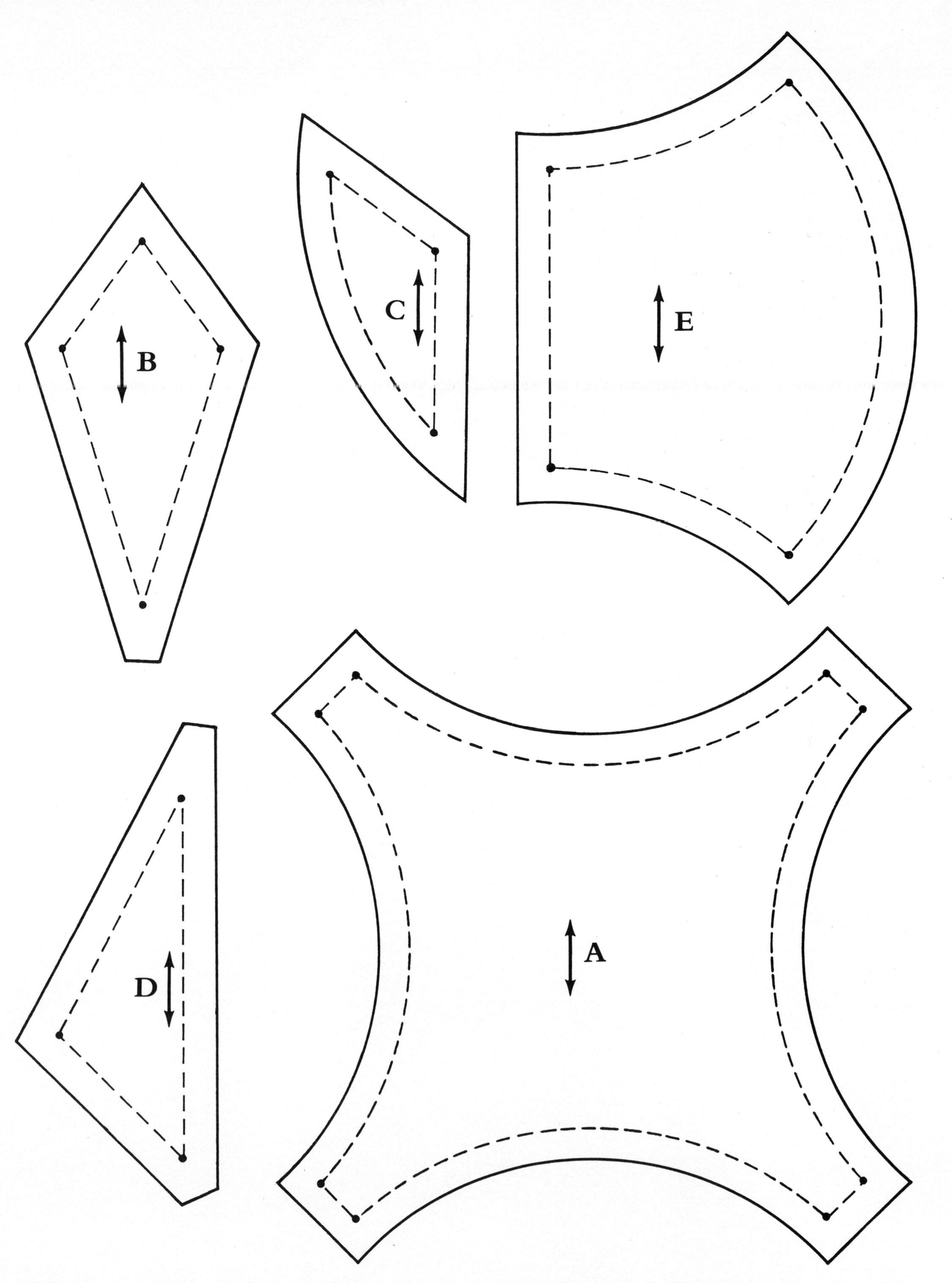
C
E
B
D
A

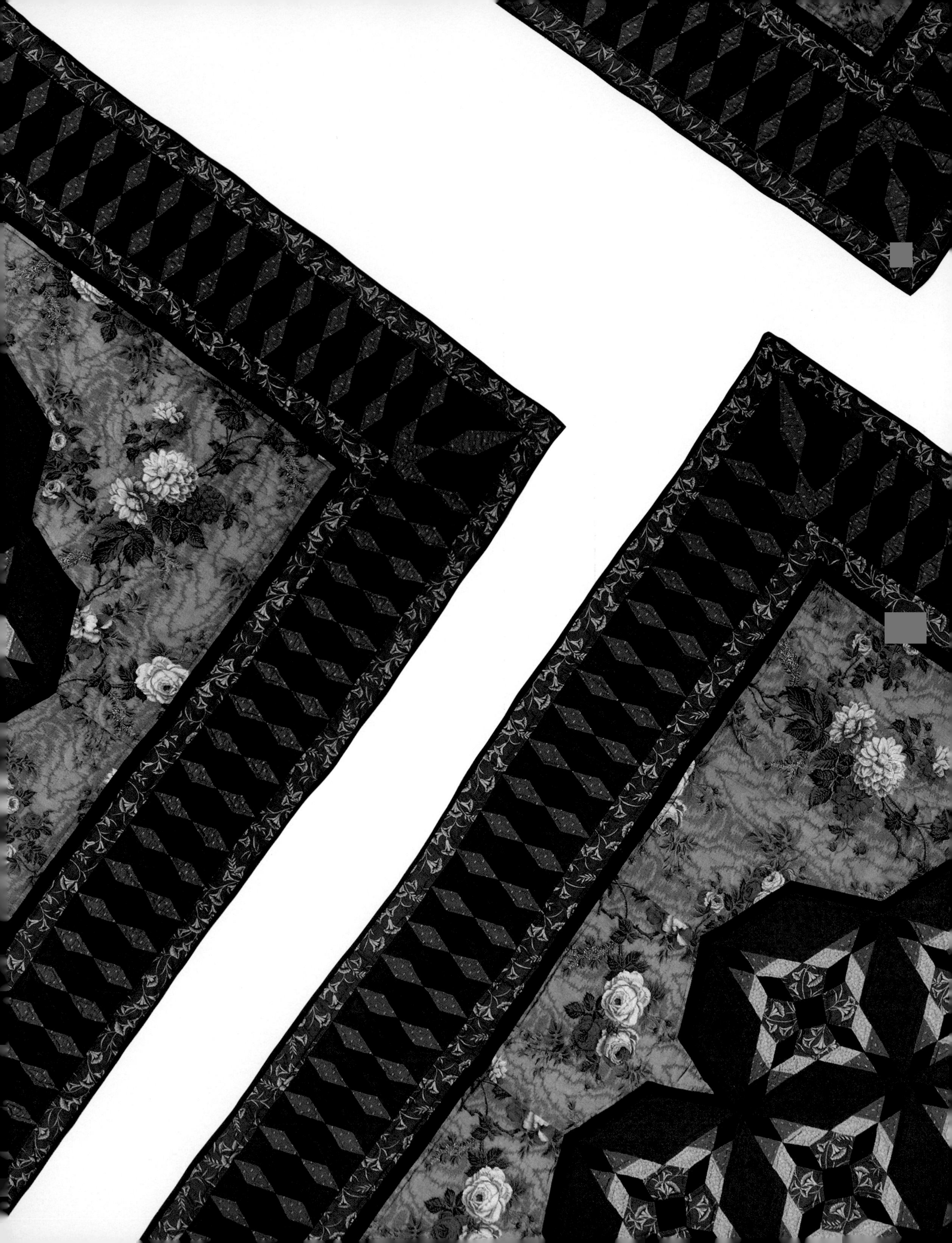

BEE QUILTERS

Friendly support and instruction
are essential ingredients—
Community projects and donations
for needy recipients,
Quilt displays and workshops—the
list goes on and on.
These are the things that
quilting bees gladly focus upon.
If I had known it was this way,
a member I would have been,
Instead of quilting all alone
with my dog and TV in the den.

Marion Glaspey, quilt coordinator for The Wetlands Quilters, is busy designing a border for their next quilt.

The Wetlands Quilters

Stone Harbor, New Jersey

Besides attracting lovers of wildlife and fishing, The Wetlands Institute is home to a dozen or so highly proficient quilters. Located on New Jersey's southern shore, The Wetlands Institute provides a spacious room just for the quilters, with windows overlooking beautiful salt marsh and an osprey nest. For seven years, these quiltmakers have met informally each Tuesday afternoon to quilt, to share recipes, to fellowship, and sometimes just to pass around a few of the latest grandchild snapshots. "They have so enjoyed the weekly get-togethers," says quilt designer and coordinator Marion Glaspey, "that they give up a week to the Christmas holiday season only with reluctance."

Learn more about The Wetlands Quilters in our "All Sorts of Samplers" chapter.

Leaf Prints

1986

The fifth of The Wetlands Quilters' raffle quilts was an adventure in simple leaf monoprinting. According to Marion Glaspey, "Many of them had never tried leaf printing before, but they all participated and had a grand time!"

Fresh leaves with intriguing shapes and sizes were selected and tested on paper or scrap fabric for their printability. Before printing, leaves were arranged on each block to arrive at the best design. Each quilter printed her own leaves on a block and then quilted around the imprint, completing each block with the lap-quilting method. (Directions below are for the frame quilting method.)

Members who worked on *Leaf Prints* were Helen Down, Marion Glaspey, Frances Maher, Mary McGuire, Elsie Mott, Ruth Murphy, Olive Prout, Elsie Snyder, Edith Soltis, and Myrtle Wilson.

Leaf Prints

Finished Quilt Size
72" x 86"

Number of Blocks and Finished Size
12 blocks — 13½" x 13½"

Fabric Requirements

Unbleached muslin	— 4¾ yd.
Rust	— 1 yd.
Orange	— ¼ yd.
Unbleached muslin for bias binding	— 1¼ yd.
Backing	— 7½ yd.

Other Materials
Fresh leaves
Textile paints in assorted colors
Small brush
Small brayer or rolling pin
Paper towels
Scrap fabric
Plastic or aluminum pie plates
Dinner plate or pot lid

Quilt Top Assembly

1. Cut twelve 14" squares from muslin for leaf printing. Using scrap fabric, practice printing a few leaves to get the feel of how much paint to apply and to determine which leaves print best. Apply paint to a leaf. (Usually, but not always, the underside of the leaf will make a better print.) Position the leaf, paint side down, on fabric and cover it with a paper towel. Apply pressure with a small brayer, a rolling pin, or with your fingers. When you have gained a bit of confidence, decide on a general arrangement for your leaves and begin printing, one leaf at a time.

When each block is finished and dry, heat-set the color by ironing on both sides.

2. Cut 16 sashing strips, 2½" x 14", from rust. Alternate 4 sashing strips with 3 leaf blocks to form a row, as shown in Setting Diagram. Join sashing strips and blocks at sides. Make 4 rows.

3. Cut 15 sashing strips, 14" x 2½", from rust. Cut twenty 2½" accent squares from orange. Alternate 4 accent squares with 3 sashing strips, as shown in Setting Diagram. Join at sides.

4. Alternate sashing-strip rows with leaf-block rows, as shown in Setting Diagram, and join rows.

5. Cut 3 borders, 12" wide, from muslin. Join to sides and bottom of quilt. Cut top border, 10½" wide, from muslin. Join to top of quilt. Use arc of acorn-and-oak-leaf cluster quilting stencil as a guide for marking scalloped edges on sides and bottom. Match midpoint of arc with center of border's edge. Use a dinner plate or pot lid for corner scallops. Leave scalloped edges uncut until quilting is done.

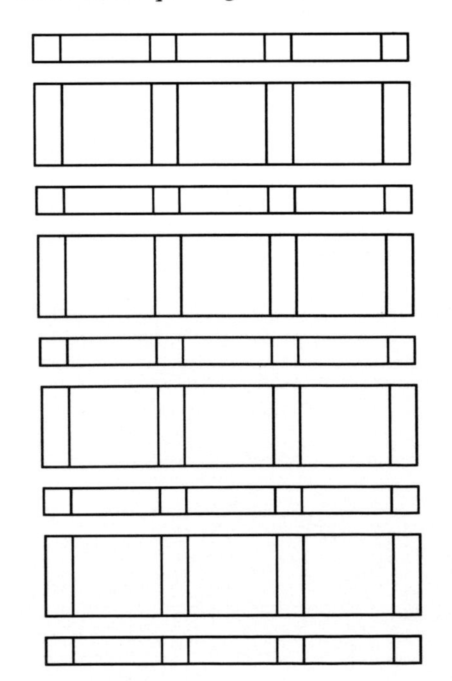

Setting Diagram

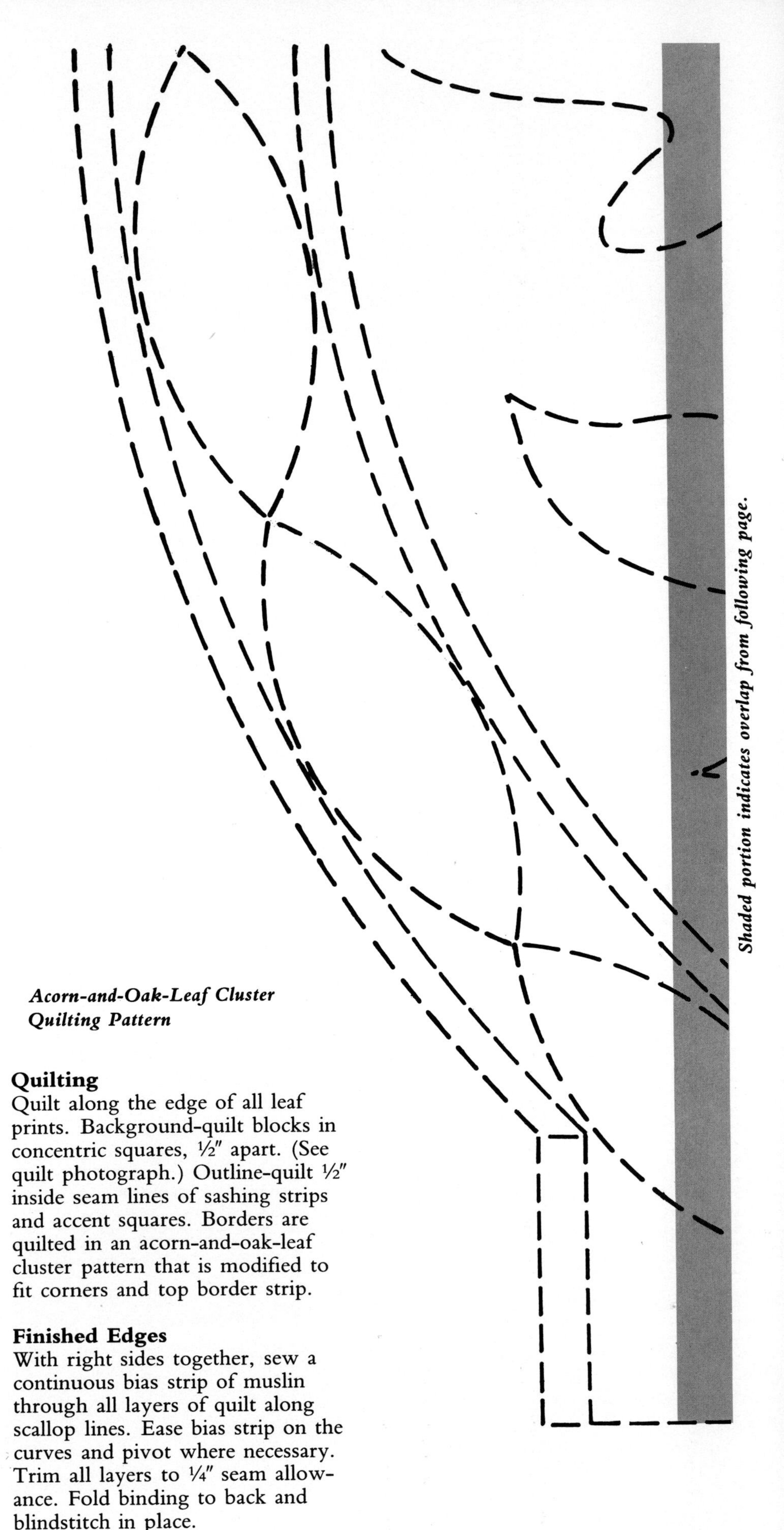

Acorn-and-Oak-Leaf Cluster Quilting Pattern

Quilting

Quilt along the edge of all leaf prints. Background-quilt blocks in concentric squares, ½" apart. (See quilt photograph.) Outline-quilt ½" inside seam lines of sashing strips and accent squares. Borders are quilted in an acorn-and-oak-leaf cluster pattern that is modified to fit corners and top border strip.

Finished Edges

With right sides together, sew a continuous bias strip of muslin through all layers of quilt along scallop lines. Ease bias strip on the curves and pivot where necessary. Trim all layers to ¼" seam allowance. Fold binding to back and blindstitch in place.

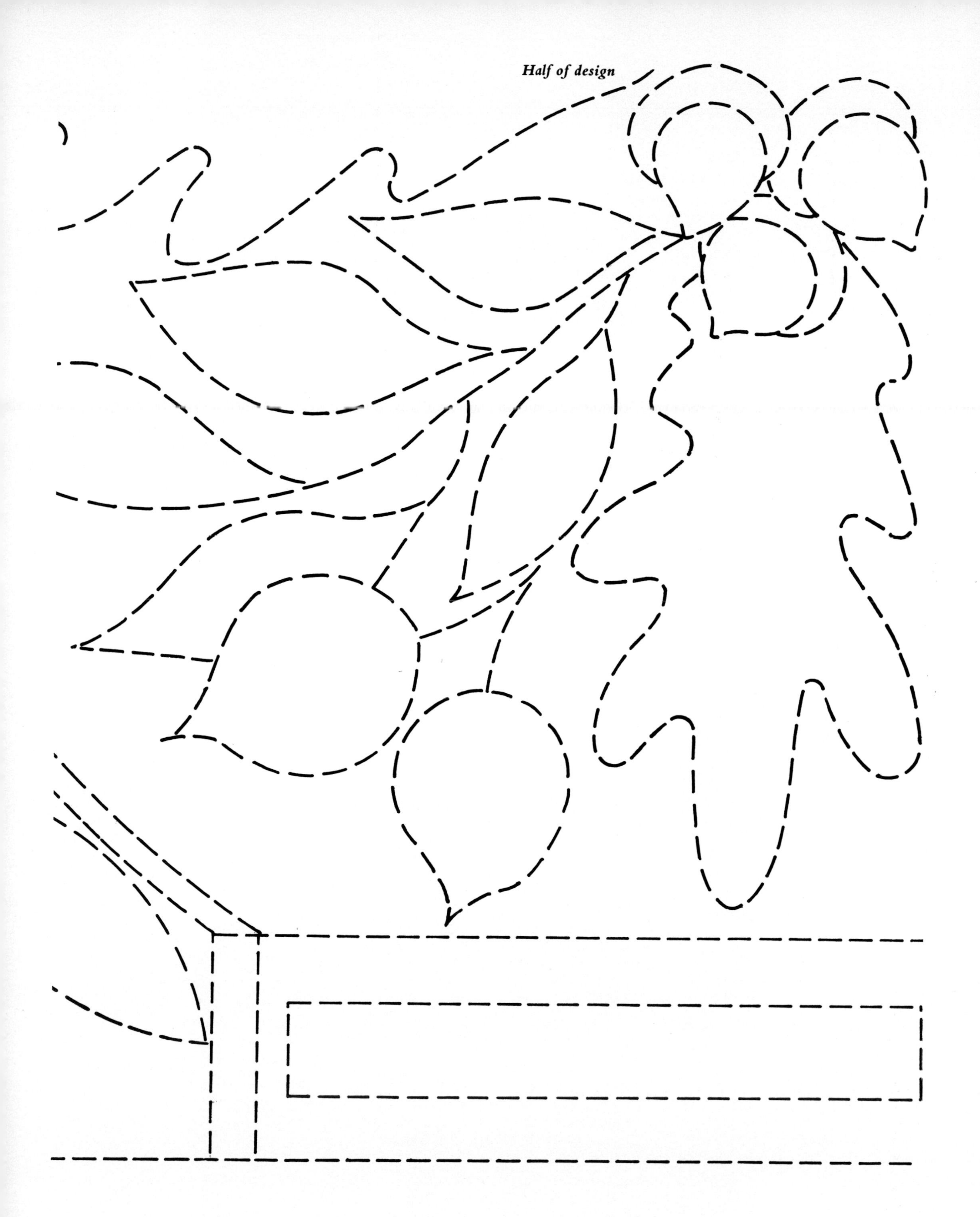
Half of design

Ozark Piecemakers (seated, left to right)—*Genella Smith, Vesta Dean, and Cynthia Bezanson, and* (standing, left to right)—*Gondy Shuler, Mary Phillips, Alleta Whittaker, and Toni Smith—surround their latest quilting achievement,* Lincoln Quilt.

Ozark Piecemakers Quilt Guild

Springfield, Missouri

While attending a quilting symposium in 1981, two enterprising ladies, Karen Soetaert and Joan Kloppenburg, put together sketchy plans for a quilt guild. Word traveled about the first meeting, and friends brought friends to bring the attendance tally to 16. Today membership rolls contain more than 200 names, according to 1988 Guild President Barbara Warren.

The guild's activities are many. Members have made and donated quilts to the Museum of Ozark's History Auction, to Springfield's Ronald McDonald House, and to a local home for retarded and handicapped people. And more than 20 quilts have been made by them for Springfield's Children's Home as an ongoing project.

Ozark Crystal

1985

It all began with a well-known television program about pioneer settlers. When Ozark Piecemaker member Juanita Bridges spied a quilt on a bed during the playing of a videotape of the show, she decided that she had to get the pattern. She stopped the tape and drafted the pattern on the spot. Guild members loved the pattern so much that they decided it would be their next guild quilt project.

With 170 guild members, teamwork for quiltmaking was essential. Once the quilt setting was decided upon, a small group traveled to the fabric store to select the material. The idea was to choose something with eye appeal, with rather strong colors, and with a floral pattern background to give the effect of an Old English quilt. Small groups then met to cut the fabric and to bag block pieces into kits for members to sew by hand at home. Quilting was done twice a week on a drop-in basis.

This pattern requires a great deal of set-in piecing; therefore, *Ozark Crystal* is recommended for experienced quilters. Since piecing accuracy is essential, hand piecing of the blocks and side and corner sections is also recommended.

Two methods for quilt assembly are given. The first method divides diamond E in half to form a triangle. With this method, the quilt top is made in blocks and should be easier to assemble. For the second method, diamond E is alternated with crystal stars and presents a large unseamed area for quilting. Fabric requirements are the same for both methods.

Members who worked on *Ozark Crystal* are Georgia Adams, Maxine Allen, Maxine Armstrong, Barbara Austin, Maryann Bagg, Betty Baker, Norma Barton, Janet Beeler,

Cynthia Bezanson, Ferrita Blunt, Maxine Bossing, Thelma Bradford, Lois Bray, Lillian Breshears, Marie Brewster, Juanita Bridges, Nina Brown, Ann Bush, Pat Butler, Mildred Carey, Linda Chamberlain, Arline Charlet, Penny Childress, Helen Corlett, Shirley Crouch, Elane Crum, Belva Curry, Martha Davis, Vesta Dean, Genelle Deaton, Ann Dowell, Lucille Edgett, Myrtle English, Dorothy Fare, Norene Fields, Mary Sue Fox, Eileen Franz, Sara Fugitt, Anna Griffin, Beatrice Harden, Wilma Hardiman, Marilyn Harris, Linda Harter, Bytha Hayter, Jeanne Helfrecht, Vivian Helm, Margarete Herring, Christine Johns, Anna Lee Johnson, Diane Keeter, Joan Kloppenburg, Janelle Knox, Betty Koeppe, Sue Lawley, Barbara Livingston, Mary Marlin, Gladyce Mars, Evelyn Mendes, Susan Monroe, Pat Morris, Anna Murray, Claire Murrell, Janet Northup, Pam O'Neal, Agnes Pemberton, Mary Phillips, Alice Podrecca, Nettie Polodna, Anita Sanker, Virginia Schenk, Dortha Shields, Gondy Shuler, Cathy Smith, Genella Smith, Sarah Smith, Toni Smith, Reva Sobotka, Karen Soetaert, Nola Sparks, Helen Spellman, Annie Stokes, Nancy Test, Joan Thompson, Sharlet Tomforde, Thelma Turner, Grace Underwood, Nadine Upchurch, Gerry Western, Flora Wetzel, Ellen Whitesell, Alleta Whittaker, Helen Williams, Kathy Williams, Margaret Wilson, Ramona Wood, and Anna Lee Young.

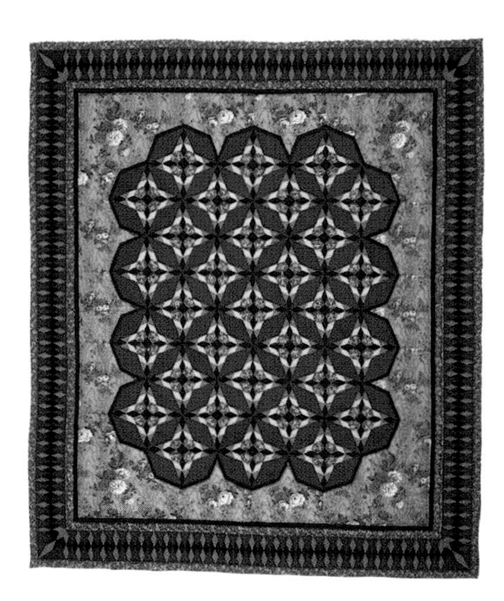

Ozark Crystal

Finished Quilt Size
81″ x 94″

Number of Blocks and Finished Size
31 blocks—9″ x 9″

Fabric Requirements

Purple	—4¼ yd.
Morning glory print*	—3 yd.
Beige print	—1¼ yd.
Taupe print	—2 yd.
Purple print	—4¾ yd.
Cabbage rose print*	—3½ yd.
Purple for bias binding	—1 yd.
Backing	—8 yd.

* — Throughout the directions, morning glory print and cabbage rose print will be designated as MGP and CRP, respectively.

Number to Cut

Template A	—31 purple
Template B	—124 MGP
Template C	—520 purple 248 beige print 276 taupe print
Template D	—248 taupe print
Template E for method one	—156 purple print
Template E for method two	—92 purple print
Template F	—4 purple
Template F*	—4 purple
Template G	—4 taupe print
Template H	—4 purple print
Template H*	—4 purple print
Template I	—264 purple print
Template J	—10 CRP
Template K	—4 CRP
Template L	—4 purple
Template M	—10 purple

* — Flip or turn over template if fabric is one-sided.

Quilt Top Assembly For Method One

1. Refer to Ozark Crystal Piecing Diagram I, and join 2 pieces (B) to opposite sides of square (A).

Join a purple diamond (C) to a beige print diamond (C) at sides twice. Join C sets to 1 unjoined piece (B). Set-in C sets by stitching from the outside edge of one side and stitching up to the seam line. Stop and backstitch 1 or 2 stitches. Remove fabric from the machine. Align the remaining sides and stitch from the center to the outside edge, backstitching 1 or 2 stitches at the start. Join taupe print triangles (D), as shown in Ozark Crystal Piecing Diagram I. Make 2 pieced shapes. Join pieced shapes to remaining sides of square (A), as shown.

Join beige print diamond (C) to taupe print triangle (D) to purple diamond (C) to form a strip, as shown in Ozark Crystal Piecing Diagram I. Make 4 and join to assembled pieces, as shown, to make a 4-pointed star.

2. Join triangles (E), as shown in Ozark Crystal Piecing Diagram II, to complete block. Make 31 blocks.

Ozark Crystal Piecing Diagram I

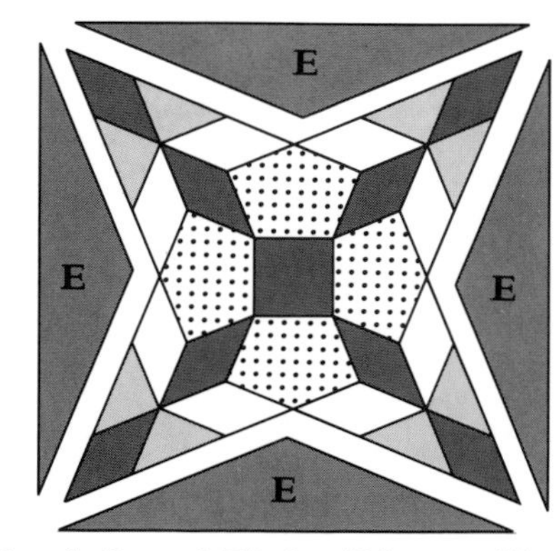

Ozark Crystal Piecing Diagram II

beige print *taupe print* *purple* *purple print* *morning glory print*

3. Arrange blocks in 7 diagonal rows, as shown in Setting Diagram I for Method One. Join blocks at sides. Join rows.

Setting Diagram I for Method One

4. Join pieces L and M to the top edges of pieces J and K, as shown in Setting Diagram II for Method One. Join purple print triangles (E) to pieces, as shown. Make 10 side sections and 4 corner sections.

Join side sections to quilt, as shown in Setting Diagram II for Method One. (See Step 1 for set-in piecing technique.) Join side sections at sides. Join corner sections to quilt.

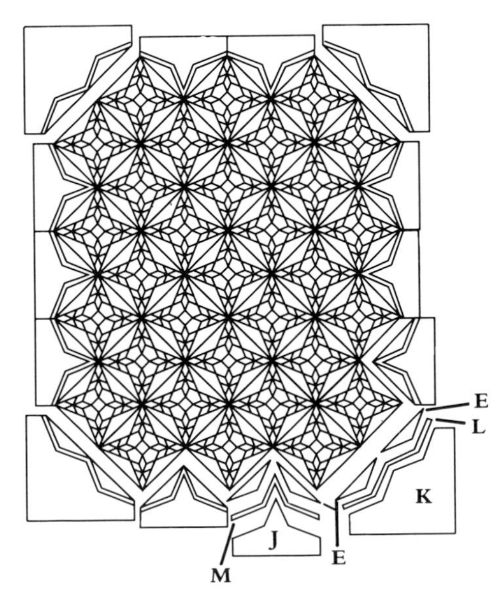

Setting Diagram II for Method One

5. Cut 4 border strips, 1″ wide, from purple. Join to quilt and miter corners.

6. Cut 4 border strips, 1½″ wide, from MGP. Join to quilt and miter corners.

7. Join 272 purple diamonds (C) to 272 taupe print diamonds (C), as shown in Border Piecing Diagram. Join C sets to C sets to form a pieced diamond. Join purple print triangles (I) to opposite sides of pieced diamond, as shown, to form small diagonal strips. Join at sides and make 2 pieced borders for quilt sides and join to quilt. Make 2 pieced borders for top and bottom of quilt and set aside.

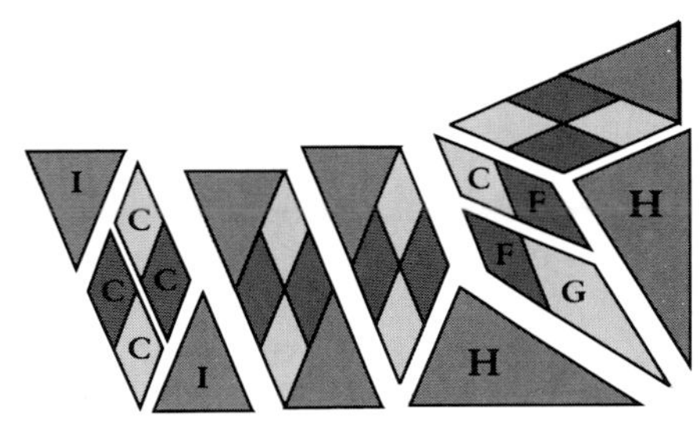

Border Piecing Diagram

Join taupe print diamond (C) to purple diamond (F), and a purple diamond (F) to taupe print diamond (G), as above. Join to form corner diamond. Join purple print triangle (H) to each side of corner diamond, as shown. Make 4. Join a corner diamond section to each end of pieced borders for top and bottom. Join to quilt.

8. Cut 4 border strips, 2″ wide, from MGP. Join to quilt and miter corners.

Quilting

Outline-quilt ¼″ inside seam line of Ozark Crystal block pieces A through D. Outline-quilt ¼″ inside seam line of outside edges of joined triangles (E) in the case of Method One or diamond (E) for Method Two. This will form a diamond of quilting. Duplicate diamond shape twice, with two lines of parallel quilting. Outline-quilt ¼″ inside seam line of outside edges of side and corner sections. Outline-quilt ¼″ inside seam lines of MGP border strips. Outline-quilt ¼″ inside seam lines of pieced border diamonds and triangles. The Ozark quilters quilted flourishes of spineless plumes along the CRP borders.

Finished Edges

Bind with purple fabric.

Quilt Top Assembly For Method Two

1. See Step 1 for Method One.

2. Alternate stars with diamonds (E) in 7 diagonal rows, as shown in Setting Diagram I for Method Two. Join at sides. Alternate diamonds (E) with star rows and join.

Setting Diagram I for Method Two

3. Join pieces L and M to the top edge of pieces J and K, as shown in Setting Diagram II for Method Two. Join diamonds (E) to pieces, as shown. Make 10 side sections and 4 corner sections.

Join side sections to quilt. (See Step 1 for set-in piecing technique.) Join side sections at sides. Join corner sections to quilt.

4. See Step 5 of Method One and continue quilt assembly as directed.

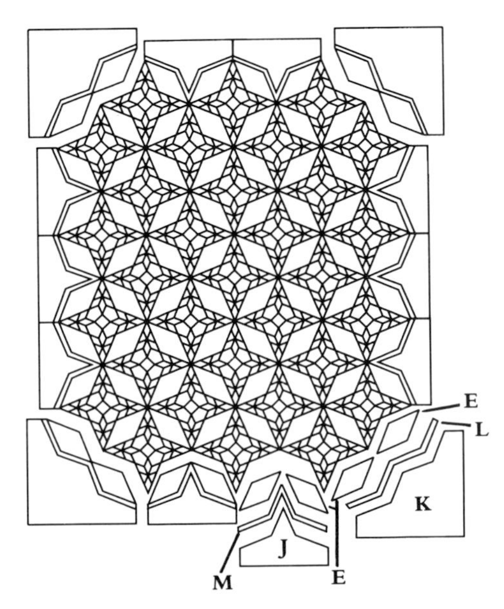

Setting Diagram II for Method Two

J

Shaded portion indicates overlap from following page.

Place on the fold.

C

Place on the fold for Diamond E.

E

M

L

H

I

♥ — ★

For L, flip piece and match ★s and ♥s to make one template.

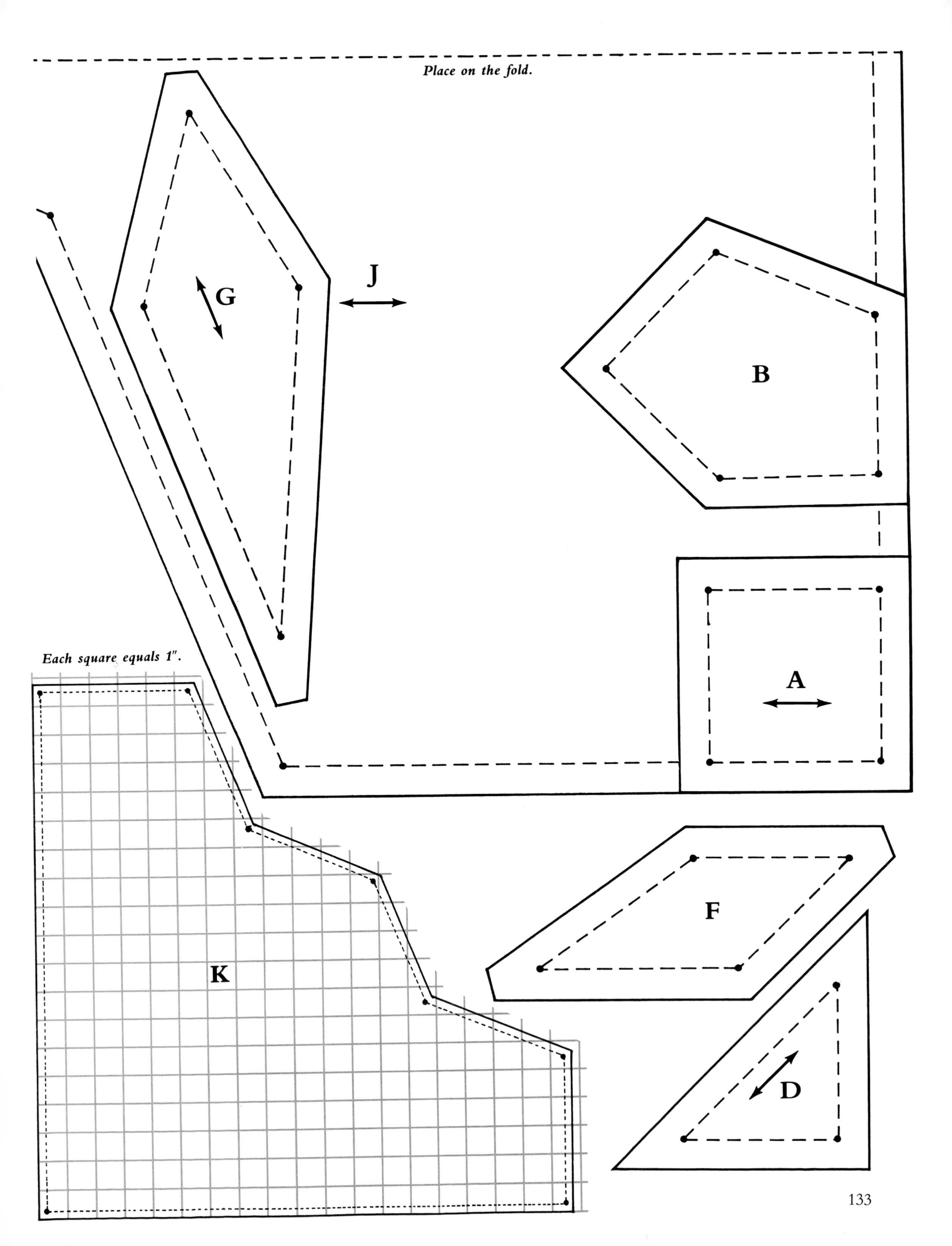
Place on the fold.
G
J
B
A
Each square equals 1".
K
F
D

Anniversary
1983

The devoted hands of 28 quilters supplied over 3,500 quiltmaking hours to make *Anniversary*. And many more uncounted hours were contributed by members to attend workshops to learn the various techniques used on this quilt.

Nancy Myers, president of Quilters' Workshop when *Anniversary* was begun in 1981, suggested that the group make a white-on-white quilt. The group agreed to use Nancy's original adaptation of a quilting pattern published in an early edition of *Quilter's Newsletter*. (See "Resources.") Nancy conducted the workshops and managed the project from beginning to end. An event in her mother-in-law's life indirectly influenced the naming of the quilt. Nancy's mother-in-law's golden wedding anniversary and all the plans associated with that occasion coincided with the making of the quilt, so the quilters decided to name the quilt *Anniversary*.

Anniversary has won numerous ribbons, has been exhibited in libraries, community colleges, and quilt shows, and appeared in the *Washington Post*.

Club members who worked on *Anniversary* are Marcia Aasmundstad, Jean Beall, Ellen Brooks, Dolores Burgess, Sandy Chaconas, Jeanne Cusin, Shirley Elliott, Judy Hanak, Cindy Hrebar, Betty Johnson, Sue Kelly, Ruth Lang, Mary Licari, Freda Malone, Joan Middleton, Jenny Mitchell, June Mitchell, Carolyn Morrow, Nancy Myers, Vi Negra, Betty Over, Joan Peake, Kathleen Randolph, Marilyn Trimble, Connie Wilcox, Susan Wolfe, Jean Zazarine, and Marianne Zmudka.

A regular rotation of members from the Quilters' Workshop of Oxon Hill spends time quilting at the home of Shirley Elliott. Shown here are members (seated, left to right)—*Cindy Hrebar, Janise Bernier, Audra Walcutt, and Shirley Elliott, and* (standing, left to right)—*Vi Negra, Connie Wilcox, Jacqueline Moseley, Nancy Wooster, and Betty Bevans.*

Quilters' Workshop of Oxon Hill

Fort Washington, Maryland

Does your guild know exactly the total number of hours members spend making the guild's quilt? Members of Quilters' Workshop of Oxon Hill were often curious to know the answer to that question. Therefore, they developed a system that would furnish that number. Members sign in and out of a logbook each time they work on a quilt. Hours of work done individually, i.e., piecing blocks at home, are estimated and then tallied with the logbook hours.

It was decided that this system also provided a more judicious method for the quilt drawing, held among members after each quilt is completed. For every 15 hours a member works on a quilt, she is allotted one chance on it. Therefore, the more hours a member works on a quilt, the more chances she has to win it.

The Quilters' Workshop has been a quilting club since 1973 and at present has 18 active members. Members stay busy working on the club's annual quilt, once or twice a week.

Anniversary

Finished Quilt Size
84" x 101"

Number of Blocks and Finished Size
20 blocks—16½" x 16½"

Fabric Requirements

White	—11½ yd.
White batiste	—6 yd.
Backing	—9 yd.

Other Materials
Polyester stuffing material
White polyester cable cord, size 16 (1/16" diameter) — 60 yd.
White polyester cable cord, size 200 (9/32" diameter) — 11 yd.
White embroidery floss
Small embroidery hoop
Tapestry needle
Knitting needle or orange stick

Quilt Top Assembly

1. Cut twenty 21" squares from white for quilt top and twenty 21" squares from white batiste for lining. Press white fabric and batiste lining thoroughly before beginning trapunto. (This will be the final pressing of the block since trapunto work should not be pressed.)

Finger-crease white square for quilt top in half twice to find the center. Center and mark square with trapunto and quilting patterns.

Baste white square to batiste lining square, making sure to place basting stitches only in areas for quilting and not for trapunto. (Areas for trapunto are the flowers, grapes, and handlebars. See photograph of trapunto block.)

2. To prepare areas for trapunto, backstitch around all flowers, grapes, and handlebars, using one strand of embroidery floss. Backstitches should be even and approximately ⅛" in length. Use a small embroidery hoop to hold work. It is important to complete all backstitching before stuffing since the embroidery hoop cannot be placed over any area that has been stuffed.

3. Turn work to the back and snip a slit in *lining only* of flowers and grapes, being careful not to cut too close to the backstitching. Fill the area with batting completely and fully, using a pointed instrument (such as an orange stick, seam ripper, or knitting needle) to aid in stuffing. Nancy reminds us that the finished raised areas should be full and firm, but not hard as a rock!

Cover the opening in the lining with very loose stitches, using white thread. First stitch across the opening and then up and down. Make enough stitches to secure the stuffing. (It is not necessary to try to close the opening.)

4. Snip a slit in lining of handlebars at points marked X1 and X2, as shown in Handlebar Diagram.

Handlebar Diagram

Thread tapestry needle with size 16 cording and pull until thread is doubled and measures 5½″ for the innermost handlebars and 3½″ for the outermost handlebars. Enter at point X1 and leave ½″ of cording outside lining at entrance point. Run needle, threaded with doubled cording, from one end of the handlebar to the other. Exit at X2, leaving ½″ of cording outside lining. Straighten fabric and cord before cutting. Push ends of cording through lining opening and fill the remainder of handlebars with stuffing. Close off opening with loose stitches, as above.

5. Work French knots onto centers of flowers, using 3 strands of embroidery floss. (See photograph of trapunto block.) Fill centers of flowers completely.

6. After trapunto is complete, check for any puckered areas. Where necessary, make very tiny snips in the lining to relieve puckering.

7. Prepare all 20 trapunto blocks for lap quilting by layering the trapunto block, batting, and backing and basting layers together. Quilt the remainder of the pattern.

8. Trim all trapunto blocks to 17″ squares. Arrange blocks in 5 rows of 4 blocks each. To join, pin backing and batting of adjacent blocks to backing to expose the top layer of fabric, as shown in Block Joining Diagram I. With right sides together, join top layers of quilt blocks at sides to form a row. Press all seams of each row in one direction. Unpin backing and batting and trim batting so that edges abut. Overlap backing, turn one side of backing under ¼″, and slipstitch to batting and backing only. (See Block Joining Diagram II.) Join rows in same manner.

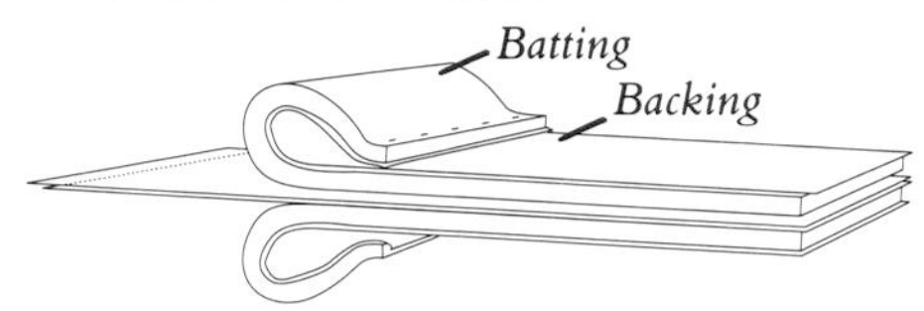

Block Joining Diagram I

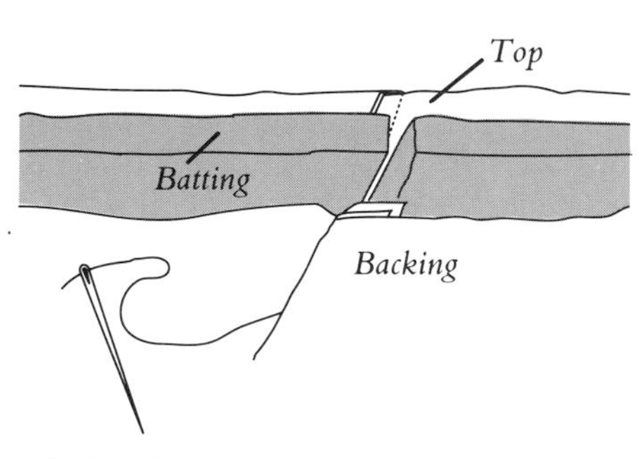

Block Joining Diagram II

9. Mark areas of quilt top where blocks meet with circular quilting pattern. (See photograph of trapunto block.)

10. Cut 4 borders, 9½″ wide, from white fabric and join to quilt with mitered corners. With right sides together, match raw edges of border with quilt front. Pin or baste in place.

Cut 4 backing strips, 9½″ wide. With right sides together, match raw edges of backing strip with quilt back and pin or baste in place. With one seam, stitch through all five layers (border, quilt front, batting, quilt back, and backing strip).

Join remaining borders to quilt in this manner and miter corners. Turn border and backing so that wrong sides face each other. Mark border for quilting with parallel lines at a 45° angle and ¼″ apart.

Cut 4 strips of batting, 9½″ wide or wider. (Be sure batting strip is wide enough so that it can be anchored by the seam that joins the binding.) Insert batting between border and backing.

11. Put quilt in a frame and quilt the circular patterns and parallel lines as marked. Repeat the circular motif of each trapunto block with echo quilting in the remaining unquilted areas of each block. (See photograph of trapunto block.)

Finished Edges

Center and cover size 200 cording with strips of white fabric, 2½″ wide. Trim one side of white fabric to ⅜″ from cording seam line. Turn the remaining side under ¼″ and press. (See Covered Cording Diagram.) With right sides together, match raw edges of quilt to front edge of cording. (See notations on Covered Cording Diagram.) Stitch through all layers as close to the cording seam line as possible. Trim any excess batting to relieve bulkiness. Turn free edge of cording strip to back and blindstitch in place.

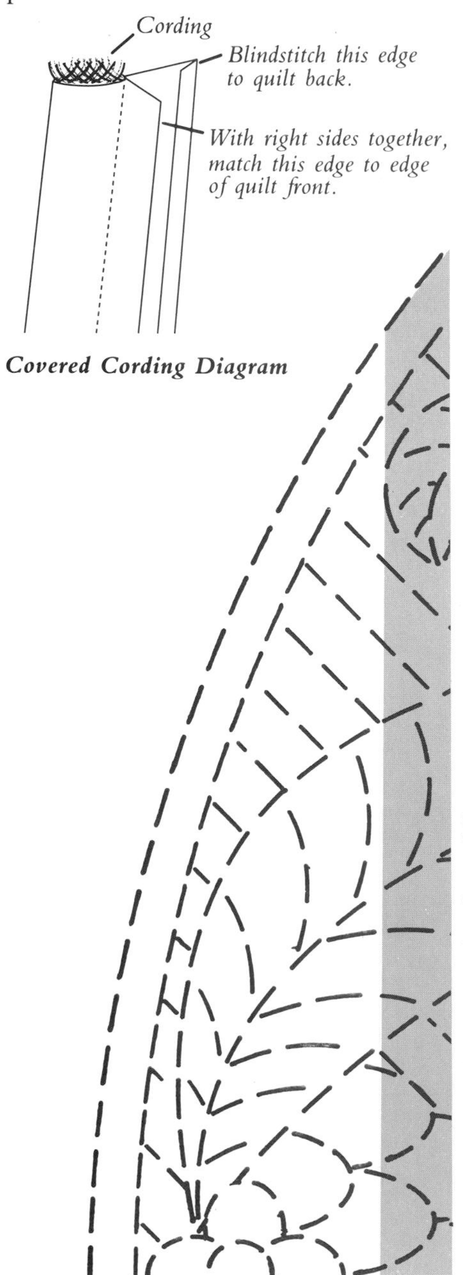

Covered Cording Diagram

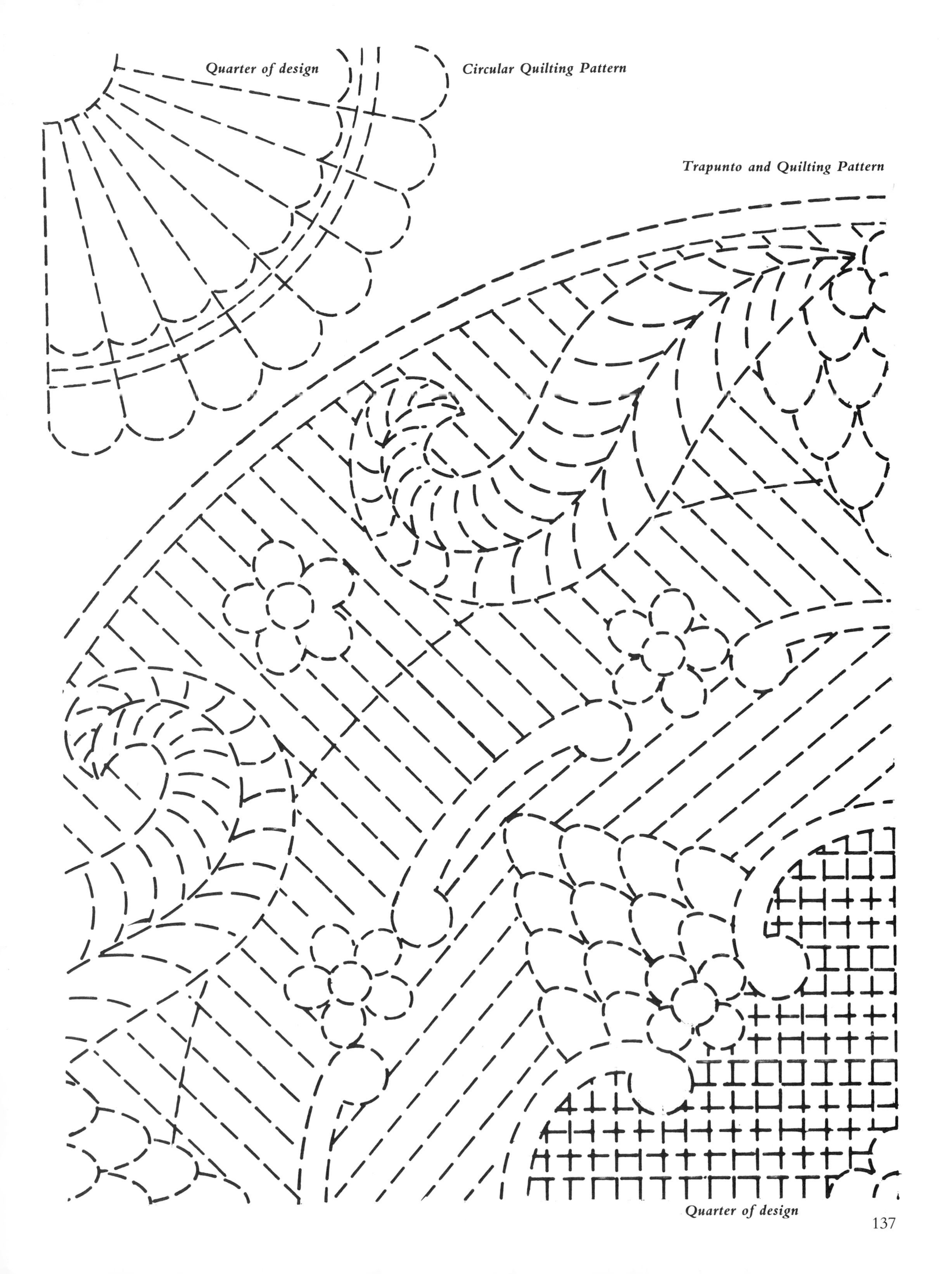
Quarter of design
Circular Quilting Pattern
Trapunto and Quilting Pattern
Quarter of design

A GLIMPSE OF YESTERYEAR

DESIGNER GALLERY

Using dazzling fabrics in glorious hues,
from cadmium yellows to azure blues—
These meticulous stitchers, originators they are,
spark our imaginations to dreams afar.
So twist 'em and turn 'em, that's what it's all about.
These one-of-a-kinds can prevent quilt burnout.
An idea, a scheme, let your thoughts unwind—
Watch out, before y'know it, you'll say,
that one-of-kind, it's mine!

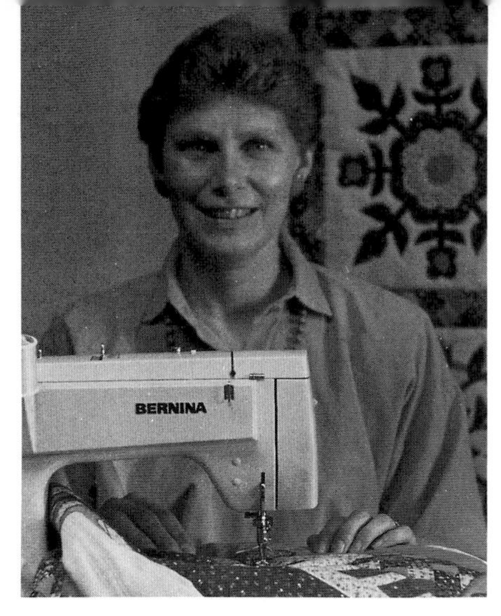

Arlis Obbink

Rock Valley, Iowa

Machine appliqué and machine quilting are "where it's at" for this Iowan. "They make quilting faster and more durable," says Arlis, "and I believe they are essential techniques for any quilter, like me, who has three active children."

As Arlis describes it, she and her family live on a little acreage in the middle of corn country. Besides making quilts and raising children, Arlis operates a small sewing and alterations business from her home and serves as a counselor for a club of girls from their church. "The club gives me the opportunity to share the Bible and sewing skills with young girls," says Arlis.

Arlis recommends purchasing ample amounts of fabric for all your quilting projects. "That way," says Arlis, "you'll have lots of fabric left over to make coordinating accessories, years after the fabric is no longer available."

Iris Garden
1986

It's springtime in Arlis's bedroom all year round, thanks to her *Iris Garden* quilt. Vibrant blossoms of bearded irises and a pair of friendly yellow birds brighten each new day, rain or shine.

Before Arlis designed *Iris Garden*, she searched existing flower patterns for something that evoked the essence of a fresh iris garden. After an unsuccessful search, she decided to draw her own pattern. "Six hours later," recalls Arlis, "I had exactly what I wanted on paper, not just a vision in my mind." With her machine-appliqué and machine-quilting techniques perfected to a science, Arlis was able to complete *Iris Garden* in two weeks.

Kathy Emmel

Arvada, Colorado

"Each time I unfold one of my quilts, I feel like I'm unwrapping a wonderful Christmas present!" says Kathy. It took a while for Kathy to discover quilting, but now she feels that all the time she spent as an artist, calligrapher, and graphic designer was in preparation for her years as a quilter.

Kathy got hooked on quilting when a friend showed her how to hand-quilt. "I loved the shadows, the hills and valleys that quilting made," says Kathy. She quilts as much as her job as a fourth grade teacher will allow her and is focusing most of her time on making all of her favorite traditional patterns. She continues taking as many quiltmaking classes as time permits and remarks, "I still have much to learn, and many quilts to design and make."

Homeward Bound

1986

Water vessels of every sort—from makeshift rafts and canoes to large sturdy sailing ships and paddle-boats—can be seen. You can almost hear the thump and creak of wagon wheels as they hammer their imprints upon the dusty plains of unknown horizons. There are images of tireless horses, faithfully pulling stagecoaches and trolleycars full of passengers to prescribed destinations. And adjacent to them is a steam-driven engine, rolling down the rails that followed the trails previously etched by forging wagon wheels. They are homeward bound. These forms of transportation — available to early settlers of the United States — are realistically portrayed in quilting on the borders of *Homeward Bound.*

Kathy's *Homeward Bound* began with her own pen-and-ink drawing of the United States. "Once completed, I knew I wanted to try it in a quilted format," says Kathy. Many kinds of needlework are incorporated in the quilt—embroidery, appliqué, patchwork, Seminole piecing, and of course, quilting. By using a satin stitch and outlining it with a backstitch, Kathy cleverly designed stylized letters that are shaped to fit the state they are naming. Scenes are appliquéd in each corner that picture the places in our country where the pioneers settled—the mountains, great plains, desert, and seashore.

Homeward Bound won the Grand Champion Ribbon at the Jefferson County Fair, Lakewood, Colorado, in 1986; a blue ribbon and the Colorado Quilt Council Award at the Adams County Fair, Brighton, Colorado, in 1986; and most recently, the Viewer's Choice Award at the Heritage Quilt Show, Denver, Colorado, in June 1988.

Fleetice has made hundreds of quilts in her more than 40 years of quilting and has exhibited many of them throughout the South, including at the World's Fair in Knoxville, Tennessee. She regularly conducts quilting demonstrations at state fairs and has become well-known for her artistry and teaching ability. "Quilting has given me much joy and pleasure," says Fleetice. "It is one of the great loves of my life."

Fleetice Coon Martin

Murphy, North Carolina

A Glimpse of Yesteryear
1985

Take a step back in time and place yourself upon the seat of a 1914 Stutz Bearcat or maybe a 1910 Packard. You hang on tight as your beau swings around the curves at the blazing speed of 10 miles an hour. That's just one of the visions that may come to your mind as you look at Fleetice's collection of embroidered vintage automobiles.

You'll find a 1874 Siegfried Marcus, a 1905 Pierce-Arrow, a 1910 Overland, a 1911 Stanley Steamer, a 1902 Studebaker Electric, a 1913 Model T Ford, a 1904 Crestmobile, and several more.

Fleetice found the designs in a library book and embroidered them in black and gold on white cotton squares. Her initial plan was to sell the collection of 20 embroidered squares at the state fair. "People wanted to buy one or two squares but not the entire collection," says Fleetice. "I wouldn't sell them that way." She took them home and decided to make a quilt with them. "I was so excited about the project," says Fleetice, "that I didn't stop until I finished."

Kathy Lee

Seattle, Washington

"I put my quilts together all over the house," says Kathy. "But my family is very patient with all of my clutter." She especially likes the freedom of expression quiltmaking affords and frequently lets a quilt design evolve as she makes it. As Kathy explains it, "It is hard for me to plan and design too far ahead, so I expand and design many of my quilts as I go." This method also inspires her to finish the project. "As the design grows, it is hard for me to put it down until I can see it finished," says Kathy.

Though she makes most of her clothes and enjoys all kinds of needlework, quilting is her favorite. "Most of my quilts hang on our walls at home, and I enjoy the warmth and color that they bring to the rooms," Kathy says.

Springtime Fantasy
1986

What a fantastic way to capture the image of your children! "The idea came from a picture taken of my two sons, Aaron and Bryan," says Kathy. (See below.)

Kathy changed the setting to a garden in spring and sat her sons under a shady tree. Then the boys chose several things they wanted to include—their puppy, Saki; two pet ducks; and a ladybug. (The frog is a "family friend," also well-known to many of you.) Extra care was taken in embroidering eyes, hair, facial and hand features, flower stems, and petals to give a textured look.

"Though my sons were not barefooted in the photograph," says Kathy, "I appliquéd them with bare feet since they love to run barefooted through the grass in the springtime. My sons were very proud to be included in this project, and they consider it their quilt, too."

Kathy's sons, Aaron and Bryan, strike a loving pose.

RESOURCES

Many of our quilters gained inspiration for their quilt designs from previously published designs and patterns. Below is a list of those publications.

Joan Nahass and Cornelia Pool's *State Quilt* — Patterns were originally published in issues of the magazine *Hearth & Home*. Augusta, Maine: Vickery Publishing Company, 1907-1912. A more recent collection of these patterns was published by Bannister B, Ford EP: *The United States Patchwork Pattern Book*. Mineola, New York: Dover Publications, Inc., 1976.

Billie Carter's inspiration for her sampler quilt was Leone D: *The Sampler Quilt*. Santa Clara, California: Leone Publications, 1980.

Photographs of Susan Stein's sampler quilts were published in "Blockbuster Sets for Sampler Quilts." *Quilter's Newsletter Magazine* 178:24-25, (January) 1986.

Judy Sogn's *Christmas Tulips* — "Rosegay." *Quiltmaker* 2:8-9, (Spring/Summer) 1983.

Linae Frei's *Draw Me* was previously published in *Erica Wilson's Quilts of America*, edited by CN Conard, pp 48-49 and 166-169. Birmingham, Alabama: Oxmoor House, 1979. The quilt also appeared in "51 Prize-Winning Quilts." *Good Housekeeping* 186:124-135 and 218-230, (March) 1978.

The quilting pattern used by the Quilters' Workshop of Oxon Hill was inspired by one published in an early issue of *Quilter's Newsletter Magazine*, edited by Bonnie Leman. Wheatridge, Colorado: Leman Publications, Inc.

For Log Cabin quilt lovers, an original *Holiday Wreath* patchwork wall hanging by Cristal Carter is available from THAT PATCHWORK PLACE, INC., P.O. Box 118, Bothell, Washington 98041-0118.